Women's Voices

Women's Voices

*New Perspectives for the
Christian-Jewish Dialogue*

Edited by
Helen Fry, Rachel Montagu and
Lynne Scholefield

scm press

© Helen Fry, Rachel Montagu and Lynne Scholefield 2005

British Library Cataloguing in Publication data

A catalogue record for this book is available
from the British Library

0 334 02986 4

First published in 2005 by SCM Press
9–17 St Albans Place, London N1 0NX

www.scm-canterburypress.co.uk

SCM Press is a division of
SCM-Canterbury Press Ltd

Typeset by Regent Typesetting
Printed and bound in Great Britain by
William Clowes Ltd, Beccles, Suffolk

Contents

CONTENTS

For our mothers

Profile of Editors and Contributors

Helen Fry is an Honorary Research Fellow in the Department of Hebrew and Jewish Studies at University College London. From 1997 to 1998 she was the Rabbi Marc H. Tanenbaum Foundation (New York) Scholar in Christian-Jewish Relations. She has written *Christian-Jewish Dialogue: A Reader* and published widely in the field of Christian-Jewish relations.

Rachel Montagu works in the Education Department of The Council of Christians and Jews and is a lecturer in Judaism and biblical Hebrew at Birkbeck College, London.

Lynne Scholefield is Senior Lecturer in Theology and Religious Studies at St Mary's College, Strawberry Hill.

Anne Clark is the Director of The Jewish Resource Centre which is part of the Centre for Research in Religious Education and Development at Roehampton University of Surrey.

Clare Jardine, a member of a religious congregation, the Sisters of Sion, is an educational consultant at the Sion Centre for Dialogue and Encounter. She is a visiting lecturer at Heythrop College, University of London.

Kathleen de Magtige Middleton is associate Rabbi at The Liberal Jewish Synagogue and teaches *chumash* at Leo Baeck College-Centre for Jewish Education.

Beryl Norman, an Anglican Christian, has an MA in Classics and a Postgraduate Diploma in Jewish-Christian Relations. She chairs the Israel Committee of The Council of Christians and Jews and lectures to groups of clergy on aspects of Jews, Christians and Israel.

Marcia Plumb is the Director of the Spirituality programme at Leo Baeck College-Centre for Jewish Education. She is also a congregational rabbi. She was ordained in 1988 at Hebrew Union College-Jewish Institute of Religion in New York. She has written on women's rituals and spirituality.

Irene Wise is an artist, designer and educator. She has initiated and established a course in Holocaust Representation at Roehampton University of Surrey.

Introduction

Helen P. Fry

In and around the field of feminist studies, much has been written by Jewish and Christian women on the challenges to their inherited patriarchal traditions. Feminists in both faiths have been working for more than three decades to change the status of women in leadership, religious learning, and ministry but also working for a more gender-inclusive language in the liturgy and prayer books. However, Jewish and Christian women have rarely met *as women* to speak from *women's* experience to formulate their own dialogue on a whole range of issues of joint concern or interest, issues which are not necessarily part of the feminist agenda thus far. The lack of women's voices on Jewish-Christian relations, means that half of the participants' experiences are unspoken and unrecorded. While women have been actively involved in improving Jewish-Christian relations for decades now, their experiences as women have not been shaping the relationship between Jews and Christians thus far. The analogy of the half-empty bookcase is particularly appropriate in describing the lack of women's voices in the Jewish-Christian dialogue. *The Half-Empty Bookcase* is an organization based in Britain which provides a forum for Jewish women to express their spirituality and challenge their inherited patriarchal traditions. These traditions, developed and recorded by men, were assumed to be the whole picture but in fact represented 'a half-empty bookcase' which Jewish women are now seeking to fill. Likewise, our group has begun to fill a space on the bookshelf of Jewish-Christian relations, not only by including the voices of Jewish and Christian women from within their respective traditions but also their experiences in dialogue with each other. It is precisely these two dimensions that are providing a new impetus to the way in which Jewish-Christian dialogue is carried forward and in this sense it is pushing the boundaries of that dialogue. The focus of this book represents some of the dialogical experiences of a particular group of academic Jewish and Christian women who have met for over eight years now to discuss issues of mutual interest, and as such is one of the few groups in Britain at this time.

It is important to clarify that we are women in dialogue and not necessarily feminists in dialogue *per se*, although there will inevitably be some overlap with feminist theology because some of the women speak as feminists working within their traditions and their spirituality has been directly transformed by feminist theology. Throughout this book we are expressing our voices as *women*, which may or may not touch on gender issues. We are meeting and dialoguing on two levels; first as women, and second as Jews and Christians and therefore it is significant to mention that our voices do not only have something worthwhile to say on women's issues. We should not be viewed as an appendix to the Jewish-Christian dialogue but have something of value to contribute as Jews and Christians even when it is not feminist-related.

The importance of the women's dialogue is discussed in more depth by Helen and Lynne in Chapter 1; however, the following preliminary pointers about the distinctiveness of our dialogue as women are helpful. We have consciously chosen to meet as a women-only group primarily because many of us have been frustrated with the often hierarchical and structured nature of the mixed dialogue groups. These are usually heavily represented by the institutions of Judaism and Christianity most of whose representatives are men, and the difficulty for women is that they have often been silenced. Not all women, all the time, but on the whole they have been silenced by a different pace, different ways of speaking and by the kind of things that are often said which are disempowering. In the wider dialogue, 'knowing' is tied up with authority and position and therefore only those in an authoritative position are able to speak and this is especially true for those denominations within our traditions that limit women's leadership roles or do not permit the ordination of women. The male-led scholarship and dialogue often assumes, sometimes unconsciously, that what has been said is all that there is to say. The women's dialogue does not make the same assumption and tends to be much more personal and egalitarian. Through the sharing of personal stories or the study of biblical texts, our voices as women have provided new insights into the dialogue process itself. Our group has created a way of working that has enabled us to find our voices and to express some experiences which could not have been shared in the wider dialogue as it is currently carried out. Helen's and Rachel's experiences of what childbirth means for them in terms of the possibility of being the bearer of the messiah is one example of that in Chapter 3. They have shared that particular experience together in a safe environment among the other women and are now empowered to share it here in the book.

Women's methods or ways of dialoguing tend to be more fluid and this means that we often present material that is partly academic but interwoven with our spiritual or religious experiences. The dialogue that follows is more open and egalitarian where each woman does not wait for permission to speak from a leader or chairperson, which all too often results in serial monologues rather than dialogue. In our group, one person comments and then another brings her perspective. There may then be a natural backwards and forwards in the discussion in which other women join in. Our dialogue is not only a response to the paper that has been presented but is also a response to every individual in the room. Our journeys as women of faith are an integral part of what we bring to the dialogue and intensely personalized stories are often told. It can, of course, be done by both men and women, but women doing it in this way, and to this extent, tends to be the distinctiveness of our ways of dialoguing. Lynne explores this further in the first chapter on women's epistemology (knowledge) where she discusses women's ways of knowing which, while not exclusive to women, tend to be less structured with an acceptance that our knowledge is partial as expressed through our experiences. We seek to show through the chapters of this book that through our joint study and dialogue, the particular perspectives of women can make important contributions to the interpretation of our traditions, texts, and theology and these are the voices that have been missing so far from the wider Jewish-Christian dialogue.

Foundations of the Group

This section will briefly outline the formation of the group which grew out of a frustration with the wider Jewish-Christian dialogue that seemed to have reached a plateau after having made so many advances in the first 50 years. Many people involved in the dialogue have spoken about how it was time to push forward the boundaries of that dialogue but nothing had really been forthcoming. Lynne and Helen often spoke together in the early 1990s about the need for Jewish and Christian women to meet to share their experiences to make a significant contribution to the Jewish-Christian dialogue and to move beyond the plateau. It was becoming apparent from conferences or dialogue weekends that in the small group sessions which had a predominantly female presence the nature of the dialogue was different. Some of those differences have been touched upon in the section above. The final impetus for setting up our women's group came after Helen and Lynne attended a conference on Jewish-Christian relations in Russia in January 1997, entitled *Theology after Auschwitz and the Gulag and the Relation to Jews and Judaism in the Orthodox Church.*

The conference should be praised as one of the first in Russia to deal with the Holocaust and Jewish-Christian relations. Western scholars were invited to participate because of their experience in Jewish-Christian dialogue; however, Helen was the only official female speaker at the conference and only then at the last minute when, on the evening before his address, a male speaker had to cancel. This reflected just how far the Orthodox Churches need to go in their basic organization of such dialogue conferences. The structure of the conference was clearly patriarchal in the use of extremely long conference tables and was hardly the round-table discussion that was promised. Questions and comments after each paper consisted of a series of extremely lengthy monologues. This confirmed for us the need for a major input into the dialogue of women's voices and experiences. It was directly after that conference that we had our first women's meeting in London, meeting initially at Kent House by kind permission of Mrs Evelyn Friedlander and the late Rabbi Dr Albert Friedlander.

The group comprises eight women who have had formal academic training and who teach and write in the areas of theology, Jewish studies or Jewish-Christian relations. We do not seek to represent our faith on an official level but rather come from a variety of affiliations and denominational backgrounds with diverse life-experiences. Some of us are single, some are married, some have children and some do not, and one is a religious sister. There are women in our group from Roman Catholic, Anglican and Reformed Christian communities and from Reform and Liberal Jewish traditions. We come together as women of faith, interested in enriching our spiritual journeys through the interaction with other women. We do not represent any particular generation, neither do we seek to be representative of Judaism or Christianity, or of Catholicism,

Anglicanism or Progressive Judaism but rather we bring a rich and particular perspective to our own traditions and the Jewish-Christian dialogue in general. It is fair to say that while this group represents an important initiative in filling in the voices of women, there are some voices which are sadly lacking; namely the orthodox and conservatives of both faiths. When the group was first formed, every effort was made to include these women but for a number of reasons, usually because of an already hectic life, they could not commit themselves to the group. It is our hope that future dialogue groups may be more successful in attracting women from a wider range of religious backgrounds. This does not negate our claims that women's voices have something new and different to contribute to the wider dialogue, rather it means that our perspectives are particular and limited and could be further enriched by the inclusion of orthodox voices from both faiths. It in no way lessens the impact of the insights which we have expressed throughout this book.

Content and Methodology

The book has been divided into three main parts: Theology, Scripture, and Spiritual Journey. Each of these areas is central to any Jewish-Christian dialogue. Theology is thinking and talking about God, Scripture is writings revealing God, and Spiritual Journey is experiencing God (including liturgy and prayer). Each of the three parts has a short introduction to contextualize the material in the chapters that follow. In choosing the material for this book, there were two main criteria: first, the material forms part of our experience as women either because it affected us directly on a personal level or it was something that we were working on in our professional capacities; and second, the material represents topics which are central to the wider dialogue between Jews and Christians and we as women, have something unique to offer to the inherited interpretations and traditions. We address a wide range of topics which are indicative of where we are as women and where we see our stories can impact on scholarly interpretation and tradition, most particularly in the genre of narrative. Our methodology often weaves the informed intellectual and academic perspective with personal experiences, described by Lynne in the next chapter as 'situated knowledge'. The weaving of autobiographical and anecdotal material with scholarly research combines styles in a postmodern approach that challenges established ways of doing theology and dialogue. This postmodernism reflects the diversity of contemporary literature, a diversity which women can now bring to the dynamic of Jewish-Christian relations and thereby push forward the boundaries of that dialogue.

Part 1 of the book is Theology and focuses on four of the central areas for any contemporary Jewish-Christian discussion: Epistemology and Dialogue, Feminist Theology, Messiah, and the Holocaust. Theology is about our reflections on the relationship between God, human beings and the natural world. Within the field of theology, and in feminist theology in particular, women have made a major contribution in recent decades to transforming the patriarchal foundations of their traditions in both Christianity and Judaism. It is something that has affected all areas of theological discussion in one way or another and so part of that is reflected in this section. Since we are dialoguing as women, feminist perspectives will impact on our theology at points but we are also dialoguing as Jews and Christians and therefore the discussions will reflect wider theological scholarship and not only be limited to feminist perspectives. Part 2 is on Scripture and the four chapters are Studying Biblical Texts, the Rape of Dinah, Mary Magdalene, and Women Prophets. It highlights important insights which we have learned from the experience of studying a number of biblical texts together. It is often the case that when we hear and study our texts in the presence of 'the other', it challenges, shapes and transforms how we understand the background to our sacred texts and how the interpretations within our respective faiths are very different. Three of the chapters in this section focus on specific women in the Bible. They have been chosen because their voices have been marginalized or silenced by the text itself or by our traditions. Part 3 is about our Spiritual Journeys. The four topics discussed here are Life Cycles, the Eucharist, Prayer, and Pilgrimage. They reflect the significant religious elements that define our lives as either Jews and Christians on the one hand and women on the other. These chapters reflect how our journeys are transformed by the encounter with 'the other'.

The process that we have adopted as a group has taken the pattern of a Jewish or Christian woman presenting a paper with a dialogue following among the members of the group. Imagine a Monday evening, on a first-floor living room in North London, in a room with comfortable chairs and sofas, surrounded by books, eight women ranging in age from 30 to 80 are gathering. They arrive in ones and twos. After a brief chat over tea, one of the women reads a paper. When she has finished there is usually a period of silence, and one can feel the thoughts buzzing around the very room itself. Then someone will respond or ask a question and thereafter begins a conversation and dialogue that continues for about an hour. Before we finish it is agreed that at the following meeting in a few weeks time, a woman from the other tradition will respond with a full paper on that same topic. The order in which the Jewish and Christian contributions appear within each chapter reflects how they were presented within the group. The ordering of the material in no way reflects any statement on the historical position of one faith in relation to the other nor any superiority of one faith over another. This point is important to us because we are conscious of the history of supersessionism and wish to make clear that no theological point is being made by the order in which the material appears in this book. We have reproduced the papers that were discussed in the group but not the dialogue itself. Some books have tried to reproduce the dialogue or discussion which has followed the main presentation, but we have often found this to be unsuccessful for the reader; primarily because while the dialogue itself might be deemed to be the dynamic of the relationship, it is difficult to re-convey it in a meaningful way on paper. An essential element of the dialogue is in the connection with 'the other', in the meeting of the soul at that moment in time, and therefore on a deep level it cannot easily be transferred to paper.

The results of our dialogue may not always be comfortable, particularly from the Christian side where the challenges seem to be the hardest regarding our liturgy, tradition or about the central figure of Christian faith, Jesus. Nevertheless, the group has been a refuge and resource for women who give so much elsewhere, and who have struggled to make their voices heard in a male-dominated forum. It has been, and continues to be a rich forum for discussion and growth. We have just touched the tip of the iceberg. There is a wealth of experience, textual interpretations and theological reflections that women can offer. Our reason for writing this particular book has been to provide a resource for others who may begin to undertake similar dialogue. Our book makes an important, hitherto undocumented, contribution to the beginnings of the women's Jewish-Christian dialogue as well as having something to say on Jewish-Christian relations in general. The next step is to encourage the formation of other women's dialogue groups whose experiences and voices can be disseminated to the wider Jewish-Christian dialogue, thus transforming the way in which dialogue is carried out. There is much work to be done to fill the half-empty bookcase.

Background Introductory Reading

See the Bibliography section for full details of these titles.

Daniel Boyarin, *Border Lines: The Partition of Judaeo-Christianity.*
Marcus Braybrooke, *Time to Meet: Towards a Deeper Relationship between Jews and Christians.*
James Dunn, *The Partings of the Ways Between Christianity and Judaism and their Significance for the Character of Christianity.*
Paula Fredriksen and Adele Reinhartz (eds), *Jesus, Judaism and Christian Anti-Judaism: Reading the New Testament after the Holocaust.*
Helen P. Fry, *Christian-Jewish Dialogue: A Reader.*
Marcel Simon, *Verus Israel.*

Part 1: Theology

Introduction

The first part of the book focuses on Theology and Jewish-Christian relations and is set against the background of, first, the sweeping changes which have been made by the churches in their teaching and preaching about Judaism, and second, the changes that feminist theologians have brought to our respective faiths. We as women come to our group consciously aware of the painful history of the Christian treatment of Jews and of the patriarchal oppression of women in our religious traditions. This dual dynamic to our history affects our dialogue because the transformation that we are bringing about has to relate to the past and to understand that past for us to be able to move effectively towards the future. In this section we are focusing on four theological topics which are central to any women's Jewish-Christian dialogue: Women's Knowledge and Dialogue, Feminist Theology, Messiah, and the Holocaust.

We are painfully aware of how the Church's theology regarding Jews and Judaism has been marked by negative teachings and stereotyping that often led to periods of forced conversions and persecution. Jules Isaac coined the phrase 'the teaching of contempt' for this. Jews were accused of deicide (that they were responsible for the death of Christ and in so doing were guilty of killing God), and there was also the Blood Libel where they were accused of killing Christian children at Passover time and using their blood to make matzah (unleavened bread). It was also believed that Jews bear the mark of Cain and that they were destined to wander the earth, like Cain, for killing Christ. The Church combined these myths with a theology which argued that Judaism had been superseded by Christianity. Christianity was believed to be the only true religion and Judaism had been rendered obsolete because the Jews had rejected Christ. Periodically,

Christian theology allowed for limited tolerance and Jewish survival because Jews were an essential part of the events of the End Times, but on the whole the history has been one of persecution. The Holocaust in the twentieth century resulted in the annihilation of six million Jews in the heart of Christian Europe. No contemporary theology, including the women's dialogue, can be carried out without turning its face to the Holocaust and an awareness that new forms of anti-Judaism once again threaten the image of Judaism in Christian teaching and preaching. In the twentieth century, major changes have been made in Church teachings; however, a new form of anti-Judaism has emerged which blames Judaism for patriarchy and the oppression of women.

During the time that we have been meeting in our women's group, a number of significant documents have been issued by the Churches on Jewish-Christian relations, including the *Alexandria Document* on peace in the Middle East, *We Remember: A Reflection on the Shoah* issued by the Roman Catholic Church, and the *Leuenberg Document* produced by the Reformed Churches. It has, however, not been all one-sided. In September 2000, hundreds of Jewish leaders and scholars world-wide signed a document, *Dabru Emet*, meaning 'speak truth' (Zech. 8.16), in which they laid out an eight-paragraph statement on Jewish thinking about Christians and Christianity. This was further explored in a book entitled *Christianity in Jewish Terms*, which marked an important step forward in formulating a Jewish theology of Christianity, something which we speak about in more detail in the final chapter. The four chapters in this part are written against the background of these significant changes. In the first chapter on Dialogue, Helen looks at the background to the Jewish-Christian feminist dialogue on the one hand and the dialogue on wider theological issues between Jewish and Christian women on the other. She outlines the historically significant results of the feminist Jewish-Christian dialogue which raised the consciousness of Christian feminists to a potent form of anti-Judaism that was emerging in their feminist theologies, centred around ideas of Jesus as the great liberator of women in direct contrast to the Judaism of the day. In the second half of this chapter, Lynne focuses on the theoretical foundations for women's epistemology (knowledge) and dialogue. She explores some of the ways in which women 'know' and how that epistemology is different from male-centred knowledge. She explains how the voices of women can make a distinctive contribution to the wider dialogue in both its content and methodology. This provides the context and foundations for the chapters which follow in this book.

Chapter 2 on Feminist Theology provides a Jewish and Christian understanding of the feminist dimension to the dialogue. It explicitly explores the significance of the work of Jewish and Christian feminist theologians on our traditions and addresses questions such as: how do we understand feminist theology? What is distinctive about the feminist dimension to faith experience and to Jewish-Christian relations in particular? Rachel and Lynne explore particular issues that touch at the heart of the feminist debate; such as leadership, ordination, language in prayer and liturgy. Chapter 3 on Messiah is pivotal for any discussion between Jews and Christians precisely because it is the key issue which divides our faiths. The concept of messiah is a shared one and yet there are such divergent interpretations of the same language. Helen begins by outlining concepts of messiah in the period up to the first century CE and argues that Jesus did not fulfil Jewish messianic expectations at that time and that, whatever his significance, it must be located elsewhere. She then looks at the issue of messiah and gender, something which has relevance to her experience as a woman of faith in the twenty-first century. In response, Rachel explains why it is difficult for Jews to accept the traditional Christian interpretation of the messiah and why Jesus was not the messiah of Jewish expectation. She also looks at how messianic expectations are meaningful for her as a Jewish woman.

No contemporary theological discussion can be carried out without reference to the Holocaust. The impact of the annihilation of a third of world Jewry within the heart of Christian Europe in the twentieth century continues, quite rightly, to be felt in Jewish-Christian dialogue. The lessons of the Holocaust cannot be marginalized and continue to bring forth new challenges to our understanding of faith and God. Chapter 4 of this section is on the Holocaust and provides reflections by a Catholic educator, Lynne, and two Jewish educators, Anne and Irene, on education and remembering the Holocaust. They explore the context of the Holocaust for reflecting together as Jews and Christians and show that this is an area which directly affects how we teach our traditions. They share their reflections on their visit to the Holocaust Exhibition at the Imperial War Museum in London. For them, understanding the Holocaust as 'a text' raises a number of important points about how experiences and stories are heard and their role in education.

Our voices, then, as women are contributing to the ongoing theological dialogue between Jews and Christians and one that is necessary as Jews and Christians work towards greater understanding and reconciliation.

1 Dialogue

Their words [the words of women] will have the same authority as the Scriptures.

Mahatma Gandhi

I Women's Voices and Jewish-Christian Dialogue

Helen P. Fry

While women have been, and continue to be, active in improving Jewish-Christian relations, it is fair to say that their voices as women have rarely been heard. Much of the structures and theology of the dialogue have been centred on the male experience, and while this does not invalidate the enormous advances and changes that have occurred, particularly regarding Christian teaching on Judaism, it means that women's voices are missing. It is essential that women contribute their experiences *as women* to push the boundaries of the dialogue. In the first part of this chapter, I will focus on two aspects of the women's dialogue: first, the raison d'être for the women's dialogue, and second, the dialogue between Jewish and Christian feminists. This second part looks at anti-Judaism in Christian feminist theology because although this has been addressed in detail elsewhere, it is still emerging in feminist writings, including those by some prominent Christian feminist theologians. For this reason, we as a group felt it to be important enough to include here to continue to raise awareness of such anti-Judaism.

The genre of the women's dialogue is very different from that of the wider Jewish-Christian dialogue in its use of story as the mode for sharing their experiences and spiritual journey. The dialogue has enabled women to shape their own spirituality and affirm their identity within a new context. Judith Plaskow, a Jewish feminist, has expressed this succinctly: 'Through the telling of my story, I reach out to other women. Through

[13]

their hearing, which both affirms my story and makes it possible, they reach out to me.'[1] The very process of story-telling has affected the way in which women express their identity. Such a mode of dialogue has been initiated solely from the women's experience, termed *situated knowledge*, and it is in this respect that it differs from the dynamics of the wider Jewish-Christian dialogue. It is a process that is as important as the feminists sharing their emerging theologies. In the United Reformed Church I have had no need to fight to express my spirituality as a woman. My tradition was one of the first to ordain women and this has always been an option for me if I felt such a calling. Also, I have never felt excluded by the male language of the prayers and liturgy, although I do feel the use of 'men' to mean 'humankind' exclusive and outdated. Language is a limited tool and as such I do not have a problem with male images of God. My spirituality is defined by who I am in relation to God and my life-experiences which for me transcend gender. Nevertheless, it would be fair to say that my mode of dialoguing seems naturally to be one of weaving my personal experiences with theological reflection and this, feminists would argue, is precisely the women's way of 'doing dialogue' and is a key element, which on the whole has been absent in the wider Jewish-Christian dialogue thus far.

There are a number of areas where women's voices could fruitfully contribute to the Jewish-Christian dialogue, including the following: prayer, education, tradition, family, Christology, redemption, the nature of God after the Holocaust, the importance of symbols, the impact of secularism on religious observance, and liturgy.[2] The area of joint textual study is a particularly enriching and popular one, as reflected in the high numbers of people who attend such studies. Another area where the voices of women need to be heard is in the reshaping of theology after the Holocaust.[3] What are their responses to the penetrating religious question: 'Where was God in Auschwitz?' Women survivors of the Holocaust have given their testimonies and in this sense their voices have been heard;

1 Judith Plaskow, 1992, 'The Coming of Lilith', in Carol Christ and Judith Plaskow (eds), *Womenspirit Rising: A Feminist Reader in Religion*, London: Harper Collins, p. 199.

2 See also Helen P. Fry, 1999, 'The Future of Christian-Jewish Relations', in Dan Cohn-Sherbok (ed.), *The Future of Jewish-Christian Dialogue*, Lewiston: Edwin Mellen Press, p. 81–96.

3 For a challenging discussion of the Holocaust and Jewish feminism see Melissa Raphael, 1999, 'When God Beheld God', in *Feminist Theology*, vol. 21.

however, on the wider scene few Jewish and Christian women have provided theological reflections on their belief in God after Auschwitz. Could this be because there is nothing new to be said theologically?[4] This is an inadequate assumption precisely because the women's way of storying is different and therefore may provide new insights into theology and spirituality after Auschwitz. Another area for the dialogue includes discussing the impact of secularism on religious observance. Women are often the transmitters of faith and so it is particularly relevant to ask whether in the shaping of our traditions our religious observance should be shaped by the secular world around us. How far should we embrace the secular world, but equally can our religious observance allow for secular freedom? This is particularly relevant in a world where religious fundamentalism has reached a new level of fanaticism and terror.

There has been little dialogue between Jewish and Christian women thus far on issues beyond the feminist debate and this is something which now needs to be addressed. So far the dialogue that has taken place has, on the whole, tended to be between feminists of both faiths and mainly focused in the USA and Germany since the early 1980s.[5] It has also been largely undertaken by liberal Jews and Christians rather than orthodox or conservative women. However, the result of that dialogue has had far-reaching implications for the emerging Christian feminist theology by highlighting the often subtle forms of anti-Judaism within it, particularly vis-à-vis its claims for Jesus. The dialogue has also provided space for feminists of both faiths to empathize with each other in their struggle for change against the patriarchal structures of their traditions and in the development of their own identity.[6] In terms of our dialogue group,

---

4 Have most human responses been developed in this respect – from the death of God theology of Richard Rubenstein to the suffering God imagery of Marcus Braybrooke and Elie Wiesel?

5 See Marie-Theres Wacker, 1991, 'Feminist Theology and Anti-Judaism: The Status of the Discussion and Context of the Problem in the Federal Republic of Germany', in *Journal of Feminist Studies in Religion*, vol. 7, no. 2, p. 109–16; Leonore Siegele-Wenschkewitz, 1991, 'The Discussion of Anti-Judaism in Feminist Theology: A New Area of Jewish-Christian Dialogue', in *Journal of Feminist Studies in Religion*, vol. 7, no. 2, p. 95–9; and Katharina von Kellenbach, 1994, *Anti-Judaism in Feminist Religious Writings*, Atlanta: Scholars Press, p. 32–7.

6 See for example Deborah McCauley and Annette Daum, 1983, 'Jewish-Christian Feminist Dialogue: A Wholistic Vision', in *Union Seminary Quarterly Review*, vol. 38; Judith Plaskow and Carol Christ (eds), 1989, *Weaving the Visions: Patterns in Feminist Spirituality*, London: Harper Collins.

anti-Judaism in our theology has not been a problem with which we have had to deal among ourselves because we have all come to the dialogue already aware of much of the traditional Christian stereotyping of Jews and Judaism.[7] However, it is a reality for many of us in our work and something that we have had to address in that context and for that reason it is something that our group has discussed.

In the dialogue, Jewish feminists have challenged Christian feminists in two main areas relating to new forms of anti-Judaism:[8] first in Christian feminist claims that Judaism killed the goddess religion and is responsible for patriarchy; and second in their proclamation of Jesus as the great liberator of women in contrast to the Judaism of his day. The first claim that Judaism has been blamed for patriarchy or 'male monotheism' creates another scapegoat from Judaism for all the negative images associated with patriarchy: images of oppression, militarism, sexism, violence and slavery.[9] This ignores the influences on Christianity itself of the surrounding patriarchal, polytheistic cultures of the Graeco-Roman world. The Christian theologian Rosemary Radford Ruether, for example, has argued that sexism, exclusivism and the subjugation of women is rooted in the dualistic and hierarchical thought inherited from the classical world rather than from Jewish patriarchy. This is not to deny that Jewish feminists have also been struggling, and continue to struggle, with patriarchy. They too have suffered marginalization which has restricted their public religious role; however, the difficulty arises when Christian feminists have blamed Judaism for the root of all patriarchy.

The male God of the Hebrew Bible has been seen as merciless, brutal, intolerant, and the destroyer of the goddess religion, in contrast to the God

---

7 We are aware of how the New Testament is still used to re-enforce myths and stereotypes about Judaism in spite of changes in Church teaching, particularly regarding the Pharisees. There is still a tendency to assert the superiority of Christianity over Judaism by casting first-century Judaism in negative terms, whether in relation to the Pharisees or to Jesus' position on women.

8 Katharina von Kellenbach, 1994, *Anti-Judaism*; Rachel Montagu, 1996, 'Anti-Judaism in Christian Feminist Theology', in Jonathan Romain (ed.), *Renewing the Vision: Rabbis Speak out on Modern Jewish Issues*, London: SCM Press; Judith Plaskow, 1991, 'Feminist Anti-Judaism and the Christian God', in *Journal of Feminist Studies in Religion*, vol. 7, no. 2; and Asphodel Long, 1991, 'Anti-Judaism in Britain', in *Journal of Feminist Studies in Religion*, vol. 7, no. 2, p. 125–33.

9 Katharina von Kellenbach, 1994, *Anti-Judaism*, p. 107–13. See also Rosemary Radford Ruether, 1987, 'Feminism and the Jewish-Christian Dialogue', in John Hick (ed.), *The Myth of Christian Uniqueness*, London: SCM Press.

of love and compassion of the New Testament.[10] This is a long-standing anti-Jewish image of the Hebrew Bible and Judaism, which surprisingly and unexpectedly emerged in Christian feminist theology in spite of the assumption that such images had been dealt with adequately in post-Vatican II teaching as well as in other Church documents. Such generalizations have ignored the multiplicity of language used about God in the Hebrew Bible, such as the images of God as forgiving, loving and compassionate. It also ignores the feminine language and imagery, for example, God hovering over us like a mother hen.[11] Interestingly, within the biblical tradition there is a lack of any polemic against the goddess religion *per se* and any critique is usually directed at the male God *Baal*. Prophetic critique is usually directed against idolatry in general, whether male or female, irrespective of gender and, as Katharina von Kellenbach suggests, this has been overlooked by some Christian feminists. The belief that Judaism was responsible for the death of the goddess (matricide) is an accusation on a par with the charge of deicide and as such represents a dangerous new development within Christian theology. The charge of matricide does not take into account the fact that Christianity waged its own war on paganism, leading to the suppression of female symbolism. Judaism has also been portrayed by Christian feminists as the prologue to Christianity and this again reiterated centuries of anti-Jewish, supersessionist theology which fails to accept the continuing existence and particularity of Judaism without conversion to Christianity. Many of the above critiques, which were first raised by Jewish feminists, have now been addressed by Christian feminists, although much of their work has yet to filter to students and preachers. Such anti-Jewish claims continue to find their way into Christian scholarship and popular religious writings.

The second area of anti-Judaism is in Christian claims about Jesus. Christian feminists have re-claimed the Jesus of history as the champion of their cause, seeing him as a feminist and therefore arguing that the historical figure challenged the Judaism of his day regarding the status of women. This is the area where it has been harder to shake off assumptions that Jesus liberated the women in the first century CE. Such claims were found in the early writings of the influential Christian feminist writer

---

10 Katharina von Kellenbach, 1994, *Anti-Judaism*, p. 97–106.

11 See Nehama Aschkenasy, 1994, *Eve's Journey: Feminine Images in Hebraic Literary Tradition*, Detroit: Wayne State University Press, as one example of Jewish literature which studies feminine language in biblical tradition.

Elisabeth Schüssler Fiorenza, for example,[12] and have found their way into popular preaching and teaching. Since the early 1980s, regarding Jesus and feminism, there has been an over-reliance on the New Testament scholar Ben Witherington III whose work overtly argues that Jesus freed women from the confines of an oppressive and patriarchal Judaism. Many of his assumptions have now been seriously challenged by a number of Jewish and Christian feminists;[13] nevertheless, an undercurrent of anti-Judaism does remain in the essays of theology students, in some feminist studies and in many sermons preached from the pulpit on a Sunday. The difficulty lies in the way that some Christian feminists have quoted a series of Talmudic texts to back up their claim that the Judaism of Jesus' day denigrated women. Jewish feminists are quick to respond that these passages may date anywhere from before the time of Jesus to five centuries later. Such polemical use of rabbinic literature to document Jesus' feminism shows no serious study of recent research on the context of Jesus' ministry or that of the emerging Rabbinic Judaism of the first century CE. The Talmud should be more appropriately compared with the Church Fathers rather than the sayings of Jesus. Rabbinic literature is as varied as the New Testament in its comments about women and its legal treatment of women's issues.[14] Jewish feminists have highlighted the often subtle anti-Judaism in such thinking where claims were based on affirming the uniqueness of Jesus by portraying first-century Judaism in unambiguously negative terms. Judith Plaskow has argued that rather than affirming the Jewishness of Jesus, Christian feminists have removed Jesus from the context of first-century Judaism and, whatever Jesus' view of women, it remains an option within Judaism rather than a radical departure from it.[15] Yet the Christian feminist movement continues to feel the need to root the liberation of women in the life of Jesus – something which is highly debatable from a historical perspective. As a group, we have discovered that it may be more helpful to root the liberation of women in the lives of women in the Bible rather than in Jesus himself. This is reflected in what

---

12 Schüssler Fiorenza's theology has now taken on board these critiques. See Elisabeth Schüssler Fiorenza, 1994, *Jesus. Miriam's Child, Sophia's Prophet: Critical Issues in Feminist Christology*, London: SCM Press.

13 The work of Amy-Jill Levine and Katharina von Kellenbach are just two examples of excellent scholarship in this respect.

14 Judith R. Wegner, 1988, *Chattel or Person? The Status of Women in the Mishnah*, Oxford: Oxford University Press.

15 Judith Plaskow, 1991, 'Feminist Anti-Judaism', p. 105.

has been written by women of our group in Chapters 7 and 8 on Mary Magdalene and women prophets, respectively.

I wish to cite two examples of the typical stereotypes that are emerging about Jesus and women which remain highly problematic. The first example is from a sermon that I heard in which the preacher stated that Jesus liberated women to pray for the first time. This seems to be a widespread popular assumption which has gone unchallenged and such a claim ignores biblical passages such as the story of Hannah praying in the Temple. Such statements about Jesus liberating women seem to ignore the obvious lack of evidence in the Gospels because nowhere does Jesus overtly challenge the patriarchal structures of first-century Judaism. Patriarchy was a product of the cultural world of the Ancient Near East rather than instituted by Judaism.[16] The second example comes from a letter written in a provincial newspaper in support of the ordination of women. The relevant part says this:

> The most popular argument [for non-ordination of women] is that Jesus did not have a woman disciple. First, it must be remembered that Jesus and his disciples were afoot in Palestine at a time when, if a woman even so much as thought about joining a bunch of itinerant preachers, she would probably have been stoned to death. Things in twenty-first-century England are a little more liberated.[17]

Such an assertion about the status of women in first-century Judaism is factually inaccurate and needs to be challenged wherever it appears. The problem is that such anti-Jewish stereotypes have now been transferred to the mind-set of the readers of that newspaper. I asked the people whom I was with at the time about this passage, but nothing struck them as particularly difficult about it and they had assumed that it was accurate. This is cause for concern because there is a tendency for Christians to feel an often unconscious superiority over Jewish faith that allows such

---

16 See Rachel Montagu, 2000, 'Women, Prayer and Ritual in the Bible', in Sylvia Rothschild and Sybil Sheridan (eds), *Taking up the Timbrel: The Challenge of Creating Ritual for Jewish Women Today*, London: SCM Press; and a number of chapters on the historical status of women and prayer within Judaism in Susan Grossman and Rivka Haut (eds), 1992, *Daughters of the King: Women and the Synagogue*, Philadelphia: The Jewish Publication Society, p. 15–83.

17 *The North Devon Journal*, 13 December 2001, p. 44, letter entitled 'What is so wrong with women clergy?'.

statements to go unchecked. This misinformation once again asserts the traditional superiority of Christianity over 'a misogynous, oppressive Judaism' – a picture that is clearly inaccurate and dangerous. The acceptance of such statements, as cited in the sermon or the above newspaper letter, is linked to belief in the uniqueness and even perfection of Jesus. An important question needs to be addressed here and should be on the agenda of the women's dialogue. It is a question that Judith Plaskow first raised: must Jesus always be unique and contrasted with the Judaism of his day for Christianity to make sense? Christian theologians are keen to affirm the Jewishness of Jesus and therefore whatever his teaching on women, it must represent a position within the diversity of Second Temple Judaism of the first century CE. The large following of women around Jesus may not have been as unusual as is often claimed because it was not extraordinary for itinerant Jewish preachers and healers to draw large crowds which included the presence of women.

For the future, it will only be possible to combat this new form of anti-Judaism by Christian feminists carrying out studies in two key areas: first, in learning about the attitude of the historical Jesus to women;[18] and second, in the awareness of the status of Jewish women in the first century CE and for this latter part we need our Jewish partners in the dialogue. Both aspects, the status of women in first-century Judaism and Jesus' attitude to women, need to be part of a joint study and dialogue programme between Jewish and Christian women; obviously this will assume a certain level of expertise from the women of both traditions. It is usually only in a study-dialogue context that such misinformation is brought to our attention and hence the importance of such studies can not be over-emphasized. The results of the joint study need to be disseminated to our students, clerics and lay people if this undercurrent of anti-Judaism is to be addressed. Because Jewish and Christian feminists have been dialoguing on this for some time now, it is easy to assume that these issues have been dealt with; but there can be no room for complacency in this respect. Christian feminists, then, need to be careful about what claims they make for Jesus and as such these claims need to be explored in dialogue with our Jewish partners to ensure that inaccurate, stereotypical images of Judaism are not being incorporated into our theology. There are Jewish and

---

18 Studies have shown that Jesus did not challenge the patriarchal structures of his day and that New Testament scholarship does not in fact justify a 'feminist' reading of the life and ministry of the historical Jesus.

Christian feminists who are working for a theology of respect – a theology which will always be open to the critical assessment of the other, an approach described by Clark Williamson in another context as *critical solidarity*.[19] The dialogue between Jewish and Christian feminists is essential to the future of Jewish-Christian relations and feminist theology.

It is important then that Jewish and Christian women dialogue, first to combat the anti-Judaism which seems to have reared its head frequently in Christian feminist theology and popular teaching; and second, to meet to discuss a whole range of religious issues. There are too few women engaged in this dialogue and so it is vital that those who are already part of the dialogue share the fruits of their encounter with other women in their communities to encourage their participation. It is essential to bring their insights to the emerging Jewish and Christian theology of the other.

II Women Knowing, Women in Dialogue

Lynne Scholefield

In this part I explore some of the ways in which we women know and some of the characteristics of our conversations which we call 'dialogue'. The sentence I have just written is not very elegant but it makes a number of points that I want to consider further in what follows. It is fairly tentative, referring to 'some ways', 'some characteristics', rather than making more categorical claims. It is firmly situated in our experiences and it refers to dialogue as 'conversation', talk between people. I want to argue that for women, dialogue is a way of knowing that is situated, inter-personal, reflective and transformative and where the outcomes cannot be known in advance. I am committed to the idea of a women's dialogue group because I share with other women the experience that women's ways of understanding the world and acting in it are different from men's ways. I am also aware how under-represented women's voices are in inter-faith dialogue. Helen has outlined the historical background to the women's dialogue and provided an important back-drop to my discussion of women's epistemology (knowing) and dialogue here. This part explores

---

19 Clark Williamson (ed.), 1992, *A Mutual Witness: Towards Critical Solidarity Between Jews and Christians,* St Louis: Chalice Press.

the distinctive contribution which we as women can make to the wider Jewish-Christian dialogue and affirms both the claim of women's difference and problematizes it.

I remember the pleasure I had on discovering that in French there were two different words for 'to know'; *connaître* and *savoir*. It still seems to me that there are significant differences between knowing a person and knowing a fact or an idea but that what both have in common is the person who knows. I am sceptical about absolute claims to knowledge or an over-emphasis on objectivity because they ignore the knowing person. Putting it like this suggests the active nature of knowing and the situatedness of the knower and therefore of the knowledge. This is important to me as a woman because it asserts my presence, my situation, my subjectivity as epistemologically crucial. Carol Gilligan drew attention to the negation of this, experienced by many women, as 'a dissociative split between experience and what is generally taken to be reality'.[20] Supposedly objective males have often made women objects of supposed knowledge in ways that have been harmful to those women such as in medicine or the law or in religions. So it is not surprising that feminist approaches to epistemology, such as Donna Haraway's for example, should stress situated knowing.[21] Neither is it surprising that our knowing should be constructed *against* patriarchal power that denies or limits the subjectivity of women and our active knowing.

Dialogue between women, then, enables knowledge to be constructed in an inter-personal, relational way. We come together as Jewish and Christian women and talk and listen to one another. Perhaps the order should be reversed to put the stress on 'hearing'. Nelle Morton argued that women hear one another into speech and that this is a divine activity but: 'the speech is our speech. It may come on stumblingly or boldly, but it is authentically our own. Through hearing and speaking women sense the possibility of doing theology out of our own experiences.'[22] As we engage in conversation our individual identity matters; we are not representatives of our churches or synagogues, and in the group we are not talking in any

---

20 See Carol Gilligan, 1993, *In a Different Voice*, Cambridge, Mass: Harvard University Press, p. xxi.

21 Donna Haraway, 1991, 'Situated Knowledge: The Science Question in Feminism and the Privilege of Partial Perspective', in Donna Haraway (ed.), *Simians, Cyborgs and Women*, London, Free Association Books.

22 Nelle Morton, 1985, *The Journey Is Home*, Boston: Beacon Press, p. 55.

official capacity. Kate McCarthy has argued that this offers a real opportunity for a new approach, at least by Christians, to dialogue. She wrote:

> When women's experience, diverse and complex as it is, is made the point of departure for theological reflection on religious pluralism, new resources emerge for a theology of religions that can genuinely encounter the otherness of the non-Christian without either subsuming that otherness or sacrificing the specific content that enlivens Christian community.[23]

Our dialogue is a dialogue of people rather than of ideas. Mary Belenky and the others named this as 'connected knowing'.[24] While both men and women are able to engage in this type of knowing, women probably do it far more than men. By saying that I am not, of course, intending to suggest some essentialist nature of 'women'. What we have learned from feminism perhaps more than anything else is to be wary of speaking for each other and minimizing the numerous differences between us in order to celebrate what women share. In some ways we are quite a diverse group and we speak from our particularities. The group is also a particular occasion and I am very aware that this group of women enables me, for example, to act as a Catholic woman in ways that I do not experience anywhere else.

During the time we have been meeting, four of us have been pregnant and have given birth. This has been a forceful reminder of our embodied nature as persons and therefore of the embodied nature of our conversations and our knowing. Haraway called this a feminist form of objectivity in which embodied vision sees the object of knowledge as an active agent. Another way to refer to this is as inter-subjectivity. Martin Buber wrote of dialogue as a subject-subject relationship of openness, directness, mutuality and presence.[25] The presence of the 'other' means that I can both speak and listen to what is new, to what has not been spoken and heard before. One of the main modes of dialoguing as women is 'storying'. What we speak is our story. We weave connections between our individual story,

23 Kate McCarthy, 1996, 'Women's Experience as a Hermeneutical Key to a Christian Theology of Religions', in *Studies in Interreligious Dialogue*, 6 (2), p. 164.

24 Mary F. Belenky *et al.*, 1997, *Women's Ways of Knowing*, New York: Basic Books, p. 112–30.

25 Martin Buber, 1958, 2nd ed., *I and Thou*, Edinburgh: T&T Clark.

our scriptural story and our community's story. When we tell our stories, we proclaim identity and make meanings of our experience. Carol Witherell and Nel Noddings in the Prologue to their book *Stories Lives Tell*, wrote:

> Like many writers on narrative, we acknowledge the central role that narrative structure plays in the formation of the self and in the construction, transmission and transformation of cultures.[26]

Here I affirm the feminist view that the identities we proclaim and the meanings we make are constructed against patriarchal power structures and as a result our stories often make visible the power structures that exist. Our stories may threaten the power of those whom the structures privilege, and so these stories, and we ourselves, may be fiercely opposed if not suppressed.[27] Stories are also powerful because they are necessarily *particular*, and it is this particularity that is expressed in this book. They remind us of who we are and the meanings we make are precisely located in space and time and therefore partial. We have to spell out our identity and to do so, we tell stories. The effects of the telling of our stories, and in turn their hearing the story, means that stories of both women are transformed. This seems to me to be both the claim of feminist writing and the point of dialogue.[28]

We tell stories about our own lives and also use stories to make sense of our lives, termed *narrative theology* in Christian theology – a hermeneutical approach where meaning is only achieved when the individual story, the community's story and the scriptural story engage with one another. The ways in which biblical stories, for example, might be transformational for women as part of Jewish-Christian dialogue is discussed in Part 2 of

---

26 See Carol Witherell and Nel Noddings, 1991, 'Prologue – An Invitation to Our Readers', in Carol Witherell and Nel Noddings (eds), *Stories Lives Tell*, New York: Teachers College Press, p. 3. Barbara Meyerhoff, on the final page of her innovative study of a centre of elderly Jews, refers to *homo narrans*, humankind, as story-teller. See B. Meyerhoff, 1978, *Number Our Days*, New York: E. P. Dutton.

27 This suppression can sometimes be found within the wider Jewish-Christian dialogue where women's voices make uncomfortable challenges to the existing structures and established ways of doing dialogue.

28 See for example Ruth Linden, 1993, *Making Stories, Making Selves*, Columbus: Ohio State Press; and Ruth Behar and Deborah Gordon, 1995, *Women Writing Culture*, Berkeley: University of California Press.

this book. Every time we tell our story there is a performance of our identity. A similar parallel in the Jewish tradition would be the Passover seder (meal) when the community's story is retold and performed and thereby becomes part of an individual's identity. For Christians, the Eucharist is a re-enactment of the Jesus story and one which becomes part of one's own identity.[29] It is interesting that for me the most concentrated performance that I give as a Christian is here in the women's dialogue group. The presence of both Jewish and Christian women both impels and empowers me into telling stories in which I am a Christian woman. In this way, my identity is created, transformed and communicated. Just as there are many ways of being a Christian, so there are many ways of being a woman, or rather, my identity is not a matter of 'being' at all. There is nothing existentialist going on. Judith Butler argues persuasively that the essentialist notion of woman is doubly problematic. It ignores the very different experiences of women who are poor, black, lesbian, handicapped, old and in this context Jewish or Christian. Even more interesting is the way in which she claims subject and gender are assumed to be fixed and existing categories when they are nothing of the sort.[30] The attention to the lived experience of people, as a way of relating to one another and as a way of knowing, is what I meant by claiming at the beginning of this chapter that women's ways of understanding the world and being in it are different from men's ways. That has been my experience of many women-only meetings and it is reinforced by my reading of feminist theory. The potential of this is what Donna Haraway describes as 'a power-charged social relation of "conversation"'.[31]

In the women's dialogue group we hear Jewish and Christian women's voices and experiences. Because women's stories have played so little part in the history and development of Judaism and Christianity it often seems that what we say has not been said before. McCarthy talked about 'hermeneutical audacity' which comes from 'the otherness, the multiple

---

29 See also Judith Butler, 1991, 'Imitation and Gender Insubordination', in D. Fuss (ed.), *Inside Out*, London: Routledge. Susannah Heschel makes a similar point about the performative nature of religious activity in the provocatively titled paper 'Jesus as Theological Transvestite', 1997, in M. Peskowitz and L. Levitt (eds), *Judaism Since Gender*, London: Routledge.

30 See Judith Butler, 1990, *Gender Trouble: Feminism and the Subversion of Identity*, London: Routledge.

31 Donna Haraway, 1991, 'Situated Knowledge'.

social location and the embodied spirituality of women's experience'.[32] This does not mean that it is unconnected with the traditions from which we come, or unrelated to wider knowledge in the areas which we are exploring with one another. On the contrary, it is part of the particularity of this group that we take learning seriously; we do study and share our understanding and our scholarship with one another. But we do it reflectively, slowly, engaging emotionally, intuitively and imaginatively as well as intellectually; heart, head and gut. This enables us to really talk, based on a 'mutually shared agreement that together you are creating the optimum setting so that half-baked or emergent ideas can grow. Real talk reaches deep into the experience of each participant; it also draws on the analytical abilities of each.'[33] There is a strong sense of co-operative learning between us, rather than competition as to who knows the most. I often come away from the group feeling inspired that encourages me, gives me courage, to name our dialogue as an occasion for the work of God's spirit. And as a result, I think we do open up new knowledge and understanding and the possibility of wisdom. This is a transformative process for us, opening our hearts and minds to one another.

In this group we women have both the freedom and the responsibility to speak for ourselves and in the process we also speak as Jews and as Christians. In a way we are spokespeople for Judaism and Christianity in a way that rarely, if ever, happens in most forms of Jewish-Christian dialogue which takes place largely between men. It is also a transformative process because what I learn from the conversations, the dialogue, makes a difference to the way I can be a Christian. For example I find much of the Catholic Easter service very difficult to respond to warmly because of the way it presents a Christological reading of the Old Testament as if this were the only way to understand these passages and ignores the wealth of biblical understanding I have begun to see through studying texts in the group. As I have listened and responded to conversation about aspects of Jewish life I have realized much more the Jewishness of Jesus and his friends. Is this a one-way process? It is a question that I would like to pose to the Jewish women. Is your understanding of being a Jew transformed in any way by dialogue with us Christians? These conversations can also be risky. We do not know where they will lead or what the consequences for

---

32 K. McCarthy, 1996, 'Women's Experience', p. 168.
33 Mary F. Belenky *et al.*, 1997, *Women's Ways of Knowing*, p. 144.

us will be. As our group has developed we have become braver about asking questions such as the one in the previous paragraph. I really do not know what your answer will be and this seems to me to be a final characteristic of women knowing and in dialogue. There is no knowing in advance how we will change as we come to know.

I will end by saying something about the ways in which I have been challenged by this group and the knowing we women have ... what – made, birthed, engendered, created, spoken, spelled, spun? I am intrigued by the similarity between talking about knowledge being the result of a 'power-charged social relation of conversation'[34] and the creation story in Genesis where God speaks and it is so. Does the idea of us being co-creators with God come in here? I feel privileged to have spent time in the group reflecting at depth about some of the most important things in our lives. I am affirmed by everyone's patience and attention while I have struggled to become aware of something and find the words to explain.

Further Reading

See the Bibliography section for full details on these titles.

Mary C. Boys, *Has God Only One Blessing?*
Helen. P. Fry, *Christian-Jewish Dialogue: A Reader*, Chapter 9.
Carol Gilligan, *In a Different Voice.*
Katherina von Kellenbach, *Anti-Judaism in Feminist Religious Writings.*
Edward Kessler *et al.* (eds), *Jews and Christians in Conversation: Crossing Cultures and Generations.*
Judith Plaskow and Carol Christ (eds), *Weaving the Visions: Patterns in Feminist Spirituality.*

---

34 Donna Haraway, 1991, 'Situated Knowledge'.

2 Feminist Theology

Say unto wisdom, 'You are my sister'.

Proverbs 7.4

I Feminist Theology and Jewish Tradition

Rachel Montagu

What is feminist theology? What is theology? In a Jewish context this is a serious question. Judith Plaskow says that 'the right question is theological';[1] while the first serious Jewish feminist studies were often focused on issues of *halachah*, Jewish law, Plaskow says that one has to look at the framework of meaning behind the *halachah* to make sense of these issues – and that is theology. Nevertheless, theology is a word which Jews habitually hold at arm's length, not quite sure whether it applies to them. Louis Jacobs, the Jewish scholar and founder of the Masorti movement, spends the first chapter of his book *A Jewish Theology* justifying doing theology in a Jewish context.[2] He succeeds of course but Christian theologians do not have to do this because theology is taken for granted as a Christian religious activity.

Judith Plaskow calls her book on feminist theology *Standing Again at Sinai* to show that whereas we have always assumed that the Torah was given to the whole Jewish people and that receiving it was one of the great covenantal moments in Jewish life, Exodus 19.15 makes clear that some recipients of the Torah are more equal than others. 'Be ready for the third

---

1 Judith Plaskow, 1982, 'The Right Question is Theological', in Susannah Heschel (ed.), *On Being a Jewish Feminist: A Reader*, New York: Schocken Books, p. 223–33.

2 Louis Jacobs, 1973, *A Jewish Theology*, London: Darton, Longman & Todd.

day. Do not go near a woman.' This does not mean 'women, don't talk to your female friends'. It means 'men and women should not have sex with each other in the next three days so that men are not impure after an emission of semen at the moment of hearing the commandments' (Lev. 15.16–18); but that is not what it says. So the language of Exodus makes the moment of receiving the Torah, which we might call a seminal moment in Jewish tradition, a moment where that which is 'seminal' is all too much the issue: women's experience is silenced and male experience described as if it described all. This bias can be seen throughout many of the stories of the Bible. Many women remain strangely nameless: Mrs Lot, Mrs Noah, Mrs Manoah, and the woman who lived in Endor, where the original Hebrew text says 'woman'. The word 'witch', which appears in many translations, reveals prejudice infusing translation and shows how often women have been described pejoratively without protest. At our meetings we have read many wonderful *midrash* (rabbinic exegesis) which show amazing sensitivity to women's perspective and to the meaning of the biblical stories about women. However, the rabbis were men and most, although definitely not all, of their discussions were men only. 'Rabbi' means having a minimum competence in, and access to, rabbinic litera-ture. When preparing sources for a talk on women in the Talmud, I was surprised to realize that I felt excluded from the material I was researching in a way that I never have when looking for sources on medical ethics or *kashrut* (food laws). The rabbinic sources on women were about me and provided more for my welfare than the biblical legislation,[3] but I could not feel myself to be in a continuous tradition to them. I could not feel that they were by my spiritual ancestors even if they were by my distant fathers. It does not matter whether the rabbis describe women as the 'daughter of the king' or as gossips who distract men from their prayers; the significant thing is that in *halachic* literature women are described by the rabbis rather than defining themselves. A feminist world-view is one where the landscape seen by a woman is a valid perspective and women are not seen as merely the equivalents or the adjuncts of men. The Progressive Women Rabbis called their series of conferences *The Half-Empty Bookcase* because they wanted to state that Jewish literature, as we have it, is written by men and so while we have plenty to read, we do not yet have the other half of

---

3 For instance, the Bible permits a husband to send away at will a wife who displeases him (Deut. 25.1–4) but the rabbis introduced safeguards for women like alimony pay-ments and delays to the divorce process in the hope that there would be a reconciliation.

the library – the books which women would have written and will write on these issues. So a feminist perspective on Judaism or Christianity would start from the belief that women's experiences are significant and need to be explicitly and particularly addressed; it is not sufficient to assume that a tradition developed mostly by men adequately covers women's religious life too. Lawrence Hoffman's book, *Covenant of Blood*, describes how Judaism developed as a religion in which men's experiences are central, focusing on circumcision, which is a key rite of Jewish life and a symbol of the covenant between God and the Jewish people.[4] While women were originally present at their son's circumcision, they were gradually marginalized from the ceremony. It is a tribute to the passionate involvement of Jewish women in Jewish ritual and spiritual life that no one actually believes that women are not part of the covenant community of Judaism. Rachel Adler goes so far as to ask, 'are women Jews?';[5] but centuries of Jewish women have taken for granted that they are part of the Jewish community and that they as individuals, as women, are part of God's covenant.

The assumed male gender of God plays its part in the way relationship with God becomes a male business. God, Torah, Israel, the key nouns of Jewish existence, are linked to the three key verbs of Jewish religion, creation, revelation and redemption. The Torah becomes the symbolic female link between God who is male and Israel who is male. We can quote those places in the Bible where women are active in the process of creation and redemption: for example, Eve saying 'I have acquired a man with the Eternal'; Ruth and Naomi assertively encouraging Boaz to redeem Ruth rather than waiting passively; and Miriam's role in the Exodus – but the male experience takes centre stage in revelation and redemption. The relationship between God and the covenant people is often seen as a friendship between chaps, patterned on the relationship between God and Moses who led the people to redemption from Egypt, and re-enacting the revelation at Mount Sinai by studying the Torah has often, though not invariably, been a club for men only.

Women are now saying that their experience of religion also needs to be

---

4 Lawrence A. Hoffman, 1996, *Covenant of Blood: Circumcision and Gender in Rabbinic Judaism*, Chicago: University of Chicago Press.

5 Rachel Adler, 1982, 'The Jew Who Wasn't There: Halakhah and the Jewish Woman', in Susannah Heschel (ed.), *On Being a Jewish Feminist: A Reader*, New York: Schocken Books.

explicitly included in the way we describe religion. Why does this process need to be named 'feminist'? Why is it not enough to say that these days there is more interest in women's issues? Judith Plaskow writes:

> Feminism is a process of coming to affirm ourselves as women/persons and seeing that affirmation mirrored in religious and social institutions. As women began to share with each other our pain as women, we start to see the systematic ways in which social ideologies and institutions have kept us from ourselves. Only when those who have had the power of naming stolen from us find our voices and begin to speak will Judaism become a religion that includes all Jews.

We cannot take for granted that we have an equal voice because for so long tradition declared our voices out of bounds and then began to listen to us, provided we sang the same tune as men, even if at a higher pitch.[6] We need to find our own voices and then to learn how to use them and then decide what we will use them for. This is a specifically feminist project and we have to be ready to name it as such. For instance the European Society for Women in Theological Research did not use the word 'feminist' in its title because for many of the women involved, the explicit use of the f-word would have been too controversial in the institutions in which they did their theological research. Because the world-view of women has not been given equal priority during the centuries of Jewish existence and we have now noticed this, we have to seriously undertake the process of rectifying that imbalance. We have always recognized in our women's group that our process of dialogue is different from that in male or mixed dialogue groups, something which Lynne has addressed in the previous chapter.

One hundred and fifty years ago women in this country did not have the vote and had only limited educational opportunities. Throughout Jewish history Jewish women's opportunities for a good Jewish education, as distinct from a basic ability to read Hebrew and practise Jewish observances, would have been very limited, unless they came from a scholarly family and were able to learn at home, just as Beruriah, wife and daughter of

---

6 See Lavinia Byrne, 2001, *The Journey is My Home*, London: Hodder & Stoughton. She speaks about the early days of ordination within the Anglican Church when women had to dress and act like men to be included in the male discourse. Now such women are finding their own voices and telling their own stories, sharing power (with men) rather than exercising power over, above and against them (p. 180f). She says that 'the role of priest is being feminized'.

distinguished rabbis or Ima Shalom, wife, daughter and sister of distinguished rabbis, did in the Talmudic period. Their demands of Judaism, their analysis of Judaism would therefore have been very different from ours.

With Ima Shalom and Beruriah, we can see that their menfolk respected their wisdom – because the learned remarks they made at home have entered the public domain and been quoted in Jewish literature, and this can only be because their male relatives quoted them publicly. But the exclusion of most women from the world of learning means that women were barred from one of the main sources of spiritual passion in Judaism: delight in study. The extraordinarily aggressive reaction sometimes shown by Jewish men today to the idea of women learning as they do, making religious decisions as they do, expressing their love of study by dancing with the scrolls containing God's revealed Torah on *Simchat Torah*[7] as they do, this surely shows a defensiveness, a jealousy about sharing their love for God's teaching with women that is disturbing in its implications.

One of the strengths of Judaism is the way in which over the centuries it has responded to the shifts in world-view in the surrounding culture. Within Judaism, the refusal to engage with the outside world and its values is regarded as a strength by those Orthodox Jews who wish to distance themselves from non-Jewish influence but as an aberration by the rest of the Jewish world.[8] If we learn at school and university to read texts critically and to analyze the position of women and the ways in which women are treated, we will not ignore those mental habits while we practise our religion. That intellectual training will have made us what we are too much for us to be able to switch it off at will. Should we not take our strongest selves to our religious life, not a truncated version of the mind we use for the rest of our lives? A creative synthesis between Judaism and feminism will have to be found if women who have learnt to recognize gender discrimination as morally wrong, never mind not politically correct, are to remain Jews and the need to make such a synthesis will also spill over into dialogue.

---

7 On *Simchat Torah*, the festival called Rejoicing of the Torah, the cycle of reading from the Pentateuch ends and at once begins again.

8 Even within the ultra-Orthodox community, the need for a creative response to the difficulties caused by marriages between *yeshivah bochurim*, nurtured by Talmud, Talmud and Talmud, with perhaps a little Mishnah, and women educated in contemporary literature and able to speak several European languages led Sarah Shenirer (1883–1935) to create the Beis Yaakov schools so Orthodox girls could have a good Jewish education and share a world-view with their future marriage partners.

One topic of importance is the language we use for both God and the community. The way in which I think of God or address God has changed over time – which I'm sure is the result of some years of using language which would not have been available to me before it occurred to all of us to ask a few basic questions about the implications of traditional god-language. I was reassured to hear Lynne say that recognizing the problems of non-inclusive language was a gradual process for her as it was for me – but it is hard now with the benefit of hindsight to realize why it took me so long. But there are many stages to this process. Using more egalitarian language for the first line of the *Amidah* and saying God of Sarah as well as God of Abraham is something that is now automatic when I pray,[9] but it leaves unchallenged the tough questions as to whether the way the *Amidah* and other important Jewish prayers describe and praise God is the way we would as women, as feminists wish to address God in whose image we are created. By adding the matriarchs we add to the role-models of relationship with God available to us as we pray but do not address whether we are comfortable with the words used to describe God acting in the world or the language of power used in the liturgy.

Written Out of History is the title of a book on the history of Jewish women, pointing out that it is not that women were not there or did not do noteworthy things, it is just that their history was not what anyone thought about when they looked back at Jewish history.[10] We also have to recognize that in some respects, Jewish history has affected our lives differently from Jewish men. The traditional Jewish explanation for the two creation stories with their slightly different descriptions of how men and women came into being is that in Genesis 1 God created Adam and Lilith (Adam's first wife) both equally in God's image, and in Genesis 2 Eve was formed from Adam. When I was first in Jerusalem I was fascinated when I discovered some childbirth amulets protecting against Lilith but then I began to ask why Lilith was a danger to babies. Aviva Cantor suggests that Lilith was the one who wanted to be equal in all ways and whom Adam asked God to replace with someone more obliging, but who became demonized in Jewish tradition at the time of the Exile when Jewish men, newly powerless and aware of non-Jewish contempt for them as

---

9 See my article in Sybil Sheridan (ed.), 1994, *Hear Our Voice: Women Rabbis Tell Their Stories*, London: SCM Press.

10 Sondra Henry and Emily Taitz, 1983, *Written Out of History: Our Jewish Foremothers*, New York: Biblio Press.

defeated, took out their anger on Lilith – the strong woman of their tradition.[11] What can be a worse way to demonize someone when your people's very survival seems to be at risk than saying that she kills babies? And what can be a more powerful way of making wifeliness seem more appropriate than dominating one's husband? So non-Jewish attacks on Jews could lead Jewish men to take out the pain this caused on their wives.

Many of the early books on women's issues in Judaism concentrated on issues of Jewish law because being able to speak with knowledge in this area has long been a hallmark of Jewish scholarly competence and because there were areas of Jewish law which were causing women to suffer or to realize that contemporary reality was treated as an absolute, yet women had in the past participated in observances from which custom now debarred them, such as wearing a *tallit* (prayer shawl). In divorce, men were allowed an initiative and room for manoeuvre denied to their wives who were left as *agunot*, tied women unable to remarry in an Orthodox synagogue.[12] The substantial changes that took place in divorce law once women began to press for change may not have released all *agunot* but do show clearly that Blu Greenberg was right when she said 'when there is a rabbinic will there is always a *halachic*, Jewish legal way'.[13]

For many years one would hear the boast that Judaism had rituals to express all religious events. Then gradually it was noticed that actually mainstream Jewish prayer books covered the male life cycle adequately but offered no ritual for experiences like miscarriage, birth, becoming a mother and menopause which are significant experiences for women. Now Yiddish women's prayer books which did contain prayers for some, if not all, these experiences have been translated and there has been an explosion of liturgical creativity in this area, which is described in greater detail in Chapters 9 and 11.

One of the most contentious issues within both Judaism and Christianity is that of women's leadership or ordination. Does ordination as rabbis matter? It is a recognition and in the Progressive world it would be curious at this point if there were not women rabbis, given that Progressive Jews

11 Aviva Cantor, 1982, 'The Lilith Question', in Susannah Heschel (ed.), *On Being a Jewish Feminist: A Reader*, New York: Schocken Books.

12 See Jack Porter (ed.), 1995, *Women in Chains: A Sourcebook on the Agunah*, New Jersey: Jason Aronson.

13 Blu Greenberg, 1981, *On Women and Judaism*, Philadelphia: Jewish Publication Society.

pride themselves on their egalitarian approach. Reading Rabbi Debra Orenstein's book *Lifecycles*, it is noticeable how a generation of women rabbis have quite simply by their existence changed many assumptions of the American Progressive world.[14] First Liberal and Reform Judaism had women rabbis, then Conservative Judaism and now there are a very few Orthodox women rabbis. It will be interesting to see how long it takes for them to be accepted in the mainstream Orthodox world. It is important to remember that there are Orthodox Jewish feminists as well as Progressive ones. In a TV documentary on women's role in Judaism, Norma Rosen complained that she had expected difficult responses to her feminism from the Orthodox world but found it deeply upsetting when Jewish feminists rejected her because of her Orthodoxy.[15] It is also important to remember that there is a huge gulf between mainstream Orthodoxy and ultra-Orthodoxy. Yet ultra-Orthodox Jews too have changed their position on women's issues in line with changed perspectives in society on women's capacity. The *yoetsot halachah*, women advisors in Jewish law, now being trained in the ultra-Orthodox world to give authoritative advice in areas like marriage and family purity where women have often been shy to consult male rabbis, are benefiting from the feminist challenge to traditional Jewish perceptions on women's role even if they live in a world where feminist ideas are not explicitly part of the mind-set.

Jewish women need to set our own agenda in the feminist process yet we would all acknowledge that Christian feminist theology has been an important stimulus to new areas of thought. Some of the most influential early books on feminism and religion were a shared Jewish-Christian project, for instance Carol Christ's and Judith Plaskow's two anthologies *Womenspirit Rising* and *Weaving the Visions*. When Leo Baeck College graduates were invited to submit essay titles for an anthology celebrating the fortieth anniversary of the College, I was uncomfortable that the editor selected the third of the three titles I offered – anti-Judaism in Christian feminist theology. Of course 'Jesus was a feminist unlike his Jewish contemporaries' and inaccurate assumptions about Jewish purity laws are infuriating and need correcting for all our sakes but I did not want to be seen as attacking in any way the development of feminist theology as such,

---

14 Debra Orenstein and Jane Litman (eds), 1997, *Lifecycles: Jewish Women on Biblical Themes in Contemporary Life*, Vermont: Jewish Lights Publishing.
15 The Channel 4 programme was called *Half the Kingdom: Jewish Feminists Speak.*

merely the anti-Judaism which has on occasion marred Christian feminism. In sharing our very similar experiences within our traditions and therefore coming to understand better what lies behind them, feminism gives an extra dimension to what we are doing as Jewish and Christian women in dialogue.

II Women and Wholeness: An Approach to Christian Feminist Theology

Lynne Scholefield

I believe that the most important and far-reaching social and theological development in the twentieth century was the growing realization and recognition that women were people too. If women are fully human, then this has serious implications for power relations in many different contexts, including within Judaism and Christianity. Feminists have been exploring and making explicit aspects of these power relations especially by drawing attention to areas where women *as women* lose out. They have also analyzed new ways in which women contribute to knowing and understanding the world and other people. In the first part of this chapter, Rachel has shown how Jewish feminists are transforming and challenging patriarchy within Judaism and, as we will see, some of the issues resonate with the work of Christian feminist theologians particularly in the areas of biblical scholarship, leadership roles, and gender-inclusive language. In my response, I will outline some of the key areas of Christian feminist theology that address what it means within Christianity to take seriously women's full humanity. This has involved exploring our ways of thinking and speaking of God, approaches to Scripture, prayer and worship, and also many aspects of the role of men and women in the institutional Church.[16] As Rachel comments, there is nothing unusual about doing theology in Christianity. What is new is the increasing number of theologically educated women who are now developing a range of distinctive approaches which fall under the heading of 'feminist theology'.

---

16 For an early, but still excellent introduction to some leading feminist theologians see Ann Loades (ed.), 1990, *Feminist Theology: A Reader*, London: SPCK.

I have been a feminist for as long as I can remember. I was educated at an all-girls secondary school and I cannot remember ever thinking of anything within academic life as a boys' subject. I am sure that I accepted the socially endorsed traditional gender roles of the 1950s and early 1960s but I did study theology at university and always expected to have a career. It seemed unfair that young men who studied theology with me could train for the priesthood while I could not. I could not see any good reason for that; I still can't. I remember writing an exam answer about 'man's inhumanity to man' without any awareness that there was anything problematic in the language. Gradually I began to be aware of how powerful language is; how it can include or exclude women and how it can almost magically make women disappear. Take the simple sentence 'Sikhs wear turbans.' Nothing wrong with that until one realizes that Sikh women do not wear turbans. 'Sikhs' = 'male Sikhs'. Men's experience is being treated as normative and women do not count. Rachel's discussion of Exodus 19.15 in the previous section is another example of this. Language is power because it shapes what people see, know and understand; it determines what we can think as well as what we can say. That is why I enjoyed Mary Daly's feminist writing so much with titles like *Beyond God the Father* (1973), *Gyn/Ecology* (1978) and *Pure Lust* (1984). Her book *Webster's First New Intergalactic Wickedary of the English Language* is about language,[17] where she weaves language that is playful, sharp and full of puns, showing the power of language very vividly. In the preface she writes that using language in these ways:

> Springs from the original be-ing of women, from which patriarchal religion attempts to 'save' us, but which is inherently Untouchable, Inviolate and Wild.[18]

And that brings us to a number of related questions for feminist theology and for me as a feminist Catholic woman; questions which have also been in the background throughout the dialogue within our group but which we have not always explicitly addressed. Here are some of the relevant questions: Can a male saviour save women? Are Christianity and patriarchy

---

17 Mary Daly, 1988, *Webster's First New Intergalactic Wickedary of the English Language*, London: The Women's Press.

18 Mary Daly, 1988, *Webster's First New Intergalactic Wickedary*, p. xiii.

inevitably connected and so are Christianity and feminism incompatible? Should the roles of men and women in the Christian Church be different? Is the Bible good news for women? How do we speak about God in an inclusive way? What are the relationships between feminist theology and Jewish-Christian dialogue? In some ways the questions are interconnected and I shall say something about each of them. I will try to explain what the issues are and give some ideas about the ways in which I approach them. Those people who know that I am a convert to Roman Catholicism sometimes ask me how I could have converted to a Church that is so patriarchal in its approach. In response, I often say that it was partly the quality of the Catholic feminist theology that attracted me and partly the dialogue between the Roman Catholic Church and Jews.[19] Most of the leading feminist theologians were Catholics and I wanted to be involved in their dialogue. I was excited by what I was reading and saw, and still see, as the possibilities within biblical and Church tradition for a challenging and liberating form of Christianity.

Long before I became a Catholic I was interested in the Catholic spiritual tradition. I lived in Norwich for some time and became aware of the writings of Julian of Norwich, Britain's best-known medieval woman mystic. I later discovered many other outstanding Catholic women writers and leaders whose lives and ideas I found inspiring. This is not the place to discuss the details of these women who are now resources for contemporary Christian women but I will name those who have had most impact on me: Hilda, abbess of Whitby; Teresa of Avila, fifteenth-century mystic and writer; Mary Ward, the founder of a women's order that refused to be enclosed and which tried to work in a similar way to the Jesuits; Clare of Assisi, friend of the more famous Francis; and Hildegard of Bingen, thirteenth-century abbess, composer, artist and extraordinary writer. Among other things, what these women indicate is that the Catholic tradition has in the past enabled women to be fully active and innovative in the life of the Church even if they had to struggle 'womanfully' to do so.

I have not (yet) despaired of finding a way to be both Christian and feminist in the twenty-first century but I do not underestimate the difficulties. Language is one of the difficulties. Every Sunday during the service

---

19 The Roman Catholic Church has also been very active in developing relations, at all levels, with Jews and Judaism, and I was also drawn to participate in this dialogue.

of Mass I am supposed to recite in the Nicene Creed that I believe in Christ who: 'for *us men*, and for our salvation, came down from heaven.' This language does not include me. It is no good saying that 'men' means 'men and women'. Even if it did, it would include me by making me invisible – by 'disappearing' me in a language trick. The Roman Catholic Church refuses to use inclusive English in its translations of texts originally in Latin or Greek and this raises each time the key question about whether women are fully included in the good news of salvation which the Church proclaims. As the Christian feminist theologian Rosemary Radford Ruether rather sharply puts it, 'Can a male saviour save women?' Is the life, teaching, death and resurrection of Jesus relevant to me or only to men? I want to argue that at the incarnation, God becomes human and that this is significant for all humanity because it shows in a very special way, the possibility, the potential of human beings for relationship with God. In Christ, God shares our suffering and death, and the resurrection shows that this is not the end of the story either for Jesus or for us. In order to believe that the incarnation, crucifixion and resurrection of Jesus Christ are relevant for me I have to believe that Jesus was, in the ways that matter, like me. Christians have to be able in some way to identify with Jesus. This is why Chinese artists depict Christ as Chinese, or African Christian artists show Jesus as an African. Some women Christian artists have made 'Christas' showing a woman on the cross.[20] But what if Jesus is not like me? What if what matters about Jesus was that he was male, not that he was human? This is part of the reason why the Roman Catholic Church believes that women cannot be priests. The argument runs along these lines: because the priest represents Jesus at the altar and Jesus was male, only men can be priests. This makes Jesus' maleness an essential aspect of his saving mission; and interestingly, his Jewishness (for example) is not treated in the same way. The early Church soon decided that Gentile converts to Christianity did not have to become Jews first, but according to some early non-canonical texts which seem to reflect widespread

---

20 Marcella Maria Althaus-Reid writes that: 'Christas have been more important than many theological books. Christas made theologians become the voyeurs of a strange God by looking at her exposed nudity transgressing the cross.' See 'Queer I Stand: Doing Feminist Theology outside the Borders of Colonial Decency', in Charlotte Methuen and Angela Berlis (eds), 2002, *The End of Liberation? Liberation in the End? Feminist Theory, Feminist Theology and their Political Implications*, Louven: Peeters Publishers, p. 30.

attitudes, women who aspired to holiness could and must 'become' men, at least if they were virgins and remained celibate.[21] By contrast, those who married and gave birth 'became' women and therefore could not be holy. The clearest examples of this are Mary Magdalene in the Gospel of Thomas, which insists that Mary should remain a disciple at the same time as she must be made male, and the story of Paul and Theckla where Theckla refuses marriage, cuts her hair, dresses like a boy and becomes Paul's close companion. I shall say more about the dualism that this implies later.

The Roman Catholic Church also claims that because it has never ordained women, there is no authority to change that now. This seems to me to be a misreading of tradition as a fixed and one-way process. There are many different strands in tradition and the Church has changed in many ways in response to reading the 'signs of the times', a phrase from the Second Vatican Council of 1962–5, which transformed the understanding of the Roman Catholic Church and re-expressed central truths for the life of the Church. The change in attitudes to Jews and Judaism by the official Roman Catholic Church is one example of a new reading of Church teaching which promotes justice and a fuller understanding of Scripture and tradition. The many positive things that have flowed from this might encourage the institutional Church to begin to risk real dialogue with women. There is also the so-called 'fact' that Jesus only chose men as his disciples and apostles. I challenge that claim in my discussion of Mary Magdalene in Chapter 7; however, the belief in different gender roles for men and women in Christianity is a strong one. This is in spite of passages like Galatians 3.28, which is often quoted to demonstrate Christianity's commitment to equality:

> There is no longer Jew or Greek, there is no longer slave or free, there is no longer male and female; for all of you are one in Christ Jesus.

I used to find that verse encouraging, as a vision of the ideal to which the Church could strive, if not a statement of present reality. However, a few years ago I heard the Jewish feminist scholar Amy-Jill Levine arguing in a lecture at a conference that for her the verse had Nazi echoes of a vision of

---

21 Daniel Boyarin, 1998, 'Gender', in Mark C. Taylor (ed.), *Critical Terms for Religious Studies*, Chicago: University of Chicago Press, p. 125.

a world where there were no Jews.[22] That made me begin to reflect that here again, women are in danger of being 'disappeared' too.

The contemporary Jewish scholar Daniel Boyarin has argued persuasively that Paul and early Christians were much influenced by the Jewish philosopher Philo. In discussing the early stories of Genesis, Philo had argued that the first Adam in Genesis 1, made in the image and likeness of God, was a spiritual being, whereas the second chapter of Genesis introduces an embodied male Adam from whom the female is constructed. Boyarin comments about this distinction:

> Bodily gender – structurally dependent on their being two – is thus twice displaced from the origins of 'man' ... The oneness of spirit is ontologically privileged in the constitution of humanity.[23]

It follows from this that women have no spiritual role *as women*. Their social, political and economic role is to be subservient to men. In the New Testament, 1 Corinthians 11.1–16 is a good example of this point. There are a number of distinctions at work here: first between spirit and body, second between virgins and women, and third there is 'equality in the spirit and hierarchy in the flesh'.[24] Both Philo and Tertullian, Christian Apologist of the third century, distinguish between virgins and women. Virgins are asexual or androgynous. There is one further twist to the argument, however, of great significance to understanding the power of gender issues in the Church – the spiritual, transcendent dimension is always described as male. Bodies of both men and women are characterized as female. It is an easy move from this to regard women as essentially embodied, and men as higher, rational and spiritual beings. This stress on the bodiliness of women, reinforced by the teachings of other Christian theologians like Augustine in the fifth century and Aquinas in the Middle Ages, has produced much fear of women. This fear provides a key for understanding much in Christian history and theology that shocks the

---

22 As a Jewish feminist New Testament scholar, A. J. Levine is a good example of the cross-over between Jewish and Christian feminist scholarship. Her commentary on Matthew's Gospel is a set text-book for students. See also Susannah Heschel's chapter 'Jesus as a Theological Transvestite', 1997, in Miriam Peskowitz and Laura Levitt (eds), *Judaism since Gender*, London: Routledge, p. 188–99. These Jewish feminist scholars contribute to, and challenge, my own understanding of Christianity.

23 Daniel Boyarin, 1998, 'Gender', p. 120.

24 Daniel Boyarin, 1998, 'Gender', p. 122–4.

contemporary reader, such as the claim that women are 'The Devil's Gateway' (Tertullian) or the waves of women (witch) burning that swept through Europe in the early modern era. This is not dissimilar to the myths surrounding Lilith in the Jewish tradition to which Rachel drew our attention earlier. Women's 'bodiliness' is, I believe, behind much of the resistance to the ordination of women in the Roman Catholic Church. It comes from a deep-seated, and often unrecognized, blood taboo. A menstruating or pregnant priest would pollute the sacred space of, and around, the altar, and therefore may be for many literally 'unthinkable'.[25] This rejection of the body is ironic in a religion that is theologically centred on incarnation, embodiment, and liturgically focused on 'the body and blood' of Christ. As a Christian feminist, I challenge the dualism that equates women with the body and men with the mind or spirit. If women are fully human then they are not spiritually second rate or second class, always subservient to men. This feminist reappraisal requires new hermeneutical approaches to reading the Bible, including the early Genesis stories, and this has been one of the most creative areas in the Christian and Jewish feminist encounter and dialogue.[26] Feminist biblical scholarship has engaged in reading Scripture in ways that proclaim women's full humanity and full participation in both the Jewish and Christian life. This involves rediscovering in the Bible those elements that challenge or critique patriarchy. The cross-over in biblical scholarship between Jewish and Christian feminists has strengthened and enabled the struggle against the patriarchal heritage.

One of the most significant Christian feminist writers is Elisabeth Schüssler Fiorenza. Her early book *In Memory of Her* takes its title from the story in Mark's Gospel (14.3–9) where a woman anoints Jesus. This can be understood as both a prophetic action that shows Jesus to be the messiah and one which anticipates his death by preparing him for burial. Jesus comments that, 'truly I say to you, wherever the gospel is preached

---

25 Despite some biblical passages which speak against women having authority in the Church, most mainstream Protestant Churches have enabled women to take on equal leadership roles with men. They are ministers, not priests. There has been so much more opposition to women in ministry from Christians in traditions that have priests, such as the Roman Catholic and Anglican Churches.

26 The Jewish scholar Phyllis Trible provides just such an interpretation in her book *God and the Rhetoric of Sexuality* (Philadelphia: Fortress Press, 1978). See also the work by the Christian feminist Anne Primavesi, 1991, *From Apocalypse to Genesis*, London: Continuum.

in the whole world, what she has done will be told in memory of her'.[27] And yet we do not even know this woman's name. There are many examples of women who, like the woman who anointed Jesus, have been ignored and forgotten. The book, *Women in Scripture*, is a dictionary of all the named and unnamed women in the Bible. Running to nearly 600 pages, it reflects the far-reaching results of, and co-operation between, Jewish and Christian feminist scholarship of the last few decades. Perhaps it would be fair to say that now Jewish and Christian feminists are no longer 'passing like ships in the night' – a phrase taken from the writings of the Catholic feminist writer Deborah McCauley who has argued that our historical experiences as Jewish and Christian women within our religious traditions were not the same and that we were passing like ships in the night and not really meeting each other.[28] That has changed in recent years and this book from our women's group is one indication of that change. Some of the biblical women can be role-models for us today but there are other stories which recount the oppression and violent treatment of women. These 'texts of terror', as Phyllis Trible calls them, can be re-told *in memoriam*.[29] This, like the efforts made to name those who died in the Holocaust, is a powerful way of contesting attempts to dehumanize the victims.[30] But there is more to feminist hermeneutical approaches than dealing with stories about women. The Bible tells us about God, and feminist theology wants to expose and challenge the view that God is male. Some of the biblical language for God is explicitly female and so helps to balance the imagery. A good example of this is Deuteronomy 32.18: 'You were unmindful of the Rock that begot you; you forgot the God *who gave you birth.*' Trible argues that this is a tame translation, which underplays the 'striking portrayal of a woman in labour pains, for the Hebrew verb has exclusively this meaning'.[31] It is even more striking when one considers the translation in the Roman Catholic Bible, The Jerusalem Bible, which reads: 'you forgot the God who *fathered* you'.

---

27 Mark 14.9.

28 Deborah McCauley, 1988, 'Nostra Aetate and the New Jewish-Christian Feminist Dialogue', in Roger Brooks (ed.), *Unanswered Questions*, Notre Dame: University of Notre Dame Press.

29 Phyllis Trible, 1984, *Texts of Terror*, Philadelphia: Fortress Press.

30 In our women's group we have discussed the story of the rape of Dinah in Gen. 34. See Chapter 6.

31 Phyllis Trible, 1982, 'Feminist Hermeneutics and Biblical Studies', in *The Christian Century*, 3–10 February, p. 117.

If we take an explicitly Christian example, Schüssler Fiorenza has used Luke 1.39–40 and Proverbs 9.1–6 to develop a feminist Christology which does not privilege male language and imagery. She writes:

> By naming Jesus as the child of Miriam and the prophet of Divine Sophia (Wisdom), I seek to create a 'women'-defined feminist theoretical space that makes it possible to dislodge christological discourses from their malestream frame of reference.[32]

Not all feminists believe that feminism and Christianity are compatible. Daphne Hampson is an example of someone who describes herself as 'post-Christian' and who has debated this issue with a number of other Christian feminists in *Swallowing a Fishbone?*[33] Christianity, she argues, 'is sexist because the past history to which Christians necessarily make reference was a patriarchal history'.[34] Christians have to refer to history because they believe that in Jesus of Nazareth, God is revealed. There is an inevitable historical particularity that has to be taken seriously. In addition, Christians are always dependent to some extent on God, or Scripture or the Church which is 'other' and which prevents women being autonomous, that is, deciding things for themselves and being responsible for who they are. The book continues with a number of very different, and often very technical, theological responses from women who continue to be Christians because they find that in some way Christianity can be liberating for them. They, and many other feminist theologians, challenge the sexism, patriarchy and oppression in language for God, in the Bible and in the Church. They also rediscover and promote women's stories in Scripture and tradition, inclusive and also explicitly feminine language for God, and equal roles for women in society and in the Church.

At the ninth International Conference of the European Society of Women in Theological Research, which Rachel mentions because of their caution in not originally using the term 'feminist', Lucy Tatman spoke passionately about the need for feminist Christian theologians to take themselves and each other seriously as embodied thinkers. 'With word

---

32 Elisabeth Schüssler Fiorenza, 1994, *Jesus. Miriam's Child, Sophia's Prophet: Critical Issues in Feminist Christology*, London: SCM Press, p. 3.

33 Daphne Hampson (ed.), 1996, *Swallowing a Fishbone? Feminist Theologians Debate Christianity*, London: SPCK.

34 Daphne Hampson (ed.), 1996, *Swallowing a Fishbone?*, p. 7.

and flesh', she finished, 'let us take each other seriously as lovers of theo-logy.'[35] This is vital work not just for women but also for Christianity and therefore for Roman Catholicism. I agree with Nancy Dallavalle in an article called 'Toward a Theology that is Catholic and Feminist' that:

> Catholic theology and the Catholic tradition are not only unjust, they are, in many cases, paltry, flat, stultified, boring – a far cry from the ideal of a richly textured tradition of symbol and gesture and speech that draws persons into a community of praise.[36]

So, feminist theology's emphasis on justice is not wrong but limited. The idea of 'catholic' should mean not only 'inclusive' or 'open to all' but 'whole'. In other words, the Catholic Church and Christianity need the full and active participation of women in order to make possible the fulfilment of Jesus' prayer: 'I ask not only on behalf of these, but also on behalf of those who will believe in me through their word, that they may all be one.'[37]

Further Reading

See the Bibliography section for full details on these titles.

Blu Greenberg, *On Women and Judaism*.
Sondra Henry and Emily Taitz, *Written Out of History: Our Jewish Foremothers*.
Ruth Linden, *Making Stories, Making Selves*.
Ann Loades (ed.), *Feminist Theology: A Reader*.
Miriam Peskowitz and Laura Levitt (eds), *Judaism since Gender*.
Judith R. Wegner, *Chattel or Person? The Status of Women in the Mishnah*.

---

35 Lucy Tatman, 2002, 'Western European-American Feminist Christian Theologians: What It Might Mean to Take Ourselves Seriously', in Charlotte Methuen and Angela Berlis (eds), *The End of Liberation? Liberation in the End? Feminist Theory, Feminist Theology and their Political Implications*, Louven: Peeters Publishers, p. 48.

36 Nancy Dallavalle, 1998, 'Toward a Theology that is Catholic and Feminist: Some Basic Issues', in *Modern Theology*, 14, 4, p. 548.

37 John 17.20–21.

3 Messiah

Are you he who is to come or shall we look for another?
(John the Baptist's disciples to Jesus).

Matthew 11.3//Luke 7.18–35

I Jesus, Messiahship and Jewish-Christian Relations

Helen P. Fry

'Are you he who is to come or shall we look for another?' This question posed by John the Baptist's disciples to Jesus succinctly epitomizes the debate over messiahship between Jews and Christians for two millennia. It sets the agenda for the discussion in this chapter: is Jesus the messiah or do we, Jews and Christians, wait for another? To narrow the question further: was he the messiah of Jewish expectation? These are relevant questions precisely because messiahship is a major point of disagreement between Christians and Jews, a disagreement which according to Radford Ruether was the root cause of Christian antisemitism in the Church.[1] Also relevant to us as Jewish and Christian women is how our experiences as women have affected our understandings of messiahship. Therefore in the second part of this section I will reflect on my own experience and the relevance of messiahship to me as a Christian woman in the twenty-first century, as well as providing some brief comments on messiah and gender. Christians do confess Jesus as the messiah, and such a claim was among one of the earliest confessions of the Church. To them, it is self-evident from the prophecies in the Hebrew Bible that Jesus fulfilled the expectations of the *one who was to come* and that John the Baptist had prepared the way for

---

1 Rosemary Radford Ruether, 1974, *Faith and Fratricide*, New York: Seabury Press. See also her chapter, 'The Adversus Judaeos Tradition in the Church Fathers: The Exegesis of Christian anti-Judaism', in Jeremy Cohen (ed.), 1991, *Essential Papers on Judaism and Christianity in Late Antiquity to the Reformation*, New York: New York University Press.

his coming. Within the Jewish-Christian dialogue today, and certainly within the wider Church community, Christians often do not understand why Jews have rejected Jesus as their messiah. This puzzlement is something that many of the women in our group have encountered when addressing a Christian audience, and therefore is something that we consciously decided to discuss together. With these comments as the background to this discussion, I will look at the issues relating to messiahship only where they are of direct relevance to, and impact on, Jewish-Christian relations.

While much progress has been made in understanding the complexity of the thought-world of the first century CE, there are diverse pictures emerging from New Testament scholarship on exactly where to locate Jesus' ministry: from a prophet of restoration,[2] to a wandering Jewish peasant cynic,[3] to a revolutionary trouble-maker,[4] or an itinerant Galilean preacher and healer.[5] All would agree, however, that the focus of his ministry was centred on the proclamation of the kingdom of God rather than on proclaiming the coming of the messiah. It is not possible to outline a full argument here of where I would locate Jesus' ministry, but suffice it to say that I have argued elsewhere that his mission can be characterized as that of an eschatological prophet who expected the imminent arrival of the kingdom of God and worked to make that a reality.[6] It is important for our discussion, in so far as is possible from scholarly research, to seek an understanding of the concepts of messiah at the time of Jesus to enable a fuller appreciation of the historical milieu within which Jesus himself was functioning and to reflect on why Jews may not accept him as their messiah.

Many Christians do not understand why the Jews of Jesus' day or the Jews of today do not accept Jesus as the messiah. There are two parts in answering this question: the first has to do with Christian claims for divinity. Jews cannot accept Jesus' divinity or the beliefs about the Trinity, in spite of Christian explanations through Church Councils and creeds to

---

2 E. P. Sanders, 1985, *Jesus and Judaism*, London: SCM Press.

3 John Crossan, 1994, *Jesus: A Revolutionary Biography*, San Francisco: Harper Collins. See also his work *The Historical Jesus*, Edinburgh: T&T Clark, 1991.

4 Richard Horsley, 1993, *Jesus and the Spiral of Violence: Popular Jewish Resistance in Roman Palestine*, Minneapolis: Fortress Press.

5 Geza Vermes, 2000, *The Changing Faces of Jesus*, London: Penguin.

6 Helen P. Fry, 1996, *Converting Jews? From a Mission to Jews to a Mission with Jews*, PhD thesis, Exeter: University of Exeter.

explain these beliefs in terms of monotheism. Second, it was not obvious to the Jews of Jesus' day that he fulfilled Jewish messianic hopes and it is to this latter topic that I will now turn. To understand this, it is necessary to examine the messianic ideas that were circulating in Palestine from the first century BCE to the first century CE. Did Jesus fulfil the messianic expectations of his day? Another way of phrasing this question would be to ask if he was the messiah of Jewish expectation. The task of answering this question is complex. Nevertheless, there are some reasonable conclusions that can be drawn from scholarship so far. To answer this we need to look at the Jewish sources available at this time.[7] The Hebrew Bible, or Old Testament, does not use the noun 'messiah',[8] although there are important passages which became overlaid with messianic interpretation: such as Psalm 2, Isaiah 7, 9 and 11, 2 Samuel 7, Zechariah 9, and Daniel 9. The Hebrew Bible does contain passages which refer to the 'anointed one', usually the priest, prophet or king; but no expectations for an eschatological, apocalyptic messiah as became part of Jewish literature from the first century BCE. Not all Jews awaited a messiah figure, and according to the scholar James Charlesworth, the vast majority probably did not in the period prior to the destruction of the Temple in 70 CE.[9] The early Jewish texts for examining concepts of the messiah are primarily the Old Testament Pseudepigrapha and the Dead Sea Scrolls.[10]

Within the Old Testament Pseudepigrapha, the key texts which explicitly use the term 'messiah' are found in Psalms of Solomon, Parables of Enoch, 4 Ezra, and 2 Baruch. In this literature, the vast majority of

7 For a more detailed analysis of the texts, see James Charlesworth (ed.), 1992, *Messiah: Developments in Earliest Judaism and Christianity*, Minneapolis: Fortress Press.

8 It does speak of an anointed one, such as the priest, king or prophet, but the term 'messiah' as a title is not used.

9 James Charlesworth (ed.), 1992, *Messiah*, p. 11–13. He also notes that Jesus' disciples were not preoccupied with his messianic status prior to his crucifixion in 30 CE. This would cohere with his statement that the vast majority of other Jews prior to 70 CE were not awaiting their messiah.

10 The Targums are too late for this research because their current form is too late for early Jewish messianic thought because it postdates 200 CE. Although the Mishnah has numerous references to messiah, they appear against the background of an emerging Rabbinic Judaism that was struggling with the messianic claims of early Christianity and the task of disentangling the early layers of the tradition from later layers is problematic. This literature does not represent the earliest strand of Jewish messianic thought which emerged shortly after the failure of the Hasmonean dynasty, and therefore it is more appropriate to turn to the texts of the Old Testament Pseudepigrapha and the Dead Sea Scrolls.

'messiah' texts do not attribute any function at all to the messiah, suggesting that the concept was undefined and fluid from the first century BCE. The texts that do provide some idea of the messiah's function suggest that he will judge and destroy the wicked, deliver God's people, and reign in a blessed kingdom.[11] Interestingly, none of these functions was attributed to Jesus by the evangelists or Paul. In early Jewish messianic thought there was no expectation that the messiah would be a miracle worker or that he would suffer and die.[12] For those that did await the messiah in the period 50 BCE to 100 CE, there was a diversity of expectations and traditions in the Jewish literature at the time from which to draw one's understanding. Some conceived of him as a descendant of David;[13] some as a warrior figure;[14] others as a non-military figure;[15] others that he would inaugurate a messianic era and then die;[16] and some that he would appear as king.[17] Even within the same books, there are contradictory pictures about the messiah; as is particularly evident in 4 Ezra and 2 Baruch.

The Dead Sea Scrolls provide another important insight into Jewish messianic ideas from the first century BCE to the first century CE. The scholarship in this area is contentious and diverse, particularly over possible texts which may have messianic overtones; however, the majority of scholars would acknowledge that the Dead Sea community, probably Essenes, had a messianic perspective, although they disagree on what point within its history the community developed these ideas. Charlesworth, for example, suggests that there are a relatively small number of overt messianic texts within the Dead Sea Scrolls and that the crucial passages are of a later origin within the life of the community.[18] Even so, it is clear that there were some messianic expectations circulating within Palestine of the first century CE even if the vast majority of Jews at that time were not waiting for the messiah.[19] The failures of the Hasmonean

---

11 See PssSol. 17; 4 Ezra 12; 2 Bar. 40.72.

12 With the exception of 4 Ezra 7 where the messiah's death marks the end of an era.

13 PssSol. 17.21–34; 4 Ezra 12.31–34. The Samaritans linked the messiah to Moses, while the writer of the Parables of Enoch linked the messiah to Enoch.

14 Bar. 72.6.

15 PssSol. 17.21–33; 4 Ezra 13.4–11.

16 4 Ezra 7.28–29.

17 PssSol. 17.21–33.

18 James Charlesworth (ed.), 1992, *Messiah*, p. 25.

19 Some scholars suggest that messianic ideas were particularly developed in Judaism after the destruction of the Temple in 70 CE and most particularly during the Bar Kochba Revolt.

dynasty precipitated the growth of messianic expectations which looked for a priestly messiah: a Davidic and Aaronic messiah. This makes sense given that the early Qumran settlers were priests who had been expelled from the Temple. Whether these expectations influenced, indirectly, the followers of Jesus is not certain because within the post-resurrection community there was no expectation that Jesus was a priestly messiah. Such ideas appear to be a later development within the Church, probably as a reaction to the destruction of the Temple in 70 CE.[20] The broad consensus emerging in scholarship suggests that early Jewish messianism was undefined and fluid. Charlesworth writes:

> The complexity of messianic ideas, the lack of a coherent messianology amongst the documents in the Pseudepigrapha and among the Dead Sea Scrolls, and the frequently contradictory messianic predictions prohibit anything approximating coherency in early Jewish messianology.[21]

Place the above discussion against the background of the first century CE and it becomes clear that there were no clearly defined ideas of messiahship into which Jesus could easily be placed by his followers. The Gospel writers clearly believed that Jesus was the messiah, but their precise understanding of this term is unclear. The New Testament scholar James Dunn suggests that the early Christians (and maybe Jesus himself) began to shape the developing messianic ideas:

> The earliest Christian thought (including Jesus?) has to be seen itself as part of the development and transformation in the messianic ideas of the period, and not merely as reactive to ideas already in existence.[22]

Did Jesus make any claims to be the messiah? Because of the nature of his ministry (his preaching and miracles), it is likely that he was asked whether he was the messiah; however, a number of New Testament scholars have argued that Jesus himself did not make any claims to be the

---

20 And even then, the priestly line for Jesus was traced through Melchizedek rather than Aaron. See Heb. 5.7. This suggests that Jesus was not actually of priestly descent and his followers did not understand him in terms of a priestly messiah.

21 James Charlesworth (ed.), 1992, *Messiah*, p. 28.

22 James Dunn, 1992, 'Messianic Ideas and their Influence on the Jesus of History', in James Charlesworth (ed.), *Messiah*, p. 370.

messiah.[23] There are a number of key texts which are important for our discussion and which I will briefly comment on here: Peter's confession at Caesarea Philippi,[24] John the Baptist's question,[25] and Jesus' trials before the High Priest and Pilate.[26] Apart from Mark 14.62 when the High Priest asked if he was the messiah and Jesus replied, 'I am', all the other passages are not an overt affirmation of messiahship, including other key texts within Mark's Gospel. In Mark 8.29 (and parallels) Jesus asked his disciples: 'who do men say that I am?' They answered that some thought he was Elijah or John the Baptist, others that he was one of the prophets. Jesus asked them who they thought he was. Peter's famous reply was: 'you are the Christ.' Matthew's Gospel has the longer response, 'you are the Christ, the Son of the living God.' The three Synoptics all agree that Jesus ordered them to keep quiet.[27] This was not a direct denial of messiahship itself but neither was it an overt endorsement of it, but reflects a struggle in the early Church with those inherited traditions that believed strongly that Jesus was the messiah and those that reacted against a messiah figure who suffered and died.

In answer to the question, 'are you he who is to come or shall we look for another?', Jesus' response was interesting and an important pointer to understanding how he defined his own ministry. He replied: 'go and tell John what you hear and see: the blind receive their sight and the lame walk and the lepers are cleansed and the deaf hear.'[28] Jesus did not affirm messiahship outright but located his ministry within a prophetic framework by alluding directly to Isaiah 61.[29] This was not the first occasion that he had used Isaiah 61; the other example was when he read from the scroll in the synagogue in Luke 4.16–21. This indicates very strongly that he did not perceive of himself as a political messiah who would overthrow the

---

23 James Dunn, 1992, 'Messianic Ideas'; Geza Vermes, 2000, *The Changing Faces of Jesus*; and E. P. Sanders, 1985, *Jesus and Judaism*.

24 Mark 8.29//Matt. 16.16//Luke 9.20.

25 Matt. 11.3//Luke 7.18–35.

26 Matt. 26.57–75//Luke 22.54–71//Mark 14.53–72; and Matt. 27.11–14//Mark 15.2–5//Luke 23.2–5.

27 Tuckett has argued that Jesus' command for his disciples to keep quiet was part of the 'messianic secret' as a motif of Marcan origin. See Christopher Tuckett, 1987, *Reading the New Testament*, London: SPCK.

28 Matt. 11.4–5.

29 The only exception is in Mark 14.62 where the High Priest asks if he is the messiah and Jesus replies: 'I am'. Elsewhere in parallel passages he replies ambiguously: 'you say that I am.'

Romans. Furthermore, if he had understood his mission in political terms, then it is doubtful that his ministry would have lasted three years. The picture of the messiah as an eschatological high priest was also not applicable to the ministry of Jesus.[30]

Looking at the 'trials' of Jesus before the High Priest and Pilate, the four Gospels agree that Jesus was crucified as the 'king of the Jews' – the plaque over the cross said as much and it is a title which the majority of New Testament scholars agree was historical to the life of Jesus. Although there is some ambiguity over the historicity of the trial scenes as they appear in the Gospel accounts, the core tradition that there was some kind of hearing before the High Priest and then before Pilate and that it was Pilate who ordered Jesus' death is deemed to be historical by most scholars.[31] Pilate directly asked Jesus: 'are you the king of the Jews?' Jesus' response in all three of the Synoptic Gospels was: 'you have said so.' Earlier the High Priest had asked: 'are you the messiah?' and Jesus had replied: 'you say that I am.' Again Jesus' response was interesting in that it was not a clear endorsement of messiahship or kingship, showing an unwillingness to accept the role of a royal messiah figure. Rather his ministry can be understood against the background of eschatological prophetic expectations as seen in his response to the question posed by John the Baptist's disciples, and as multiply attested in his teaching on the kingdom of God.

There are a number of passages where the term 'son of David' is used but these usually appear in passages where he is healing the sick and performing various miracles.[32] There is some debate among scholars over whether he was understood as a royal figure, the son of David, the anointed king of Israel.[33] There were some Jewish expectations for a Davidic, royal messiah as reflected in passages such as 2 Samuel 7.12–14; Jeremiah 23.5, 33.15, Isaiah 11.1–2; Haggai 2.23; Sirach 47.11; and 1 Maccabees 2.57. Nowhere, with the exception of John 4.26, does Jesus claim messiahship on his own initiative. The early Christians wanted to claim messiahship for Jesus but could not overtly pin the claim to the lips

---

30 These expectations were found among the Qumran community. See 1QS 9.11; 1QS 2.11–22.

31 E. P. Sanders, 1985, *Jesus and Judaism*, p. 309ff. See also E. P. Sanders, 1993, *The Historical Figure of Jesus*, London: Penguin.

32 With the exception of the infancy narrative of Matthew's Gospel and the shout of 'hosanna to the son of David' on his entry into Jerusalem (Mark 8.29 and par.).

33 Doris Donnelly *et al.*, 2001, *Jesus: A Colloquium from the Holy Land*, New York: Continuum.

of Jesus himself. If the early Christians could have definitively claimed messiahship based on what he said in his own lifetime then they would have done so, and as Dunn writes:

> The silence of the synoptic tradition is striking: it confirms an unwillingness to retroject material beyond what Jesus was remembered as teaching back onto the Jesus tradition.[34]

The messianic proclamations about Jesus are often phrased within a context that are more readily seen as reflections of early Christian confession rather than historical to his ministry. Certainly the early Church came to understand him as their long-awaited messiah in the use of *christos* as a title for him.[35] It was precisely the issue of messiahship which defined some of the early Christological differences between Jews, Jewish Christians and the emerging Gentile Church. A tantalizing question still needs to be examined: 'why did Jesus' followers claim above all that he was the messiah?'[36] If we can answer this question, we may be nearer to understanding one of the earliest Christological claims and the faith of the first Christians. The scholar N. Dahl has suggested that it was in part due to the claim (not necessarily by Jesus himself) that he was the king of the Jews, coupled with the resurrection experiences. Although Jesus himself did not positively accept the title of royal messiah, 'king of the Jews', it is likely that Pilate ordered his death because he was perceived as a political threat and was put to death as the 'king of the Jews'. The resurrection appearances *on their own* were not sufficient to make this transformation:

> The resurrection experiences would not have led the disciples to affirm that Jesus was the promised messiah unless he had been crucified as an alleged royal messiah ... The appearances of the risen Christ were of crucial importance for the radical Christian transformation of the concept of 'messiah', but they can only have had this effect because they convinced the disciples that God had vindicated the crucified king of the Jews.[37]

---

34 James Dunn, 1992, 'Messianic Ideas', p. 375.

35 In particular, see the early Christian confession of Jesus as 'Lord and Christ' in Acts 2.36.

36 James Charlesworth (ed.), 1992, *Messiah*.

37 N. Dahl in James Charlesworth (ed.), 1992, *Messiah*, p. 391.

For Christians, the delay of the coming of the kingdom and the failure of Jesus to implement the messianic age became translated on to the belief in his second coming. The vast majority of Christians today await that coming with eager anticipation and expectation. I find some concluding reflections by James Dunn on the messiahship of Jesus helpful:

> He [Jesus] must be seen as part of the stream of Jewish messianic reflection and one of the most important currents within that stream during the first half of the first century CE broadening the stream and quite soon becoming the occasion of it splitting into two different channels.[38]

What can now be said to us about Jesus and messiahship? Since there were no clearly defined (or even diverse, but coherent) Jewish concepts of the messiah in the first centuries BCE and CE, it is problematic to state, as many Christians do, that Jesus was the messiah of Jewish expectation. It is even more problematic to 'blame' Jews for rejecting their messiah. We have to look again at our traditions and the challenges which scholarship now presents to us. Was he the one who was to come or do we look for another? For the vast majority of Jews today (and centuries past) Jesus was not, and cannot be, the messiah of *Jewish* expectation because of Christian claims for divinity. They have developed their own messianic ideas, partly shaped by Rabbinic Judaism in contrast to the dominant Christian claims for Jesus. Jews still await either a messianic figure or a messianic era of peace and prosperity. It is important for Christians to recognize that whatever his Christological significance Jesus was not the messiah of Jewish expectation. Interestingly this is one of the points which, I believe, as Jews and Christians we can agree upon. I suggest that in the light of New Testament scholarship and the Jewish understanding of messiahship, Christians must understand that Jesus was not the messiah of the Jews; however, this does not mean that they should abandon other Christological claims, but that his significance lies elsewhere. Jesus as a figure of faith will always define the boundaries between two distinct and separate faith communities. In what sense can the Church still use *christos* as an appropriate title for Jesus? Perhaps Jesus can be Christ in the sense of the biblical concept of the 'anointed one', anointed to carry out a particular task as God's

---

38 James Dunn, 1992, 'Messianic Ideas', p. 381.

prophet, although not exclusively as *the* only messiah. The Roman Catholic theologian John Pawlikowski has made a significant and poignant comment about messiahship and Jewish-Christian relations:

> If the Christian churches continue to retain the term *messiah* in reference to Jesus, as they no doubt will, it is incumbent upon their members today to recognize the redefinition of the term that took place in the course of the first century and thereafter when *messiah* became one central way of expressing belief that in Jesus, God became human. Such an understanding will go a long way in removing the traditional charge against Jews that in not accepting Jesus as the Christ they are being blind to their own messianic prophecies.[39]

Does the concept of messiah have any relevance to me as a Christian woman in the twenty-first century? I have concluded that from a historical-critical perspective it is unlikely that Jesus was the messiah, still less the messiah of Jewish expectation; nevertheless, that Jesus is central to my faith is not in doubt. I am quite comfortable to accept that his significance for my faith is not founded upon claims of messiahship and this may explain my experience when I was carrying my first son. When I was pregnant, I was surprised to find myself asking: what if this baby is the messiah? It was a legitimate question for me at that time and the fact that it surfaced at all did cause me some surprise because traditionally for Christians the messiah has come in the person of Jesus. It is not usual to have any thoughts about being the bearer of the messiah – in contrast to a Jewish woman for whom this could still be a reality because in Judaism, the messiah is still awaited. For me as a Christian woman, it should not have crossed my mind, but it was reinforced by the fact that I had my own 'annunciation'. When I was looking after a friend's three-year-old boy and getting him ready for bed one night at our flat, in the quietness he suddenly looked at me and said, 'You will have children soon.' I was so surprised by his comment because I was awaiting the results of my pregnancy test. I had been married for nine years with no plans until then for a family. Although this little boy and I were close, we had never discussed

---

39 John Pawlikowski, 1991, 'Jesus – A Pharisee and the Christ', in Michael Shermis and Arthur Zannoni (eds), *Introduction to Jewish-Christian Relations*, Mahweh: Paulist Press, p. 193.

the issue of whether I would have my own children. I replied, 'Sometimes people do not have any children at all and that's fine.' He looked at me again and said, 'Yes, you will have children very soon.' He was right because I was expecting a son, and by the same time the following year I was expecting twin boys. It was a profoundly moving experience, nothing supernatural as such, just a simple intuitive statement. I am not sure whether these experiences are common among other Christian women, but it would be worth researching. The experience of the 'annunciation' was forgotten as the time for the birth approached, but I had another experience which I have not felt able to share in the context outside of the women's group. I was rather proud when the Registrar who was delivering my son asked what his name was and declared (just as the head was coming out): 'I feel he is going to do something great with his life.' In the coming months, that little child had a charisma and spirituality which many people seemed to tune into. My Hindu friend thought he was a little guru. At the time, it went over my head – I was busy with the day-to-day activities of looking after him. I came to see in my own experience the traditional biblical prophetic pattern of annunciation, something unusual at the birth, and a recognition by others of something special about that child. What was I, as the mother, to make of it all? I could understand how Mary, Jesus' mother, may well have felt around the time of his birth. How can one explain such things? Perhaps as women, we are so close to the life-giving process that we occasionally experience such spirituality.

Has this experience changed my understanding of messiahship? In some sense *yes*, but not because I honestly believe that my son is the messiah. A shift has occurred in that I no longer actively pray for the coming of the messiah because it would suspend life as we know it and, as a mother, I fervently want to see my boys grow up and fulfil their potential. This is an unexpected transformation for me in terms of my faith. When I attend a Jewish liturgy, I notice that Jews fervently pray for the coming of the messiah. Do Jewish women in our group who have had children feel the same way? Has childbirth transformed their messianic understanding in the same way as it has for me? On the issue of being the bearer of the messiah, I knew that I was carrying a boy from the ultrasound scan, but would I have had the same experience if I had been carrying a girl? This raises the issue of messiah and gender. For many feminists, the whole concept of the messiah is problematic precisely because it is founded on patriarchal notions of kingship and male leadership. The Christian feminist theologian Rosemary Radford Ruether first raised the question of whether a male messiah (or saviour figure) can save women.[40] I do not have difficulty with messiahship and patriarchy *per se*, primarily because I believe in a messianic era rather than a messianic figure. In asking whether a male messiah can save women, it is equally valid to ask: can a female messiah save men? The gender of the messiah is not, for me, the central issue for us as women. More important to me as a Christian in dialogue with Jews, and specifically with Jewish women, is how they understand Jesus in relationship to the Jewish notion of messiah and not in relation to patriarchy. Whatever Jesus' significance, it does not lie in concepts of messiahship but in the personal transformation that his teaching effects in people's lives – whether men or women – and that understanding is not gender specific. It is my belief that for Jews, the transformation comes through Torah.

In conclusion, the figure of the historical Jesus has always fascinated me and captivated my imagination. What was that Galilean man saying and doing in the context of first-century Palestine? The charisma of Jesus the Jew is an indispensable part of my faith and still fires my enthusiasm and imagination. The quest for the true figure beneath those layers of text and tradition continues to provide a dynamic to my faith that is unparalleled in any other aspect of my religious quest in this life.

II The Coming of the Messiah: A Jewish Response

Rachel Montagu

Messianic expectation when taken in too large a dose throughout Jewish and Christian history has often proved unhealthy for both communities, but messianic hope is essential in some measure for the health of our faiths. Too much messianic expectation can destroy people's religious balance, but too little can render them hopeless. In response to Helen's explorations of messiahship, I will look at Jewish understandings of messiah and the history of messianic hope which touches on some of her

40 Rosemary Radford Ruether, 1981, *To Change the World: Christology and Cultural Criticism*, London: SCM Press, p. 45ff.

conclusions. I will also comment on the question of messianism and gender which she has raised.

Messiahship is an area which is complicated in Jewish-Christian dialogue, not just because of our differing beliefs about the identity and role of the messiah but because of generations in which Christianity has had an unacknowledged but definite influence on Jewish teaching; either because Jews wished to differentiate themselves clearly from Christianity or because Christian persecution triggered a response.[41] For instance it is likely that the role of the messiah in the process of redemption in Jewish thinking is downplayed in the Passover seder precisely because of the ways in which the concept of messiah developed in Christianity with the Eucharist, based on the last supper of Jesus which was probably a Passover meal. For Jews, the Eucharist is often associated with the Easter liturgy when, particularly during the medieval period, Jews suffered persecution at the hands of Christian mobs after the services. It is also very difficult for Christians to understand why Jews do not believe that Jesus is the messiah when this is something so central to their own beliefs. Jews cannot accept that Jesus was the messiah because we are not living in a perfect world, and Jews believe that the role of the messiah is to usher in a time of perfection and peace. Also, for Christians, Jesus' role as messiah is very much bound up with the forgiveness of sin,[42] which is not part of Jewish thinking about the role of the messiah at all, and that difference can also generate misunderstanding. There are texts in the Hebrew Bible which Christians consider to be messianic prophecies about Jesus but this is again an area of potential misunderstanding. So, for example, Jews do not read texts like that of the Suffering Servant in Isaiah 53 in any messianic way but as a metaphor for the sufferings of the Jewish people as a whole. Another example is Micah 5.2 (5.1 in the Hebrew text). Jewish discussions often describe the messiah as the son of David but this does not prove Jesus to be that Davidic messiah. If you have grown up hearing these texts interpreted in that way, then they carry that meaning but they do not automatically convey that sense to Jews, certainly not in such a way as to cancel out the manifest blemishes and difficulties of the non-messianic world we live in.

The sources on the messiah in Jewish literature are extraordinarily

---

41 See David Daube's St Paul's lecture *He That Cometh*, and Michael Hilton, 1994, *The Christian Effect on Jewish Life*, London: SCM Press, p. 30–46.

42 Matt. 9.1–8.

varied and contradictory on some levels,[43] more so than most topics in Judaism. Helen's chapter is particularly helpful in focusing on the fact that messianism was fluid and not clearly defined in the first centuries BCE to CE as Christians have often assumed from the biblical texts. Some rabbinic sources suggest that the messiah is brought by human effort although it will always be God who ultimately decides when the messiah arrives. Some suggest that the messiah comes for the Jews alone and not for all humanity. This is a puzzling concept. The *haggadah* that I used as a child had a picture of all Egypt in darkness except for a tiny patch where the Jews were dancing. A world-view like this illustration would be necessary if only part of the world is to be in messianic bliss. Do we gradually evolve to the messianic age or will there be catastrophies – the traditional 'birthpangs' of the messiah?

Some sources suggest that the messiah is a political figure and some that the messiah will be a spiritual leader. Other sources focus on the individual who is the messiah whereas others move away from the individual and look in general terms to a Messianic Age. Which do I personally believe in? On some I believe, as Louis Jacobs, the scholar and founder of the Masorti movement in Britain, put it when commenting on the afterlife that, 'religious agnosticism in some aspects is not only legitimate but altogether desirable'.[44] For instance I sometimes feel there is an irritating degree of intellectual snobbery attached to the position that there will be a Golden Age and not an individual who is the messiah to proclaim its arrival, as tradition suggests. The Messianic Age is the standard Progressive Jewish view, although there are classical sources for it before the development of Reform Judaism. How can the Progressive Jews who assert this be sure? It is perhaps a way of dealing with a certain embarrassment at attempting to define who the messiah will be. Precisely the same point applies to the Lubavitch Hasidic certainty about the messianic role of their late rebbe, Menachem Schneerson;[45] something that in his lifetime they pushed beyond any normal Hasidic passion to perfect the world and respect their

---

43 Norman Solomon's way of dealing with these varying views by dividing the Jewish teachings on this topic along seven parameters is especially helpful. See Norman Solomon, 1991, *Judaism and World Religion*, London: Macmillan, p. 134–5.

44 Louis Jacobs, 1973, *A Jewish Theology*, London: Darton, Longman & Todd, p. 321.

45 Hasidim are ultra-Orthodox Jews. Each group follows their own rebbe or teacher. The dynasty of Lubavitcher rebbes originated in the Russian town of Lubavitch in the early nineteenth century. The late rebbe Menachem Schneerson died in the 1990s.

own rebbe. How could they be so sure? Interestingly, other Jews were certain that Lubavitchers who had increasingly worked themselves into a messianic frenzy during the years of the rebbe's final illness would collapse emotionally when the rebbe died and this did not happen – they continue to work to bring the Messianic Age and some continue to promote the rebbe as the messiah and pray for his return to complete the redemption of the world.[46]

The evolutionary position that we will gradually evolve into a perfect world is harder to believe now than at the end of the nineteenth century when it fitted beautifully with the general enthusiasm of the period for progress – the wonders of the new technology of the industrial revolution and so on. Now after the Holocaust and aware of the ecological pressures on the planet and the stresses of our society we are no longer so confident that technology is an unmatched good or that we are succeeding in evolving into a better world which will develop smoothly into the age of total perfection. It can be difficult to live in a state of constant fervent expectation but it is deadening to live with no hope for the future at all. The hope for the messiah is part of optimism for the future and that is why it is such an important part of Jewish thinking. In the Mishnah (the first rabbinic code, written down around 200 CE), the first chapter, where the ostensible subject is prayer, begins by referring back 130 years to the Temple Period and ends by looking forward to the days of the messiah.[47] Even when discussing prayer regulations the rabbis deliberately linked their innovations to the traditional worship held in the Temple. They knew that they needed to generate a state of mind that could overcome the despair and horrendous experiences of the previous generation in the destruction of the Temple in 70 CE and the failed revolt against the Romans in 132–5 CE led by Bar Kochba whom many of his contemporaries had believed to be the messiah. Saying that the messiah would come was a way of giving people the sense that Judaism, even after the destruction of the Temple, still had

---

46 See David Berger's book *The Rebbe, The Messiah and the Scandal of Orthodox Indifference* (Littman Library, 2001) for a fascinating discussion of the Lubavitch movement and the extent to which belief in the rebbe as messiah distorts traditional Judaism and how the longing to continue believing in a beloved messianic candidate may override rationalism and traditional messianic beliefs.

47 *Mishnah Berachot* 1.1: 'From what time may one recite the *shema* in the evening? From the time that the priests enter [the Temple] in order to eat their offerings until the end of the first watch ... 5 ... The sages, however, say: the days of your life refers to this world; "all the days of your life" is to add the days of the messiah.'

a purpose and a future. Maimonides, the medieval Jewish philosopher, set out the role of the messiah in his *Laws of Kings*:

> If a king arises from the house of David who studies the Torah and pursues the commandments ... and observes the written and oral law and he compels all Israel to follow and strengthen it – this man enjoys the presumption of being the messiah. If he proceeds successfully, defeats all the nations surrounding him, builds the Temple in its place and gathers the dispersed of Israel, then he is surely the Messiah. But if he does not succeed to this extent, or is killed, it is evident that he is not the one whom the Torah promised.[48]

It is interesting that Maimonides and other medieval Jewish writers, who were unable to accept Jesus as messiah because of the continuing imperfections of the world, still recognized that Christianity had succeeded in weaning its believers away from paganism. Some considered Christianity to be monotheistic on the basis that while Jews must not identify any human being as more in God's image than the rest of humanity, Christians' recognition of the existence of God outweighed their associating that God with Jesus.[49] Given the profound hostility of much early Christian writing about Judaism, this seems a very rational and pragmatic attitude – or as Elliott Dorff describes it: 'the fact that Maimonides couples his denunciation of Jesus and Mohammed as false prophets with the thought that they nevertheless performed the valuable function of preparing the larger world to think about God, the Torah, the commandments and the messiah is nothing short of astonishing.'[50]

Messianism may be essential for keeping a sense of purpose and hope in

48 Maimonides, *Mishneh Torah Laws of Kings* 11.4. See David Berger, 2001, *The Rebbe*, p. 152 and following for a selection of other medieval sources on Jesus' claim to be messiah.

49 Commentary on Babylonian Talmud *Sanhedrin* 63b, Rabbi Isaac (twelfth century): 'although [Christians] mention the name of Heaven, meaning thereby Jesus of Nazareth, they do not at all events mention a strange deity, and moreover, they mean thereby the Maker of Heaven and Earth too; and despite the fact that they associate the name of Heaven with an alien deity we do not find that it is forbidden to cause Gentiles to make such an association ... since such an association is not forbidden to the sons of Noah.' Rabbi Menachem HaMeiri of Provence (early fourteenth century): 'Christians recognize the Godhead and believe in God's existence, His unity and power, although they misconceive some points according to our belief ... Idol-worship has disappeared from our lands.'

50 Elliott Dorff, 2001, 'Understanding Election', in Tony Bayfield, Sidney Brichto and Eugene Fisher (eds), *He Kissed Him and They Wept*, London: SCM Press, p. 70–71.

life but the word *messiah* has led to grief and tragedy so many times in Judaism. There have been many false messiahs who have filled people with hope and then their hope has been betrayed. There was a brilliant play on in London some years ago with Maureen Lipman acting one of the tragically disappointed believers in Shabbetai Zvi, a seventeenth-century messianic claimant. Many followed him to Palestine where, when offered the choice between death and conversion to Islam, he preferred life as a Muslim, thus betraying his followers, many of whom then suffered terribly. Israel deported some whom they suspected of preparing themselves for a messianic frenzy at the beginning of the millennium year in 2000.[51] It would only have taken one lunatic on the Temple Mount and heaven knows what could have happened. Louis Finkelstein, in his book about Rabbi Akiva, who was martyred by the Romans during the Bar Kochba revolt, says that: 'Messianism was useful as a consolatory doctrine; it was pernicious as a guide to practical policy.' He then quotes the aphorism of Jochanan ben Zakkai, rabbi of the first century CE, that: 'if you are about to plant a tree and someone tells you that the messiah has come, finish your work and then go forth to meet the messiah.'[52] The Bar Kochba revolt, which had at first seemed so successful and likely to restore the destruction wrought in 70 CE when the Temple was destroyed, ended in the martyrdom of many leading rabbis and dispersal of the people. Since no wise sayings are attributed to Bar Kochba in rabbinic literature but there are many references to his physical strength, his attraction as a leader was presumably based entirely on charisma and military prowess.[53] Bar Kochba, supported by Akiva, was at the centre of the Jewish world and his failure must have made the hopes of his generation for freedom from Rome and rescue by God seem entirely hopeless; however, as the American Jewish scholar Jacob Neusner points out, the Mishnah was published only 70 years after his revolt yet it barely mentions him but concentrates on what is possible to achieve in the future.[54]

---

51 Gershom Gorenberg, 2000, *The End of Days: Fundamentalism and the Struggle for the Temple Mount*, New York: The Free Press.

52 Louis Finkelstein, 1975, *Akiva: Scholar, Saint and Martyr*, New York: Atheneum, p. 60–61.

53 Aharon Oppenheimer, 1997, 'Leadership and Messianism', in Henning Graf Reventlow (ed.), *Eschatology in the Bible and in Jewish and Christian Tradition*, Sheffield: Sheffield Academic Press, p. 162.

54 Jacob Neusner, 1984, *Messiah in Context: Israel's History and Destiny in Formative Judaism*, Philadelphia: Fortress Press, p. 31.

Rabbi Jochanan ben Zakkai saved Judaism by smuggling himself out of Jerusalem in a coffin during the Roman siege and thereafter gained permission to set up a school of Jewish studies which the Romans did not perceive as a threat in the same way as the warriors opposing them in a spirit of messianic self-righteousness. Rabbi Jochanan believed that the study of Torah, not messianism, was the preferred path. Centuries later, the great Maimonides believed that the study of Torah was the whole purpose of the messianic age:

> The wise men and the prophets did not long for the days of the Messiah to seize upon the world, nor to rule over other faiths, nor to be glorified by nations, nor to eat, drink and have a good time, but to be free for Torah and its wisdom, free from oppression and distraction so that they might be free for the life of the world to come. When that time is here, no one will go hungry; there will be no war, no fanaticism and no conflict, for goodness will flow abundantly and all delights will be as plentiful as the countless specks of dust, and the whole world will be only concerned with the knowledge of the Eternal. Then the people of Israel will be truly wise for they will know what is hidden from us and they will attain that knowledge of their creator that it is humanly possible to attain, as it is written in the prophets, For the earth will be full of that knowledge of the Eternal as the waters cover the sea.[55]

I had great difficulty with this particular passage during the time immediately after I stopped working as a congregational rabbi. I was still doing some teaching but I was no longer doing any of the pastoral work which was one of the aspects of my rabbinical career that I enjoyed most and I missed it terribly. I am in favour of a world in which there is no war and no conflict, but I realized then that we tend to define ourselves by our work and for all of us who work in caring professions and feel a sense of vocation there is an inherent problem with the Messianic Age. In the Messianic Age our caring which is part of our sense of who we are will no longer be required. Is studying Torah in a perfect world enough to compensate us for this?

In the Jewish liturgy we pray: 'May the messiah come soon in our days.'

---

55 Maimonides *Mishneh Torah Laws of Kings* 12.4–5. See David Hartman, 1993, *Epistles of Maimonides: Crisis and Leadership and Discussions*, Philadelphia: Jewish Publication Society, p. 166–86 for a discussion of Maimonides' messianic beliefs.

What do these words of expectation mean in my life? How easy is it to live life in the constant expectation of the messiah coming or do I live life with my horizons limited to working through the shopping lists, the laundry, and reminding the children to tidy up? Sometimes I feel a sense of imminent glory, of powerful expectation but this is something that usually gets lost again in the welter of daily obligations. There is a rubric in some traditional prayer books before the blessing for doing some of the commandments, 'I am ready and prepared to fulfil the positive obligation of – e.g. count the days between Passover and *Shavuot*[56] – in order to reunite God and the *shechinah*';[57] and I really like that because it does focus one for a moment on the hope that our own actions can have a positive redeeming effect on the universe around us. Sometimes the moment during *havdalah*[58] when we sing 'May Elijah the prophet, the Tishbite come soon with the messiah, the son of David' feels like a dramatic moment of expectation – and sometimes it doesn't.

Helen has raised the interesting question of messiah and gender. She refers to Radford Ruether's question 'can a male messiah save women?' and raises a further question 'can a female messiah save men?' These questions illustrate for me the key differences between Jewish and Christian understandings of messiah. These two questions have no context in Judaism because the messiah is not a saviour-figure and, as I said earlier, does not save people from sin but is the heralder of the perfect age. Because we still await the arrival of the messiah and do not know who it will be, the gender of that person is not predetermined. However, I realize from this discussion how the last 20 years of feminist language has conditioned me always to use neutral or inclusive language for God. Feminists have reminded us that God is beyond gender and that this point must be reflected in the language we use. When we speak about the human messiah who must be either male or female, it is obvious that one gender will not be represented in the messiah. Perhaps this is an argument for believing in the Messianic Age rather than a human messiah.

As well as the major beliefs about the nature of the messiah ushering in an age of peace and perfection, Judaism has some minor beliefs about the

---

56 Shavuot is the festival of the Giving of the Ten Commandments which occurs seven weeks after Passover. See Lev. 23.15.

57 God's indwelling presence, who followed the Jewish people into exile when the Temple was destroyed and will be reunited with God in the Messianic Age.

58 The ceremony which ends the sabbath.

messiah. There is a tradition which says that he will be born on *Tisha b'Av* and therefore the beginning of redemption will occur at the same time as the anniversary of the time of the destruction of the Temple; his name will be Menachem and that he will be born already circumcised. (I have used 'he' here but in fact one of the many claimants to be the messiah in Jewish history was a woman, the daughter of Joseph.[59]) I was surprised to learn that during Helen's pregnancy she had a similar experience to my own about carrying the messiah. It was surprising for me because, as she herself says, it is not usual for a Christian woman to experience such things because, according to Christian beliefs, the messiah has already come in the person of Jesus. During my second pregnancy I wondered if I was carrying the messiah. That was because I was given 1 August as a revised expected date of delivery and was appalled to notice that it fell on *Tisha b'Av* that year.[60] Menachem was already a possible name for the baby because it was my grandfather's Hebrew name. Discussing names on email with my brother, whose wife was also pregnant at the time, I mentioned Joshua as a possibility and then thought: Joshua Menachem, due on *Tisha b'Av*, wait a minute ... When my waters broke three days before *Tisha b'Av* and we started three days of waiting for me to go into labour, I was afraid that, against my conscious wish to get this baby safely born, my body was resisting – not wanting the baby to appear before *Tisha b'Av* and therefore to have a dreary Hebrew birthday for the rest of its life.[61] I did not dare to look at the messianic implications. And although in the end my son was born on *Tisha b'Av* and although his Hebrew name is Isaac Menachem, we did have to get a *mohel* to come and circumcise him – so perhaps we should not raise our messianic hopes too far.[62] The possibility of being the bearer of the messiah is a poignant idea for women;

59 *The Encyclopedia Judaica* makes references to a female messianic figure (young prophetess) in Baghdad around 1120–21. See 'Messianic Movements' in *The Encyclopedia Judaica*, vol. 11, p. 1422. For further studies, see S. D. Goitein's article in *The Jewish Quarterly Review*, 43, 1952/3, p. 57–76.

60 I did not have the same experience with my first child because he was due in October, at least two months after *Tisha b'Av*.

61 *Tisha b'Av* is kept as a solemn fast day commemorating the destruction of the first and second Temples and many other tragedies in Jewish history and the nine days preceding it are also a time of mourning when celebrations are forbidden for observant Jews.

62 The *mohel*, the person who performs the circumcision, in Isaac's case obviously felt that date and name were enough because he said 'perhaps he is the messiah' as we waited to begin the ceremony.

I remember years ago reading an article by the American Jewish feminist Aviva Cantor in which she movingly expressed her thoughts when considering terminating a pregnancy. Her worries included her concern that perhaps it was the messiah she was carrying and her protest that Jewish women who abort should not have to feel that extra guilt.

These thoughts do fit with the Jewish belief that in every generation there is a messianic figure in waiting; if the generation is good enough to deserve the immediate coming of the Messianic Age it would be no good having to wait 20 years for the messiah who is needed now to reach adulthood. Once I spent shabbat at Kfar Chabad, the Lubavitch village near Lod airport in Israel. My hostess took me to visit her mother who as soon as I had been introduced asked, 'Do you keep shabbat?' Her daughter explained that this was because of her mother's passionate belief in the tradition that if all Jews keep shabbat perfectly two weeks running then the messiah will come immediately. This tells you a lot about Jewish sabbatical observance throughout the ages as well as about the Lubavitch sense that anything they can do to influence someone to keep the commandments should be done in case it helps bring messiah. The idea that the messiah is there and can be revealed if only we do what we must to make a world fit for his coming is the thinking behind one of my favourite Talmudic stories about the messiah:

> Rabbi Joshua came upon the prophet Elijah as he was standing at the entrance to Rabbi Simeon ben Yochai's cave. He asked him: 'When is the messiah coming?' He replied: 'Go ask him yourself.' 'Where shall I find him and how shall I know him?' 'Before the gates of Rome. He is sitting among poor people covered with wounds. The others unbind all their wounds at once, and then bind them up again. But he unbinds one wound at a time and then binds it up again straightaway. He tells himself: "Perhaps I shall be needed [to appear as the messiah] and I must not take time and be late." So he went and found him and said: "Peace be with you, my master and teacher!" He replied: "Peace be with you son of Levi." He asked: "When are you coming master?" "Today." Then he returned to Elijah and said to him: "He has deceived me, he has indeed deceived me. He told me, 'Today I am coming' and he has not come." But Elijah said, "This is what he told you '[I will come today], if you obey his voice!' " '[63]

---

63 Babylonian Talmud, *Sanhedrin* 98a, quoting Ps. 95.7.

Or as Rabbi Nachman of Bratslav (1772–1811) universalized it to apply to all of us: 'no duty is more sacred than for us to cherish the spark of messiah in our souls and save it from extinction.' I conclude with Norman Solomon's words: 'we must be genial, patient and humble. Pragmatic as well, and level-headed. Even when talking about messiah. *Especially* when talking about the messiah.'[64] But perhaps we can be hopeful enough as well as level-headed to say, 'May the messiah come soon, speedily in our days.'

Further Reading

See the Bibliography section for full details on these titles.

James Charlesworth (ed.), *Messiah: Developments in Earliest Judaism and Christianity.*
John Crossan and Jonathan Reed, *Excavating Jesus: Beneath the Stones, Behind the Texts.*
Paula Fredriksen, *Jesus of Nazareth King of the Jews: A Jewish Life and the Emergence of Christianity.*
Gerd Theissen and Annette Merz, *The Historical Jesus: A Comprehensive Guide.*

---

64 Norman Solomon, 1991, *Judaism and World Religion*, p. 169.

4 The Holocaust

Dialogical imagination attempts to bridge the gaps of time and space to create new horizons, and to connect the disparate elements of our lives into a meaningful whole.

Kwok Pui-Lan[1]

I The Holocaust and Dialogical Imagination

Lynne Scholefield

In this section I am writing about my dialogue with the Holocaust and with Holocaust museums and memorials in the context of Jewish-Christian women's dialogue. I am not particularly discussing women's experience in the Holocaust or Holocaust theology.[2] As I discussed in the chapter on 'women knowing, women in dialogue', what we have to say is expressed not only in prepositional or traditional theological language, but also in stories and other imaginative ways. Here, as a Christian, woman educator, I want to weave some fragments about the Holocaust in order to try to speak as and for myself in the face of, or in the presence of, Jewish women whose lives and whose families' lives have been touched much more directly by the Holocaust itself. I have chosen very deliberately to write about 'weaving fragments'. Weaving is a traditional women's activity and provides rich possibilities for imaging women's knowing. Fragments (of glass) are sharp and they cut; one of the first occasions for

---

1 I am indebted to the writings of the Asian feminist theologian Kwok Pui-Lan for some of the ways in which I present what I have to say here about the Holocaust. Kwok Pui-Lan, 1995, *Discovering the Bible in the Non-Biblical World*, Maryknoll: Orbis Books, p. 13.

2 For an excellent discussion of the role of gender in the Holocaust see Dalia Ofer and Lenore Weitzman (eds), 1998, *Women in the Holocaust*, New Haven: Yale University Press. For an innovative and feminist approach to Holocaust theology see Melissa Raphael, 2003, *The Female Face of God in Auschwitz*, London: Cassell.

the deliberate destruction of Jews and Jewish life in Nazi Germany was 'Kristallnacht' (night of the broken glass) in November 1938.

Among other things I am interested in the way the Holocaust affects our understanding of Judaism and Christianity and the relationship between them, and our understanding of who we are and how we should live. I am also concerned with a number of issues related to what it means to tell the truth about the Holocaust. What educational difference does it make to me if I learn about the Holocaust? I propose a particular understanding of the Holocaust centred on the power of story and I am interested in the educational potential of stories about what happened in the Holocaust and what transformation takes place when we 'hear' these stories. In the second part of this section I will look at how my own story has been affected by the Holocaust. I suggest that the Jewish commitment to education can be understood as a form of spiritual resistance to Nazism. I name Holocaust education as a form of spiritual resistance to all that made the Holocaust possible and suggest that through our educational and dialogical encounters with the stories of the Holocaust, perhaps our own stories can be transformed.

'Story' is important because it tells me who I am. If you listen to stories, they will also tell you something about me. In our women's group, we have learned from one another, through our stories, about who we are and who we might become. Education and dialogue must offer stories that challenge the limits of our self-understanding and empower us to tell our own stories. Study of the Holocaust will be educational if it enables us to engage at some depth with Holocaust stories. I find that 'storying' gives me a way of approaching the Holocaust as a 'text' and so drawing on the Jewish method of biblical interpretation called *midrash*. As the Jewish writer Avivah Zornberg writes in her book on Genesis:

> The aim of interpretation is ... to make the reader aware, in the current that runs between his/her lived situation and the text of the way in which we are, at key instants, strangers to ourselves ... On the one hand we are reassured to find ourselves, with our most radical dilemmas, reflected in these ... texts. On the other hand, the midrashic strategy will not allow us to rest in a formalized, serenely fixed image of human life.[3]

---

3 Avivah Gottlieb Zornberg, 1995, *Genesis: The Beginning of Desire*, Jerusalem: The Jewish Publication Society, p. xv.

The 'texts' of the Holocaust include the, mainly written, work of those caught up in the events: perpetrators, victims, rescuers, bystanders, survivors, resisters. There are many artefacts such as photographs, cartoons, paintings and drawings, and children's exercise books from the Holocaust which also tell a story. The museums that house these artefacts are part of an ongoing story about the Holocaust and there are also the concentration camps and extermination camps themselves. I shall be telling some stories about visits to museums and camps later. Histories, poetry, plays, fiction, films and other different forms of reflection and interpretation of the events continue to be produced and some of this is explicitly theological. However, it would be wrong to think that there is a simple and uncontroversial 'Holocaust story'. Even the word that people use to refer to the events of 1933–45 is contested. Many Jews and some Christians refuse to use the word 'holocaust', meaning 'burnt whole', because of its usage in the Septuagint (the Greek translation of the Hebrew Bible) to translate *olah*, what is brought up, that is a sacrifice, a burnt offering pleasing to God. *Churban* meaning 'catastrophe' was the term used to refer to the destruction of the First and Second Temples and some Jews use it for the Holocaust. Growing in usage is the Hebrew word *Shoah* which also signifies catastrophic destruction. I will continue to use 'Holocaust' because it is the term used by many of the victims, is widely employed and understood, and is capitalized to indicate the uniqueness of the events.[4]

To be 'a lesson in living',[5] Holocaust education must wrestle with questions of truth. There are arguments which are really about the canon of Holocaust texts. What should count as a 'Holocaust text'? What is truthful? What is allowed? There have been serious disagreements between some Jews and Christians over the Carmelite convent at Auschwitz, the beatification and canonization of Edith Stein and the story which is to be told about Pope Pius XII,[6] all of which have de-stabilized the progress in Catholic-Jewish relations in recent decades. For me, the argument about truth has been most sharply focused by the debate about the authenticity

---

4 For a much fuller discussion of this issue see Isabel Wollaston, 1996, *A War Against Memory?*, London: SPCK.

5 This phrase is used in a review of the republication of Etty Hillesum's *An Interrupted Life: The Diaries and Letters of Etty Hillesum 1941–1943*. At the end of the review Anne Karpf wrote: 'Her book is a lesson in living.' *The Jewish Chronicle*, 16 July 1999, p. 16.

6 See for example Carol Rittner and John Roth (eds), 1991, *Memory Offended*, New York: Praeger; and J. Cornwell, 1999, *Hitler's Pope*, London: Viking.

of Binjamin Wilkomirski's book, *Fragments*, subtitled *Memories of a Childhood 1939–1948*.[7] 'Telling stories' is often a euphemism for 'telling lies' and although Wilkomirski's book won the *Jewish Quarterly* Prize for non-fiction, it is probably fiction;[8] however, it has raised very complex issues about story, identity and truth. More attention needs to be given to questions about what it means to tell the truth about the Holocaust. Recent developments in gender studies have enabled scholars to recognize the importance of gender issues in arriving at more truthful accounts of the Holocaust.[9] Long before the particular example of Wilkomirski, the trustworthiness of survivors' testimonies has been of concern. I have never heard a survivor talk about his or her own experiences but I did recently hear Irene Opdyke (a Polish Catholic rescuer, honoured as a Righteous Gentile at Yad Vashem) tell her story at the Holocaust Museum in Houston. This very elderly lady has told her story many times, perhaps always in the same words. It is a moving story and she received a standing ovation but was I the only one who was uncomfortable with the 'performance'? Now, I am beginning to tell a fragment of 'my story' and to explore my responses to a Holocaust text. There are intellectual aspects which interest me about what it means to tell the truth about the Holocaust but there is also the much more disconcerting awareness that Irene's story is a challenge to me. Would I have had her courage, her luck, her ability to be 'more than she thought she was' or not?[10] It is an uncomfortable question for me.

The Holocaust must, surely, make most people uncomfortable, and yet the recent story of the Holocaust seems to be one that increasing numbers of people who have no direct link to Holocaust events want to hear. The United States Holocaust Memorial Museum in Washington is attracting four or five times the number of visitors that were expected and every

---

7 Picador, 1997.

8 Elena Lappin has provided a good summary of the case in 'The Man with Two Heads', *Granta*, 66, Summer 1999, p. 7–65. BBC1 showed a documentary about the case on 3 November 1999 entitled 'Child of the Death Camps: Truth and Lies'. It was over an hour long and in 'prime time', 9.30–10.35 pm. These details are relevant to something I shall say later about the Holocaust, Britain and the Millennium.

9 See for example Carol Rittner and John Roth, 1993, *Different Voices: Women and the Holocaust*, New York: Paragon House.

10 The phrase 'to be more than I thought I was' comes from a fascinating account of a journey from Florida to Mexico made by Nunez Cabesa de Vaca in 1528. See Haniel Long, 1969, *The Marvellous Adventures of Cabesa da Vaca*, London: Souvenir Press.

American city seems to have its own Holocaust museum. I recently visited the Holocaust Memorial in Boston. This is a city with several historic graveyards on the 'Freedom Trail'. The guide tells stories of a number of people buried there who were active in the American War of Independence and this 'freedom story' is continued and developed in 'Holocaust', which has been built on a leafy street very close to the 'Freedom Trail'. The memorial consists of a row of six glass towers with a path running from one end to the other. Steam comes up through grills under the towers. When I visited there was a survivor telling his story and showing photographs. There are a number of inscriptions which connect together freedom, America and the flag.

In Britain the official Holocaust memorial exhibition opened at the Imperial War Museum in 2000 and I think the date is significant. The first Holocaust Memorial Day was planned for early in 2001, and 2000 also saw the Deborah Lipstadt trial at the Old Bailey,[11] and a major international scholars' conference in Oxford and London called 'Remembering for the Future 2000 – the Holocaust in an Age of Genocides'. Although the events of the Holocaust occurred more than 50 years previously, it was only as thinking about the millennium took place that it was seen to be significant for British self-understanding. All this activity, and the BBC television film referred to earlier, suggests that, for decision makers in Britain, remembering the Holocaust and seeing it as having lessons for the future is important. Of course, as I am trying to show, I think that that is true.

Anne and I visited the Holocaust Exhibition at the Imperial War Museum. One of the survivors who tell their story in the exhibition was Hugo Gryn who sadly died in 1996. On a television programme he told how in the camp he felt completely abandoned by the people who could have helped him. For him the problem was not 'Where was God?' but 'Where was man [sic]?' The exhibition helped me to see more clearly the human and historical background, especially the deliberate racist and specifically antisemitic developments in education in the 1930s. I found the exhibition very restrained and carefully thought out. Although there were many voices to listen to, it left me, in the end voiceless. Anne and I had very little conversation afterwards. What is there to say? As with every

---

11 David Irving, a Holocaust denier, took Lipstadt and her publishers to court for the critical remarks she had made about him in a book. The judge found in her favour and his summing up included a significant legal judgement about the importance of telling the truth about the Holocaust.

Holocaust museum and camp I have ever visited, it left me very angry at the awful waste of human life and potential, and the stupidity of the whole thing, aware of the drivenness of those involved, and overwhelmed by the concreteness of the evil.

One of the things that going to see the exhibition with a Jewish woman made me strongly aware of again was that I, as a Christian, have a choice, in a way in which she, as a Jew, does not, about whether to claim that the Holocaust has significance for me, about whether it is, in any way, 'my story'. And if I do claim this, is this too audacious? Will it offend or insult Jews? And yet the Holocaust has affected my story. In 1994, I went to Poland as part of a Jewish Studies delegation. In Warsaw we visited the Jewish Museum where there is an exhibition of items saved from the Ghetto. We saw exercise books used by children in the days before they were loaded on to trains and sent to their deaths in an extermination camp. These children would not have a future, they would not live to experience adult life, but it was still seen as important that they receive an education. One of the Jewish delegates summed up this commitment to education as 'the distilled essence of teaching'. Those words haunted me. What could I as a teacher and educator learn from the Warsaw Ghetto?[12]

When I went to Auschwitz my 'reading' of it was affected, in one particular way, by my own story. We were guided round the site by a quietly spoken and reflective man. Unlike some guides he did refer to Jewish victims at Auschwitz and not just at Birkenau. He did not hurry us and we could try to take in the meaning of the piles of shoes, glasses and suitcases, the places where people slept, were marched around and were shot or hanged. Finally we walked through a gas chamber and stopped by the ovens that had burned the corpses. One member of the group was a cantor and she sang *kaddish*, the Jewish prayer for the dead. Most people in the group were crying; a few had lost relatives in the camps. No relative of mine had been killed but it was as if I was saying *kaddish* too for my mother who had died the year before. My father had not wanted any fuss and she had been buried quickly with no funeral service or gravestone. He had also cleared the house of anything that would be a reminder of her. Somehow,

---

12 I explored the question of the important ideas about education in Jewish thinking in my PhD thesis (*A Tale of Two Cultures: A Dialogical Study of the Cultures of a Jewish and Catholic Secondary School*, 1999, unpublished, University of London) and argued that both education and Holocaust texts are forms of spiritual resistance to the dehumanization attempted by the Nazis.

in the gloom of the crematorium at Auschwitz, it was licit to mourn her and to remember her, just as we were ensuring those who had died in the Holocaust were not forgotten. These are my own stories and reflect visits to the camps and to museums. Other people, who are also not Jews, tell stories which illustrate the potential power of reading Holocaust texts.

Often when people talk about the Holocaust they refer to *The Diary of Anne Frank*.[13] Mo Mowlam claimed that when she was Northern Ireland Secretary the example of Anne Frank had inspired her efforts to bring peace to Ulster.[14] One woman I interviewed during the course of my research on the Holocaust and education talked about the impact of the book on her over a long period of time and of her identification with Anne. She was impressed with how Anne could confide her thoughts and feelings to 'Kitty' whom she addresses in her diary, and how she coped with the cramped living conditions. She said:

> I suppose it identified a way of growing up. Externally I would have learned what people can do to survive, how they did survive, how they can still read and culturally go on. Remember, her dad carried on teaching her, and that in that situation there was no loss of spirit. She maintained herself, she carried on ... You know some books change you? It was a very strong changing influence on me ... That it was okay to grow up and that people you disliked, you were probably quite right to dislike them.

She told me how the book had stimulated her to read more books by Jewish writers and books about the war. She confirmed the power of bringing together textual and personal story when she said, 'It's where it linked with my story I suppose, where there were intersections, that I read on. So I read more about being Jewish because I was Catholic. I read more about the war because my dad was in it.'

Ruth Linden, in her book *Making Stories, Making Selves*, began to record the stories of Holocaust survivors without considering what the implications would be for understanding ethnographic research, the process of writing, and for her own life.[15] In the epilogue she wrote:

---

13 Originally published in 1953 there have been many editions of the diary, in many languages. A new 'definitive edition' was published in 1997 by Penguin Books.

14 Bernard Josephs, 1999, 'Mo Mowlam's "inspiration"', *Jewish Chronicle*, 22 January, p. 9.

15 Ruth Linden, 1993, *Making Stories, Making Selves*, Columbus: Ohio State University Press.

I had no idea how I would be changed over a period of years by working with survivors and their texts, nor that, in the process, my own Jewish identity would be refigured. I did not expect to write a book that would represent my own life alongside the stories of Holocaust survivors. Nor did I expect I would discover that 'self' and 'other' are inseparably fused in a dialectic of situated knowing.[16]

Most of what I have discussed here are fragments of stories about encounters with the Holocaust. They are mainly from women, including myself. I want to end with some comments that make more explicit the links that I perceive between the Holocaust, education, women's voices and spiritual resistance. Put simply I believe that encounter with Holocaust stories can help us to be 'more than we thought we were'. When I was in hospital a friend brought me Victor Frankl's book, *Man in Search of Meaning*, to read.[17] It might seem an odd choice but it was just what I needed during long sleepless nights since it addressed fundamental human experiences and choices. It affirmed that there was meaning to be found even in the most meaningless situations, and that our individual actions can, indeed, make a difference. I see this life-changing experience as education. When the teachers and children in the Warsaw Ghetto continued with education this too was a form of spiritual resistance to all the de-humanizing efforts of the Nazi regime. Writing their story was a form of resistance for many. Rachel Brenner has described the writing of Edith Stein, Simone Weil, Anne Frank and Etty Hillesum in just this way. She argues that studying their and others' stories of their struggle might empower our struggle:

> I propose that it was their struggle to preserve faith in the reality of a faithless world, to continue to love the world despite its lovelessness, that infused meaning into the lives of these women ... The struggle of the four women to preserve the humanist ideal demonstrates remarkable foresight into the ethical predicament of post war society. Their resistance leaves us with a complex legacy of searching for the meaning of life in a reality of senseless brutality, unimaginable hatred and atrocious death.[18]

May the memory of these and all the others be a blessing.

---

16 Ruth Linden, 1993, *Making Stories*, p. 147.

17 V. Frankl, 1984, *Man in Search of Meaning*, New York: Washington Square Press.

18 Rachel Feldhay Brenner, 1997, *Writing as Resistance*, Pennsylvania: The Pennsylvania State University Press, p. 10–11.

II Consider That This Has Been: A Personal Response to the Holocaust Exhibition at the Imperial War Museum by two Jewish Women Educators

Anne Clark and Irene Wise

Where one burns books, one will, in the end, burn people.

Heinrich Heine[19]

Heine, a Jewish poet, died almost 50 years before the Nazis seized power, yet his statement rings with chilling prescience, from Berlin's Opernplatz (where his own books were burned on 10 May 1933) to Auschwitz. Heinrich Himmler, head of the Gestapo and organizer of the mass murder of the Jews, intended to destroy all evidence of the Nazi crime. He claimed that: 'The Final Solution ... would be a page of history that would never be written, it would never be spoken about, as though it had never taken place.'[20] As Jewish educators, we have a responsibility to speak about that crime and fill that page of history, refuting the Nazis with every word we write. We have a responsibility to history and to the dead; we carry that burden of memory so that our words become a memorial to the people who perished. Writing about the Shoah (Holocaust) is the antithesis of Heine's maxim, creating a powerful form of practical and spiritual resistance: Holocaust education strives to reclaim the dignity and memory of a lost generation. The Holocaust Exhibition at the Imperial War Museum plays an important role in this process and, as Lynne has argued in the first part of this chapter, can be seen in Jewish terms as a text to be read and interpreted. In our response, we will look at how the exhibition became the focus of a three-dimensional dialogue between us: first, it was the means through which Irene and Anne conversed with each other; second, the means through which we dialogued with Lynne; and finally the means through which we 'conversed' with the past, present and future.

---

19 The poet's ominous words feature in a large inscription on the wall at the Imperial War Museum Exhibition. They are taken from the play entitled 'Almansor. Eine Tragödie' in Heinrich Heine, 1823, *Tragödien, nebst einem lyrischen Intermezzo*, Berlin: Ferdinand Dümmler, p. 148.

20 In his speech to SS group leaders at Poznan on 4 October 1943.

Understanding the Shoah as 'text', like other texts in Judaism, is a helpful way of speaking about the testimonies and stories that emerged. In much the same way as Lynne understands her personal encounter with stories from the Holocaust as a 'text', in this section we will weave our understanding of such texts within the context of education. The traditional model of texts in Judaism has the Torah at the centre, surrounded in turn by rabbinic, medieval and modern commentaries. Textual study creates a dialogue between students and scholars across the centuries, 'a symposium of generations'.[21] All opinions are retained so that successive generations can use the material to inform their own lives. As Jewish educators, we lay great store on this inter-generational conversation and on the value of asking questions and on the significance of memory. We begin with our individual stories.

Anne's Story

These words that I command you today shall be upon your heart. Repeat them to your children; speak of them when you sit in your house, when you walk along the way; when you lie down, and when you rise up.

Deuteronomy 6.6–7

I was brought up in the shadow of the Shoah. My parents were refugees from Nazi Germany who came to this country shortly before the Second World War: some of my relatives were murdered by the Nazis. My childhood in North-West London was coloured by my parents' accounts of their experience of discrimination in pre-war Germany. They never lost their deep-seated fear of inadvertently transgressing against the mores of this country. They were terrified of offending their hosts and being cast adrift once again. All the significant adults in my life at that time were refugees and survivors. When I visited the Holocaust Exhibition at the Imperial War Museum, I was aware of taking with me my late parents, their refugee friends and the members of my family who did not survive.

My father never fully integrated into British society and never learnt the

---

21 This image was used during a talk given on his birthday by Rabbi Joseph Soloveichik (1985).

English language properly. Though he lived an observant Jewish life, he had not done much Jewish study. At some level, I think that my work as a Jewish educator is a form of reparation for the opportunities he missed. My passion for Jewish learning springs too from my sadness at the near-destruction of European Jewry. I feel acutely aware of my place as a human link in what Jews call 'the chain of tradition'. This continuity began with Moses at the time of the Revelation at Sinai some 3,500 years ago and stretches across the generations, right up to the present day and hopefully, way into the future.

I have an image of myself as sitting in the centre of a potentially ever-widening sphere of influence. Starting in my own home, I felt compelled to take very seriously the Torah's command to pass on Jewish customs and traditions to my children, just as my parents passed on their rich heritage to me. I chose to be a Jewish educator in order to communicate my enthusiasm for the teachings and rituals of Judaism to a larger circle of Jewish children and adults, as well as to non-Jews. I strongly believe that encounters with sensitive, articulate Jews, coupled with increased understanding of Jewish values and practices, help to combat prejudice and antisemitism. In this connection, I particularly value my work with students and teachers of religious education. I try to give them a positive experience that they will pass on to others and to future generations.

Irene's Story

Consider that this has been
I commend these words to you
Engrave them on your hearts
When you are in your house, when you walk on your way,
When you go to bed, when you rise.
Repeat them to your children.
Or may your house crumble,
Disease render you powerless,
Your offspring avert their faces from you.

Primo Levi[22]

---

22 From 'Shemá', translated by Ruth Feldman and Brian Swann, 1995, in Hilda Schiff (ed.), *Holocaust Poetry*, London: HarperCollins, p. 205.

I grew up in Surrey where my parents were active in the local synagogue but most of my friends were not Jewish. I was not conscious of knowing survivors or exiles, although in retrospect I realize a few were part of our community. The Holocaust was not discussed. Yet, at ten years old, my mother took me to see the film of Anne Frank and I read Leon Uris's novel *Exodus*. Now I work as artist and educator, teaching Holocaust representation to non-Jewish students. I deal particularly with visual awareness and how that relates to meaning. Walking around the exhibition, I automatically considered how I would teach from the display and how I might direct and facilitate my students' own looking. None of us is a *tabula rasa*, we bring to every experience that which has gone before. After my visit, I realized that subconsciously, I had brought with me many others also involved in Holocaust education and cultural representation: other artists, writers and educators; as well as survivors, historians, film makers and curators. Somehow all these friends and colleagues were present in my head, along with the images, films and texts recently discussed with my undergraduates. Constantly at the back of my mind was the earnest face of my youngest student. The people I carried with me to this exhibition were the living.

Our Story

We authors are from very different backgrounds and each has a different approach. Anne, from a refugee family, deeply affected by their experience of the Holocaust, brings a cerebral, religious perspective. Irene, from a British family mostly silent on the Shoah, brings an aesthetic and secular viewpoint. Yet there are similarities between us. We are women of a similar age. Born a few years after the Shoah, we grew up in the midst of the repercussions and trauma of the post-war years. We are both members of a Progressive synagogue; and both regard ourselves as ambassadors for Judaism, feeling a responsibility to bear witness for the past. We came to the exhibition in friendship and through this, learnt from each other. Anne appreciated the colours, textures and symbols, as seen through Irene's eyes while Irene gained insight into the religious dimension through the lens of Anne's vision.

The Artist's Eye

One single Anne Frank moves us more than the countless others who have suffered just as she did but whose faces have remained in the shadows. Perhaps it is better that way: if we were capable of taking in all the suffering of all those people, we would not be able to live.

Primo Levi[23]

Our initial impression of the Imperial War Museum Exhibition was one of life, emphasized by the warm, natural wood lining the walls of the first room. Here, and throughout the exhibition, survivors' testimonies are presented in colour film, while black and white footage and photographs portray extinguished Jewish life. The threat of National Socialism is heightened in vivid film and posters, their dramatic reds indicating danger, blood and death. Otherwise, colour is restricted throughout the exhibition: monochromatic walls and floors reflect the sombre theme, becoming their darkest on the lower level with the presentation of mass extermination. The lighting, size, scale and situation of images and exhibits have been considered: everything is placed to heighten its significance. Sometimes, silence and absence speak louder than word or image. Primo Levi reminds us that consciousness is raised through empathy with one individual. We were touched by a display of paper playing cards, made in her cell by Margot Schloss, who had been denounced as a Communist. Neatly torn, the cards' values and suits were pricked out with a pin. Emblematic of stoic endurance, they add meaning to the solo games of patience for which they were made during her time in solitary confinement.

Tension builds towards the last exhibit on the upper floor. Melancholic strains of Jewish prayer reach us from across the gallery, and behind us, the conflicting rasp of Nazi rants: but here is silence. We stare at a stark white dissection table. Among the cacophony and plethora of images, for the first time we gaze at something empty. Now we are left to our imagination, where emptiness speaks loudly to us because we know the grisly truth of human sacrifice. The torture table appears to jut out over the abyss, as it edges towards the pale, angular staircase. The limed wood of the banisters are stripped of colour, drained of life, leading us into the lower area, as if down into hell.

---

23 Primo Levi (1986) written on a wall in the Anne Frank House, Amsterdam.

Claude Lanzmann, in his film *Shoah* (1984) ensures that survivors never confront a perpetrator: he creates boundaries between them by interspersing interviews with filmed landscape. The Imperial War Museum Exhibition displays a similar sensitivity, brilliantly demonstrated in the long glass cabinet representing Sobibor. The town's large railway station sign is placed at the centre of the display, on a stark shelf. Its black and white lettering, in this context, signifies death. To the right of the sign, sits a lone Star of David: fashioned from two rusting metal triangles, its rough edges create the symbol both of the Jewish religion and of its persecution. Whoever made it surely wanted to reclaim the badge of Judaism, to celebrate its true significance. On the left of the railway sign, sit a lamp and a black telephone from the station both indicating the technology employed for the final journey to death. Next to these are grouped a chipped beer mug and some green glass beer bottles: these vessels obviously belonged to the oppressors and remain virtually intact. On this shelf, victim and perpetrator are kept separate by the railway sign between them. Hung across the front of the glass case, hard, dark metal rectangles name Nazi officials, with their photographs. White type coolly describes, in their own words, their contribution to genocide: one was the man who fitted the false showerheads. The perpetrators are kept outside of the cabinet, apart from those they persecuted, while the metallic sheets bear down towards the bottom of the glass case. Here, below the shelf with the railway sign, lie fragments of objects that once belonged to the victims. On view are odd beads and buttons; twisted, broken combs, forks and spoons; rusted tin mugs; tiny glass bottles; a crushed red thimble; and remnants of toothbrushes – the shards of shattered lives. A couple of blue beads and rusting blue fragments, together with the red toothbrushes, add touches of colour (resistance) in an otherwise muted display.

Every exhibit presented is authentically of its time, the only exception being the all-white model of Auschwitz. This is not the white of innocence – it is simply colourless: life and humanity have been bleached out of it. Any colour here would be kitsch (in poor taste) and reduce the model to a child's toy. This cold whiteness reminds us of the camp's deathly purpose, but it is not just symbolic. Survivors have written of the agonizingly long roll calls, standing throughout severe weather. In summer, the unremitting sun cruelly burned unprotected skin. Memoirs recall grey rain, freezing snow and sunlight without shade – all draining colour from the bleak landscape. This model, although in miniature, manages to portray the hugeness of the actual place by including tiny figures. From them we gain a sense of scale through seeing the camp in relation to the size of human beings within it. As we leave the exhibition, we note again the filmed colour testimonies of survivors and the fresh wooden walls of the final room, echoing those of the first. Starting with life, we are ending with life.

Educators' Insights

> Those who cannot remember the past are condemned to repeat it.
>
> *George Santayana*[24]

The Imperial War Museum has taken its remit very seriously, presenting an exhibition impressive in its range and depth and carefully planning its education programme. Schoolchildren meet with one of the museum's trained facilitators when they first arrive and once again for a debriefing at the end of their visit. They view the exhibition with an audio guide that draws attention to personal stories, significant details and the use of language; it also invites emotional response. The focused guidance helps the young visitors to make sense of their experience; otherwise there is so much to see that one risks seeing nothing.

The exhibition opens with a room entitled 'Life before the Nazis'. Significantly, the word 'Jewish' is not included here; and throughout the exhibition the richness of pre-war European Jewish life remains understated. The emphasis has been placed on the Holocaust itself and it would be hard for any museum to convey fully the enormous loss of culture and civilization that was destroyed alongside the murdered six million. The exhibition focuses on 'the destruction of the Jews and the suffering of others'[25] – an approach which writer Peter Novick finds more Christian than Jewish. Novick suggests that in such commemoration: 'suffering is sacralized and portrayed as the path to wisdom – the cult of the survivor as secular saint.'[26] He compares the display of Holocaust memorabilia to that

---

24 George Santayana, 1905, *The Life of Reason*, vol. I:12, New York: Scribners, p. 284.

25 Robert Crawford, 2000, *The Holocaust Exhibition at the Imperial War Museum*, London: The Imperial War Museum, p. 3.

26 Peter Novick, 1999, *The Holocaust in Collective Memory*, London: Bloomsbury, p. 11.

of holy relics, which could have the connotation of martyrdom for the innocent victims.[27] Jews do not see suffering as a path to holiness, but only as evidence that we humans, as God's partners, have not yet completed our task of perfecting the world. The message of Judaism, Novick reminds us, is not to extend mourning but to choose life. Indeed the *kaddish* (the sacred prayer used for remembering the dead) does not mention death at all, but affirms life: 'May great peace from heaven and the gift of life be granted to us ...'

A documentary in *The Longest Hatred* alcove provides a history of antisemitism, charting the path from religious hatred to racial hatred, culminating in persecution under the Nazis. Elsewhere, there are displays of antisemitic publications, posters and cartoons. Overall, the exhibition tends to underplay the complicity of the Church; instead, it highlights sympathetic Christian responses to the tragedy, both in Europe and in the safety of this country. We read the words of the Roman Catholic Archbishop Clemens August Count von Galen, who preached in 1941 that: 'Once human beings have the right to kill other "unproductive" human beings ... then none of us is safe.' Through a telephone handset, we hear the voice of the Archbishop of Canterbury urging the British Government and others in 1939 to seek out a place of safety for the refugees from Nazi Europe. Reminding his cinema audience that asylum is needed for 'multitudes of Christians as well as of Jews', he proposes that such settlement should be in 'the open spaces of the earth' rather than in Britain. The exhibition maps the restrictive immigration quotas imposed by the free world, including Britain. Greater emphasis could have been given to the fact that this policy cost the lives of many Jews.

Lynne has spoken about memory and remembrance. From a Jewish perspective, it is important to note that the key word of the Hebrew Bible is not history but memory. The twentieth-century Jewish scholar Yosef Hayim Yerushalmi has highlighted that: 'only in Israel and nowhere else is the injunction to remember felt as a religious imperative to an entire people.'[28] Indeed, the word *zakhor*, 'remember' in its various forms, occurs 169 times in the Hebrew Bible often in complement with the

---

27 He speaks about: 'fetishized objects on display like so many fragments of the True Cross, or shin bones of saints.' Peter Novick, 1999, *The Holocaust in Collective Memory*, p. 11.

28 Yosef Hayim Yerushalmi, 1982, *Zakhor* (Jewish History and Jewish Memory), Philadelphia: The Jewish Publication Society of America, p. 9.

command not to forget. *Zakhor* signifies more than a consciousness of the past. *Yizkor* (the name given to the traditional Jewish prayer for the dead) is associated in the Torah with the future;[29] for example, 'God remembered Rachel' and gave her a child (Gen. 30.22). 'We remember for the sake of the future, and for life.'[30] But the years following the Shoah were characterized by forgetting, both in terms of the dearth of Holocaust memorialization by governments and the silence of survivors. The deeper the trauma, the longer it takes to deal with it. Second-generation writer Lisa Appignanesi notes:

> Haunted by loss, all [they] wanted to do was forget, to live in the relative safety of the present and build a better future ... Forgetting seemed a far better recipe for life, than the endless repetitive business of remembering ... But once new lives had been established and forgetting had become entrenched, active remembering ... became possible, particularly since a new generation, untouched by war now needed not so much to remember as to learn.[31]

As Lynne has mentioned, in the last 20 years there has been a vast growth in collective remembering of the Holocaust; most significantly in Britain the Government instituted an annual Holocaust Memorial Day in 2001. Thousands of monuments and museums have sprung up all over Europe and America, drawing in many visitors. Yet the success of the exhibition at the Imperial War Museum cannot be judged by the large numbers it attracts, but rather by the personal and political responses it engenders. Remembrance alone is not enough. The lessons of the Holocaust remind us of the consequences of prejudice: this should impel us to take a stand against all forms of discrimination at both individual and governmental levels.

Jewish scholar Matis Weinberg points out that the Hebrew word *zakhor* not only means to remember and to remain aware of, but also 'to speak of'. He writes: 'Speech is not a *tool* for awareness, it is an integral *component* of

---

29 This was highlighted by Lord Jakobovits, former Chief Rabbi of the United Hebrew Congregations of Great Britain and the Commonwealth and quoted by the current Chief Rabbi Jonathan Sacks in *The Chief Rabbi's Haggadah*, London: HarperCollins, 2003, p. 29.

30 Jonathan Sacks, 2003, *The Chief Rabbi's Haggadah*, p. 29.

31 Lisa Appignanesi, 2002, untitled essay in Ben Barkow, Katherine Klinger and Melissa Rosenbaum (eds), *Storeys of Memory*, London: The Wiener Library, p. 15.

awareness.'[32] Speaking aloud is essential for keeping alive the memories of the Holocaust through survivor testimonies, the dissemination of information and the telling of tales. Nobel Laureate Elie Wiesel tells the following poignant story: When the great Rabbi Israel Baal Shem Tov saw misfortune threatening the Jews, he would go to a certain place in the forest, light a fire and recite a special prayer. Successive generations of rabbis forgot in turn how to light the fire, how to say the prayer, and finally, how to find the place in the forest. All that they remembered was how to tell the story. And that was enough.[33]

Conclusion

One who saves a single life ... saves the world entire.

Mishnah Sanhedrin 4.5

We can only comprehend the scale of the concentration camp through the tiny, modelled people at the exhibition. Similarly it is through individuals and their stories that we can begin to grasp the enormity of the Holocaust – and this is something that Lynne has also highlighted. The loss is tempered by details of the personal narratives that affirm life: small moments of humanity in the face of terror. Similarly, we are encouraged by the testimonies of survivors, who went on to forge productive and creative lives after the war. What we have gained most from our visit together as Jewish and Christian women to the Imperial War Museum is a strengthened friendship between us, born out of our struggle to engage with each other. The dialogue that we have created between ourselves and with Lynne will be incorporated into our educational work and taken into the future. This is the essence of dialogue: human connection that reaches into the wider community. This project has strengthened our identities not only as Jews, but as Jewish educators. Our work defies what the Nazis tried to achieve. Every word we have written here is an act of resistance.

The authors wish to thank Aviva Dautch for her help with this piece.

---

32 Matis Weinberg, 1999, *FrameWorks: Exodus*, Boston: The Foundation for Jewish Publications, p. 100.

33 The complete text makes up the Preface to his book *The Gates of the Forest*, New York: Schocken Books, 1982.

Further Reading

See the Bibliography section for full details on these titles.

Lisa Appignanesi, *Losing the Dead: A Family Memoir.*
Rachel Feldhay Brenner, *Writing as Resistance.*
Dan Cohn-Sherbok, *Holocaust Theology: A Reader.*
Albert H. Friedlander, *Out of the Whirlwind: A Reader of Holocaust Literature.*
Esther Fuchs (ed.), *Women and the Holocaust: Narrative and Representation.*
Peter Novick, *The Holocaust in Collective Memory.*
Dalia Ofer and Lenore Weitzman (eds), *Women in the Holocaust.*
Melissa Raphael, *The Female Face of God in Auschwitz.*
Helmut Schreier and Matthias Heyl (eds), *Never Again! The Holocaust's Challenge for Educators.*
Dina Wardi, *Auschwitz: The Limits of Dialogue.*
Isabel Wollaston, *A War Against Memory?*

Part 2: Scripture

Introduction

Part 2 of the book explores the dynamics of studying biblical texts together. It is an area that has been extremely fruitful and enjoyable for the group. The idea of studying texts together is not new. At various points throughout our histories, especially in the medieval period, Christian scholars and clerics would sit at the feet of the rabbis and learn something about Jewish exegesis and study the original Hebrew text. Within the last 100 years, biblical scholarship has taken a major shift which has enabled Christians to appreciate for the first time the Jewish roots of their faith and the Jewishness of Jesus. Jewish and Christian scholars have worked together in this respect so that now it is not unusual for Jewish scholars to be commenting on and writing about the Jewish Jesus or the apostle Paul. Through this work, they have learnt much from each other about the development of early Christianity and Rabbinic Judaism as well as the partings of the ways between them in the first few centuries of the Common Era. The work in this area continues to bring forth new understandings to our traditions; however, within the context of a women's group, biblical texts often pose difficulties because of the patriarchal nature of many of the stories. As women we approach the Bible, as we do with theology, on two levels: first, as Jews and Christians with a painful history of conflict over who holds the true interpretation of the shared texts; and second, as women struggling with a patriarchal heritage which has excluded women's voices. These dimensions bring a very particular uniqueness and dynamic to our study of texts which can bring a new impetus to the wider Jewish-Christian relationship.

One of the major break-throughs in the contemporary Jewish-Christian feminist dialogue has been in the area of biblical scholarship. Feminists

[87]

from both faiths are reclaiming the text and bringing new readings to their traditions. They have highlighted how, all too often, the experiences and stories of biblical women have been marginalized and silenced. For our group, studying biblical texts which focus on particular women has been liberating in our challenges to the patriarchal heritage. Our sacred texts have been almost exclusively written by men, with one or two possible exceptions, and that poses difficulties for us because our stories are written out of history. We are not complacent about the differences between our scriptural texts and our different ways of interpretation and that is reflected in the following chapters. What we show here is how we can deepen our own faith by learning about how 'the other' interprets Scripture, while also allowing 'the other' theological space in their exegesis. We listen to their Scriptures and interpretations and, as Lynne wrote in Chapter 1, as we do so we proclaim our identity and make meanings of our experience.

In Chapter 5, Kathleen and Lynne explore the dynamics that come into play when Jews and Christians study the Bible together. This is not limited to studying the Hebrew Bible or Old Testament. Both women argue that it is important for Jews to study the New Testament with Christians to enable Jews to gain a deeper understanding of Christian exegesis, but also because the New Testament may shed light on the Judaism of the first century CE. Kathleen looks at the study of Torah and oral tradition, exploring how Jewish interpretation is different from Christian exegesis. Lynne reminds us about the differences between the Old Testament and Hebrew Bible and argues that Jews and Christians have used them very differently. Chapters 6–8 are based around biblical women whose voices have been marginalized or neutralized, either by the sacred text itself or by the subsequent traditions. Much of the scriptural studies by feminists thus far have focused on biblical texts which have a woman as a central figure, and this is true for our group primarily because part of women's contemporary faith has first to reclaim the traditions about its women before moving to other narratives and texts. We have chosen the figures of Dinah and Mary Magdalene in Chapters 6 and 7 and the women prophets of the Bible in Chapter 8 because their lives have largely been overshadowed in contemporary feminist scholarship by the great figures of Eve, the Matriarchs, and Mary the mother of Jesus.

Chapter 6 looks at the story of the rape of Dinah in Genesis 34, a woman who was violated by men and the subsequent tradition which has not been sympathetic to her plight. Kathleen seeks to make sense of the tradition and to recover something of Dinah's own voice and her side of the story. In response, Helen affirms Kathleen's outrage at Dinah's treatment and also seeks to reclaim Dinah's voice by focusing on her name, meaning 'judgement', as the silent condemnation of her brothers for killing the Shechemites. In Chapter 7, Lynne looks at the New Testament figure of Mary Magdalene, the first witness to the resurrection of Jesus and one of the most important disciples during Jesus' lifetime. She shows how the Christian tradition has silenced and dismissed the testimony of Mary Magdalene by labelling her incorrectly as a prostitute. Rachel begins her response to Lynne by highlighting how difficult it is for a Jew to read the New Testament. She then explores some of the ways in which Mary's reputation as a prostitute has been carried through the Christian tradition in a way that is different from how other Jewish women and sexuality have been portrayed in the Bible (citing Tamar and Rahab). She also explores some of the ways in which the New Testament can provide insights into the position of Jewish women at the time of Jesus and argues that Judaism was not as oppressive towards women as is often made out in contemporary Christian preaching and writings. Chapter 8 focuses on the women prophets (prophetesses) in the Hebrew Bible and New Testament. Rachel and Clare argue that these prophetesses can be reclaimed as contemporary models for women's leadership in the synagogue and church.

In studying the Hebrew Bible, Old Testament and New Testament together our studies have highlighted how there is often a gap between what is reported in our texts on women and practice at that time. The central stories in our Scriptures are largely male-centred, told by men and passed on by men; however, there are occasions when we glimpse a more active role for women than is reported. This is especially true for the women whose lives we have studied here. This section begins to uncover their voices and restore them to a prominent place within our traditions.

5 Studying Biblical Texts

God may intend Jews and Christians to hear very different messages
through one and the same text.

George Lindbeck[1]

I Studying the Bible Together: Transforming Tradition and Hermeneutics

Lynne Scholefield

The times when we have studied biblical texts together have been among
the most interesting and enjoyable sessions that we have had. The Bible
is clearly important in both Judaism and Christianity and exploring it
together has been exciting although what we have actually done has been
fairly simple and straightforward. Here I will briefly discuss how we have
approached the texts in our women's group and also reflect on some of the
things that I, as a Christian, have particularly valued and been challenged
by. We have studied texts from the Jewish and Christian Scriptures.

Our Bible study sessions have taken the form of one of us preparing an
introduction to the material and then working slowly through the passage,
often verse by verse, explaining ways in which it has been interpreted
in our tradition. During the study, women in the group ask questions,
make comments or highlight connections with other texts or beliefs and
practices within their traditions. At points, we have drawn on insights
from contemporary feminist biblical hermeneutics and from Jewish and
Christian traditions. It is very important to me, as a convert to Roman
Catholicism, to explore the richness of the Christian tradition. This does
not mean accepting everything from the past which for me is not how

---

1 George Lindbeck, 2000, 'Postmodern Hermeneutics and Jewish-Christian
Dialogue', in Tikva Frymer-Kensky *et al.*, *Christianity in Jewish Terms*, Colorado:
Westview Press, p. 111.

tradition operates; rather the tradition contains 'traditions' and even then only some traditions. It provides limits or boundaries to help discern what is Christian. I became a Catholic partly as a result of the influence of a number of people whose work I admired, one of whom wrote:

> A tradition acts as the interpreter of experience: it provides a particular light, by and in which, to see things and it has a language it teaches to its followers.[2]

For me tradition also has a maieutic function: it gives birth to what is coming next. By helping us to recognize what is important from the past, tradition enriches our options for the future. One of the most important aspects of the Christian past for me is the shared root of Christian and Jewish development and this involves, to some extent, shared Scripture. So, it is interesting to explore the dynamics of reading texts together as Jewish and Christian women. The Bible is a major part of the Christian tradition and I encounter it mainly through Catholic liturgy where readings from the Bible and preaching, loosely based on the texts, form part of most services. In this case the Bible is *heard* rather than read or studied. Psalms and other biblical songs are also a familiar part of liturgy both in the Mass and also in the daily office (daily service). There is some continuity in the Gospel readings each Sunday and following a different pattern, in the daily liturgy; however, the readings from the Old Testament and from the Epistles (letters) in the New Testament are not continuous. They are often quite short and only certain verses are read, with others missed out. This means that liturgically there is little sense of the whole of any narrative or of the ideas and issues in a particular biblical book. Some books are hardly ever used and so remain virtually unknown to many Catholics, even among those worshippers who attend church regularly.[3]

There are, of course, many different ways of approaching Scripture within Christian tradition. Unlike some Christians I do not have a habit of daily private Bible reading but I have always been interested in the Bible

---

2 A. McCaffry, 1993, 'The Priesthood of the Teacher', in P. Jarvis and N. Walters (eds), *Adult Education and Theological Interpretation*, Malabar, Florida: Krieger Publishing Company, p. 60.

3 For a very interesting critique of Catholic use of Scripture in liturgy from a feminist perspective see E. J. Smith, 1999, *Bearing Fruit in Due Season: Feminist Hermeneutics and the Bible in Worship*, Collegeville: The Liturgical Press.

and used it in different ways in my own life and in teaching. Most of the textual studies for me are now carried out in three contexts: the first is using Benedictine approaches to prayerful study of Scripture, the second is in the context of Jewish-Christian dialogue, and the third is helping teachers and trainee teachers to find creative ways to understand the Bible and use it in the classroom. The majority of these Catholic teachers and trainees seem never to have had the opportunity to study the Old Testament although they are more familiar with the New Testament. All this has opened up much of the Old Testament which I had not previously studied, including the Pentateuch or Torah.

In both Judaism and Christianity, the Bible is understood as a revelatory text whether seen as the literal Word of God or as a text recorded by human hand but nevertheless a vehicle by which God is made known to us. In the Roman Catholic Church, after the reading of an Old Testament passage or one from the Epistles in the New Testament the reader says: 'This is the Word of the Lord' and the congregation replies 'Thanks be to God'. The Bible is understood as revelation but what does that mean? I believe that God speaks in and through the Bible but not in a simple, literalistic way. It has to be interpreted. Christians affirm that the Bible is the Word of God because it makes known Jesus Christ who is the Word of God; Christ is the hermeneutical principle for the whole Bible. That is why the Christian Bible is arranged as it is.[4] The last book in the Old Testament is the prophet Malachi who proclaims the coming of the messiah. Turn over the page and there is Matthew explaining how Jesus is the promised messiah. Catholic approaches to the Bible were transformed by the Second Vatican Council. The relevant document is called *Dei Verbum* or 'Word of God'. In this document there is a beautiful line which says that: 'in the sacred books [God] ... comes lovingly to meet [God's] children, and talks with them' (Chapter VI: 21).[5] This document affirmed the importance of the Bible for Catholics and there has been a real flowering of Catholic biblical scholarship in the years since the Council.[6] However,

---

4 For a full discussion of the Jewish and Christian Bible as literature see G. Josipovici, 1988, *The Book of God*, New Haven: Yale University Press.

5 All the documents are available in English in A. Flannery (ed.), 1992 rev. ed., *Vatican Council II – The Conciliar and Post Conciliar Documents*, Dublin: Dominican Publications.

6 See for example Raymond Brown, Joseph Fitzmyer and Robert Murphy (eds), 1990, *The New Jerome Biblical Commentary*, London: Geoffrey Chapman.

the weakest part of the document is Chapter IV on the Old Testament which 'mainly repeats traditional Christian formulas, with no sensitivity towards Judaism'.[7] This weakness has to some extent now been recognized and other Catholic publications have encouraged the very dialogue between Catholics and Jews of which our group is a part, affirming the importance of Jewish perspectives on the Bible. One example is the American Catholic Bishops' *Guidelines on the Presentation of Jews and Judaism in Catholic Preaching* called *God's Mercy Endures Forever* which ends: 'Be free to draw on Jewish sources (rabbinic, medieval and modern) in expounding the meaning of the Hebrew Scriptures and the apostolic writings.'[8] It must be borne in mind that this comes from the American Catholic Bishops rather than the Vatican, nevertheless its significance is far-reaching for Catholic understanding and interpretation of the Bible. Most importantly, in 2002 the Pontifical Biblical Commission published the document *The Jewish People and their Sacred Scriptures in the Christian Bible*, with a preface by Cardinal Ratzinger, in which the Commission stated that:

> The horror in the wake of the extermination of the Jews (the Shoah) during the Second World War has led all the Churches to rethink their relationship with Judaism and, as a result, to reconsider their interpretation of the Jewish Bible, the Old Testament ... Christians can learn much from Jewish exegesis practised for more than two thousand years ... it is hoped that Jews themselves can derive profit from Christian exegetical research.[9]

There is much scholarly discussion by Jews and Christians, largely in the United States, about the significance of this document.[10]

In the group we have studied texts from both what I have been calling the Old Testament and the New Testament. This raises the whole contentious issue of how to name these books. Do we refer to the Jewish Scriptures as 'Hebrew Bible' and Christian Scriptures as 'Old Testament'

---

7 Robert Murray, 1991, 'Revelation (Dei Verbum)', in Adrian Hastings (ed.), *Modern Catholicism: Vatican II and After*, London: SPCK, p. 76.

8 See Eugene Fisher (ed.), 1990, *The Jewish Roots of Christian Liturgy*, New York: Paulist Press, p. 196.

9 Pontifical Biblical Commission, 2002, *The Jewish People and their Sacred Scriptures in the Christian Bible*, The Vatican: Libreria Editrice Vaticana, English ed., section 22, p. 50.

10 See for example the summary of 13 studies produced by Joan Cook available at http://www.bc.edu/research/cjl/meta-elements/texts/articles/cook.htm.

and 'New Testament' or 'First Testament' and 'Second Testament'? In well-meaning Christian attempts to recognize and value the Jewish roots of Christianity it has become commonplace to speak of 'the Hebrew Bible' or the 'Common Testament' or 'the Shared Testament' instead of the Old Testament when referring to the Christian Scriptures which we share with Judaism. However, studying texts with Jews has convinced me that the Jewish and Christian texts are not the same. All too often, it appears that Jews and Christians have at least part of the Bible in common but the discovery that this is not the case has perhaps made the textual study so much more interesting. In an attempt not to denigrate the 'other' we have collapsed the differences between them. There are key differences, first, in the construction of the two Bibles, second, in the ways that they are used in worship and finally, in the ways that they are interpreted. As well as learning from Jews about Jewish approaches to the text, my Christian understanding of the Bible has been enhanced by learning to recognize something of the distinctiveness of Christian constructions of biblical understanding. The most valuable aspects that I have learned from Jewish-led study have been to pay close attention to the actual details of the text and to go slowly with it. Christians usually read the Bible in translation while Jews read the original Hebrew. Jews tend to work at a much slower pace, working through each word and sentence carefully to bring out the layers of meaning within the Hebrew itself. Again and again, I have been amazed at the richness and complexity of the literary text as expounded by one of the Jewish women in our group as she explains the meanings of words and the connections with other sections of the Bible. An early twentieth-century Jewish writer, Franz Rosenzweig, writing about the translation of Scripture, highlighted the fact that the words of the translation are a 'shell beneath which one day something holy, something holy for me, may be revealed'.[11] In the same article he discusses how Martin Luther, the Christian theologian of the Reformation, in his great German translation of the Bible had failed to make room for the original Hebrew.[12] Rosenzweig also noted that Luther only feels compelled to 'give

---

11 Franz Rosenzweig, 1994 ed., 'Scripture and Luther', in Martin Buber and Franz Rosenzweig, *Scripture and Tradition*, Bloomington: Indiana Press, p. 66.

12 See Franz Rosenzweig, 1994 ed., 'Scripture and Luther', p. 49–50. For an interesting discussion of this article see O. Eisenstadt, 2001, 'Making Room for the Hebrew: Luther, Dialectics and the Shoah', in *Journal of the American Academy of Religion*, September, 69(3), p. 551–75.

the Hebrew some room' for those parts of the Old Testament that Luther believed 'practised Christ' and therefore were the living Word of God. Elsewhere, and this is the majority of the Old Testament text, Luther, the translator, sends 'the Hebrew words packing'.[13] My experience of studying Bible with Jews has taught me something very different from the traditional Christian selectivity of Old Testament texts. It enables me to 'make room for the Hebrew'. I have come to recognize that 'wrestling' with texts, as Jacob wrestled with the angel in Genesis 32.22–32, is a pretty active thing to do; not without its risks in the engagement with the holy but ultimately liberating and life-enhancing. Although our Bibles are different we share many stories and as we reflect on the connections between a story and our experiences and our religious traditions, we learn from one another as well as more about ourselves and each other.

Studying texts with Jews has increased my sensitivity to, and understanding of, Judaism. Although Jews and Christians are both called 'people of the Book' this description fits Jews much better than Christians. Studying the Bible with Jews has opened up for me ways of interpreting the texts which reveal new layers of meaning and possibility. I am particularly conscious of the different ways in which Jews use the Hebrew Bible and Christians use the Old Testament. There are significant differences which we should not sweep away in our anxiety to 'paper over' the potentially difficult areas. This point can be demonstrated from some of Helen's comments on messiahship in Chapter 3. On the whole I am persuaded by her argument; however, I think that she has underplayed the way in which the early Church made use of the Old Testament to explain Jesus' significance. Jesus may not be the messiah of Jewish expectation, as she so eloquently argues, but a re-interpretation of the Old Testament was the prime focus of the early Christian explanation of Jesus' significance for their faith. Matthew's Gospel, for example, is full of messianic prophecies to demonstrate the community's belief that Jesus was the promised messiah. The early Church used the Old Testament selectively and differently from other Jews at that time, but we need to address the issue of how Christians used the Old Testament then and continue to do so today. Jews and Christians use the texts differently, but can Jews recognize Christian hermeneutics as authentic? The Reform Rabbi, Tony Bayfield has issued just such a challenge regarding the New Testament when he writes:

---

13 Franz Rosenzweig, 1994 ed., 'Scripture and Luther', p. 50.

Is it possible for us, without betraying our own faith and path we chose at the partings of the ways, to acknowledge that in the New Testament, in the life and death that it portrays, is revelation?[14]

I think that this might be a very tough issue for Jews in constructing a contemporary approach towards Christianity. The challenge is not only difficult for Jews but also to Christians. Christians often find it hard to accept Jewish readings of the Hebrew Bible/Old Testament, especially those texts which Christians understand to be pointing to the coming of Christ. The document mentioned earlier, *The Jewish People and their Sacred Scriptures in the Christian Bible*, raises the following comment which is of huge significance given the history of Christian supersessionism:

> Christians can and ought to admit that the Jewish reading of the Bible is a possible one, in continuity with the Jewish Sacred Scriptures from the Second Temple period, a reading analogous to the Christian reading which developed in parallel fashion.[15]

Can Jews and Christians both accept that they have differing, but authentic, interpretations of the same text? This remains one of the key challenges for the future of the dialogue and one where, I believe, women are making significant progress in their studies together.

Turning now to the kind of texts that we have chosen in our group, we have usually chosen narrative sections of text that particularly interest us because they involve women. The ideas of narrative theology suggest that the Bible can only be understood when there is interaction between the biblical story, our personal story and the community story (or tradition). In Chapter 1, I discussed the importance of story and identity in our experiences as women and this is relevant for our approach to studying texts together. Much has been written by feminist biblical scholars about the patriarchal nature of the biblical texts and we have been able to draw on those insights as well as bring our own interpretations and stories to the

---

14 Tony Bayfield, 2000, 'Response', in Marcus Braybrooke, *Christian-Jewish Dialogue: The Next Steps*, London: SCM Press, p. 124.

15 This very long document is available on the Vatican website at: http://www.vatican.va/roman_curia/congregations/cfaith/pcb_documents/rc_con_cfaith_doc_20020212_popolo-ebraico_en.html. See also *The Jewish People and their Sacred Scriptures in the Christian Bible*, section 22, p. 50.

texts. Our choice of texts as a group of women is significant because the texts are ones which expose patriarchy in the Old and New Testaments and in the way that they have been traditionally interpreted in our traditions.[16] We have not limited our study to texts in the Torah or Old Testament, but have also looked at stories of women in the New Testament. They are usually texts which focus on particular women whose voices have been silenced or marginalized by the written texts or our subsequent traditions. We have also studied women whose lives have been overshadowed by the great figures of Eve or Mary the mother of Jesus. It is important for us as women to reclaim the voices of other so-called 'minor' figures in our Scriptures and this is something that our group has started to do. As the feminist scholar Tikva Frymer-Kensky has written, the great biblical women can often eclipse the lives of others: 'The lives of great women do not always illuminate the lives of others, and the enormous shadow of individual great women can block other women from the limelight.'[17]

Studying a New Testament text with Jewish women is particularly interesting in a different way. There is always the heightened awareness of the Jewish context of the first century CE. There is now a wealth of literature and scholarship on Jesus the Jew and Paul the Jew but much less is heard in Christian writing and preaching about Jesus' disciples, Mary the mother of Jesus or the other women around Jesus *as Jews*. In particular, exploring the Jewishness of some of the women in the New Testament and their connections with earlier biblical traditions has given me a strong and powerful image of them.[18] This is particularly true for the women that we have studied in our group and who appear in more detail in Chapters 7 and 8 of this book. There is another dimension to the study of the New Testament with Jews. Since the New Testament books were written in a situation where Christianity and Judaism were going through a very painful process of separation from one another (the gradual partings of

---

16 For very helpful feminist commentary on the Bible see for example Alice Bach (ed.), 1999, *Women in the Hebrew Bible*, London: Routledge; C. A. Newsom and S. H. Ringe (eds), 1992, *The Women's Bible Commentary*, London: SPCK; K. Pui-Lan and Elisabeth Schüssler Fiorenza (eds), 1998, *Women's Sacred Scriptures: Concilium 1998/3*, London: SCM Press; and Sandra Schneiders, 1999, *The Revelatory Text: Interpreting the New Testament as Sacred Scripture*, Collegeville: The Liturgical Press.

17 Tikva Frymer-Kensky, 2002, *Reading the Women of the Bible: A New Interpretation of Their Stories*, New York: Schocken Books, p. xxvii.

18 For a very creative, interesting and close reading of the texts of six New Testament women see Margaret Hebblethwaite, 1994, *Six New Gospels*, London: Geoffrey Chapman.

the ways), some of the texts contain anti-Jewish polemic and therefore in the context of dialogue it is very important for me as a Christian to recognize the immense harm that this has caused to Jews in Christendom. Helen explored some of the anti-Judaism inherent in Christian feminist theology in the first part of Chapter 1 and I am reminded of this in the context of women's dialogue here. Some Christian feminists have perpetuated anti-Judaism by presenting Jesus as far more enlightened than others of his day in his treatment of women. They suggest that Jewish women had a rotten time in the first century and that Jesus was radical in his positive approach to them. As a Christian feminist, I want to affirm that Jesus is 'good news' for women but without demonizing first-century Judaism. In fact, I think the New Testament contains hints of a fuller role for women as disciples at the beginning of the Christian story than the early Church was able or willing to maintain. Not only that, I think that the New Testament is potentially a very important source for helping us understand the diversity of first-century Judaisms that were emerging alongside the diversity of first-century Christianity.

II Studying Torah: A Jewish Response

Kathleen de Magtige-Middleton

For a long time it has been my assumption that my love for, and the sense of obligation to, study Torah is something inherently Jewish; something that is so engrained in the Jewish way of life and living that it has become second nature. The Torah, its regular reading and the study thereof stands at the core of our worship. Through my dialogue with Christians, and Christian women in particular, I have discovered that it is often true for their experience too. In my response to Lynne, I will explore some of the ways that Jews read the Torah and then look at studying texts as a Jewish woman within an inter-faith context.

The primary importance of Torah study can be best demonstrated by a reading which appears in the Shabbat Morning Service of our prayer book, and which enumerates those actions which: 'bring benefit here and now but whose full value can be measured only in the light of eternity.'[19]

---

19 *Siddur Lev Chadash*, p. 131.

All nine actions mentioned are decidedly ethically inspired; however, ethics alone are not enough as the text concludes with a Talmudic supplement: 'And the study of Torah leads to them all.'[20] The text presumes that only through knowledge of the Torah, which in general does not only stand for biblical text, but for the entire corpus of traditional rabbinic texts, one will come to greater understanding and thus also greater observance of the commandments, one of which is Torah study itself. The entire corpus of traditional texts, study of which all fall under the generic Hebrew expression *Talmud Torah* (Torah study) is truly amazing, extending from the Bible known as the Written Torah (or *Torah shebichtav*), down to the many volumes of the so-called Oral Torah (*Torah sheb'al peh*) comprising exegetical, midrashic, mishnaic, talmudic and halachic texts which were collated, studied and commented on over many centuries. All texts of this corpus, no matter how much they may vary in kind, are in some way or another interrelated and akin in the fact that they all connect, respond, react or draw from one single source text: the Torah itself.

Confident knowledge of the entire corpus requires years of diligent study and repetition and never ends. *Torah lish'mah* (studying Torah for its own sake) is one of the highest virtues in Judaism, and this traditional emphasis on study makes one think that any Jewish individual should be in some way or another preconditioned for the study of Jewish texts and for the love for it. However, though this may be so for male Jewish individuals, for a Jewish woman this may not necessarily be the case, as in fact the halachic requirement to study Torah traditionally only counts for Jewish males, while women are exempt from this obligation.[21] Although exemption does not necessarily preclude women from study or from knowledge of the law by which they are equally bound as men, it means that they are not required to study Torah as an end in its own right. Therefore, to study Torah in such a way as a Jewish woman in an interfaith context challenges the traditional understanding of *Talmud Torah* on two different levels. First of all, study of the Torah not only seeks to find, but also adds to the tradition a women's voice, or perspective, to a

---

20 *Mishnah Pe'ah* 1.1, supplemented by Babylonian Talmud *Shabbath* 127a.

21 Babylonian Talmud *Kiddushin* 29a; Women are exempt from commandments which fathers specifically are commanded to do for their sons (*mitzvoth ha-ben al ha-av*), which are circumcision, redeeming the firstborn, teaching Torah and a skill, and arranging his marriage.

text where it had been to a large extent absent. It is therefore not surprising that the texts we choose to study in our inter-faith group were texts which touched us as women – either because a woman's voice was distinctly present, or on the contrary, because she was distinctly absent; like for example the biblical narrative of the rape of Dinah which will be discussed in the next chapter. Second, the inter-faith setting added an extra dimension and often surprising depth to our study together and gave it yet another perspective, a different voice again, to the text and its traditional interpretations. This voice of tradition, our own Jewish or Christian traditions that is, was often intellectually challenging as we were frequently in conflict rather than in agreement with it. However, being confronted with a different faith's perspective with its own salvation history, and therefore often entirely different theological interpretations and conclusion, was often even more challenging.

From a Jewish perspective it is relatively easy to accept many differences of opinion in our own tradition, as is so well expressed in the famous Mishnaic dictum of the *Tanna Ben Bag Bag*: 'Turn it [the Torah] and turn it, for all is in it',[22] yet it remains often too challenging an idea that the Torah could equally include the different theologies of the two different faiths. Lynne has raised the question of whether Jews can accept Christian interpretation of the Torah as valid, even if we ultimately disagree with that interpretation. Personally I must admit, I have as yet not emotionally reconsolidated with this possibility and am therefore still seeking an answer for the true meaning of inter-faith text study for myself. One of the main challenges on the way to a satisfactory answer to this question is the question whether the Christian Old Testament and the Torah are in fact the same texts, which stand at the core of our faiths, and indeed whether the Bible takes the same core position in our respective faiths, as we so often claim. Over the years it has become my conviction that this is not the case. Although we may use exactly the same biblical text to study from, or even use a traditional Jewish method of study, as we have done in our group (the traditional midrashic method of studying the text verse by verse with the aid of different traditional and modern interpretations through which we sought to fill up the 'narrative gaps' in the text), I have realized that it is not necessarily our different traditions' interpretations in which we differ but the very difference in which our faiths use, view and

---

22 *Mishnah Avot* 5.22.

even print the book. It is a complexity of cultural, theological, liturgical and historical influences which have determined and differentiated our faith's distinct attitudes towards the Bible, determined the language in which we read it, our attitude towards it, even the order in which the various books of the Bible have been printed and all these slight differences challenges the common assumption that we are all studying exactly the same text. First of all, there is the difference in language, something which Lynne touched on earlier. For Jews, no matter which translation we may choose to study the Torah in, the only authorized and authoritative text is the Hebrew. Though there are many different translations which all add their own particular interpretation to the text, the core, authoritative text is for Jews always the same and therefore there cannot be any dispute as to which translation, which authorized version one uses and which tradition one follows.

Of greater influence is of course the disparity in the order of the different books of the Bible, which adds a distinct emphasis to the message of the Bible as a whole. The Hebrew Bible consists of three parts: Pentateuch, Prophets and a section of miscellaneous texts known as Writings which end with the book of Chronicles. The order is not simply chronological but thematic: for example Chronicles begins with the origin of humankind and ends with the promise of redemption and the return from exile. This ending reconnects beautifully with the very beginning of the Bible, the book of Genesis. The Christian Old Testament on the other hand is chronologically ordered and this distinction in the order of the books changes the entire message of the book, its perspective and future. Thus the Torah seeks restoration of exile through reaffirmation of the covenant and punctilious adherence of its commandments, as meticulously set out in the Oral Torah. In the Christian Bible restoration of the broken divine-human relationship and fulfilment of the covenant can be found in the New Testament; and through this the Old Testament has become no longer the core text but only the prelude that leads into the New Testament. For Christians therefore the New Testament links back to the Old Testament, but the Old Testament can only be truly appreciated in the light of New Testament salvation history.

The theological difference and core value of the Old Testament to both faiths could best be illustrated by the difference in liturgical use of the text. In the Roman Catholic and Orthodox Christian traditions, for example, the Gospels are normally read in public only by ordained priests and deacons, indicating their core importance. The fundamental importance of the Torah in Jewish life finds physical expression in the reverential treatment of its text. Few Jews could find it in their hearts to discard a piece of Torah text among the rubbish, or drop a Torah Scroll on the ground, or take a copy of the Hebrew Bible with them into the bathroom. The difference in liturgical use eventually resulted in a distinct difference in knowledge and familiarity with different parts of the Bible within Judaism and Christianity. Some passages in the Torah or Old Testament are not known to all members of our group, especially parts of Leviticus, and led to a discussion regarding the importance and meaning of reading certain parts of the Torah and indeed of reading it in our group. Although our core texts are different, studying them together opens up new dimensions which we would not have come to if we had studied them with members of our own faith. This, for me, is one of the benefits of Jews and Christians studying biblical texts together.

The study of texts stimulates a person's inquisitiveness and inspires one to formulate one's own thoughts in response to the text and one's own tradition. Studying texts within my own tradition has, to me, always been more than just an intellectual exercise. It is an exciting journey into the world of the text because every text captures within itself its own dimension of Judaism and its own angle on the tradition. Through the words a distant yet faintly recognizable world filters through; the world-view of the author, together with the values of those who kept the text, transformed it and reinterpreted it. It has time and time again shown that the naïve and uninformed preconception that Judaism is a monolithic faith is really a fallacy. Each text reveals something of the individuality of its author (or authors) and every single piece of text opens a new port of insight and a deeper connection with, or possibly even a greater distance from it. On a spiritual level, I have often felt closer to God while studying than while I have been conducting a service or praying with my congregation. Textual study in an inter-faith setting on the other hand is different because there is still an element of being in conversation with one's own tradition and therefore there is still a spiritual dimension to it, although maybe to a lesser degree, for the inter-faith setting adds a degree of vulnerability and surprise. The fact that the Bible is such a different book in value and message to both our faiths, adds at the same time familiarity and challenge into the deepest core of one's religiosity.

In the context of a women's Jewish-Christian dialogue group, the study of texts speak to us personally. Our individual responses to the text emphasize our own individuality within our traditions and in relation to each other. They help us to formulate where we stand and what we accept of our traditions and for some within our group that means wrestling together with our patriarchal heritage. Depending on how much authority we individually attribute to the text that we are studying, the text itself can act as a 'safety-net' within inter-faith encounters. In effect, I believe studying a shared core text in a trusted and open environment, as we have done provides a glimpse of the deepest level of insight and understanding, not only into the text or even our traditions but to the voice of 'the other'. When we share a common text, our differences become highlighted and it is in these differences and our personal responses to these differences that we appreciate and understand the true commonalities and distinctions of our faiths. That level of insight ultimately strengthens us all in our own faiths even when we struggle with our own traditions.

Further Reading

See the Bibliography section for full details on these titles.

Judith S. Antonelli, *In the Image of God: A Feminist Commentary on the Torah*.
Alice Bach (ed.), *Women in the Hebrew Bible*.
A. Brenner and C. Fontaine (eds), *A Feminist Companion to Reading the Bible*.
Ora Wiskind Elper and Susan Handelman, *Torah of the Mothers: Contemporary Jewish Women Read Classical Jewish Texts*.
Tikva Frymer-Kensky, *Reading the Women of the Bible: A New Interpretation of Their Stories*.
B. Holtz, *Back to the Sources: Reading the Classic Jewish Texts*.
Ross S. Kraemer and Mary Rose D'Angelo (eds), *Women and Christian Origins*.
Jonathan Magonet, *A Rabbi's Bible*.
Carol Meyers, Toni Craven and Ross Kraemer (eds), *Women in Scripture*.
Sandra Schneiders, *The Revelatory Text: Interpreting the New Testament as Sacred Scripture*.

6 The Rape of Dinah

And Dinah, the daughter of Leah, whom she borne to Jacob, went out to see the daughters of the land. And when Shechem, the son of Chamor the Hivite, prince of the country saw her he took her and lay with her, and defiled her.

Genesis 34.1–2

I The Rape of Dinah in Sacred Text and Tradition: Voicing Our Outrage

Kathleen de Magtige-Middleton

Among the biblical women, Dinah is one of the most enigmatic characters in Scripture as her brief but violent history is inextricably coupled with Israel's patriarchal history. I chose this text for our group to study because this story, along with its rabbinic reaction and commentaries, is so obviously outrageous and patriarchal that it cries out for a contemporary exegesis which reclaims Dinah's voice. I approach the text as a Jewish woman, with a difficult history of exegesis of this story, who is also seeking to understand it in dialogue with Christian women. Surely for both of us, it raises the question of how we as women deal with such difficult texts. In this chapter, Helen and I will seek to understand this text within our traditions and reclaim it within the women's Jewish-Christian dialogue. It is important to note that we as women have reclaimed our identity and our female voice and have passed the stage of defending the marginalization in our tradition. We have begun to fill the bookcase with our history and with the unheard and hidden stories of the women in the Bible. It is now vital that we face the text itself, our holy texts, where women are being treated outrageously and where women are marginalized and abused and I want to see what this does to me. How can I as a woman face these texts as part of my religious heritage? I can understand how the tradition has

[105]

interpreted it in both Judaism and Christianity, but also I can see how through this process I and other women can learn from it. In the first part of this chapter I will examine some of the traditional Jewish responses to the text, often verse by verse, the detail of which may be new to many Christian readers.

Studying scriptural texts can sometimes be likened to a treasure hunt with only an old faded map to guide. Biblical Hebrew is a language which at times appears ambiguous and is open to multiple interpretations. The text is often subtle, sometimes subversive and tantalizingly brief. No matter how well we think we know the text, it remains an ancient literature, initially composed for and within an ancient culture that we cannot study without being influenced by the multi-layered baggage of our own modern world-view, our traditions and the many centuries of exegetical interpretations. Exegetical traditions are in general most obtrusive when the obvious meaning of the text is less clear. This happens often when studying the female characters in Scripture. Women's names are hardly ever given an etymological explanation (as is usual for their male counterparts) and their roles are often ambiguous. Even when their roles are pivotal to the story they are generally hidden within the narratives of their husbands, sons, fathers or brothers. The reason for this is obviously clear since the text itself is a product of a patriarchal society in which all the texts written about women were written by men. 'We have only male blueprints for female behaviour. The stories are men's imaginings about women: the good wives who support men's dreams and the seducers who lead men astray.'[1]

Within the patriarchal narrative Dinah does not have a real persona for she has no voice and is lacking in any individual characteristics. We do not even know whether she was attractive or not. Her role seems to be purely functional and, as soon as her role has been fulfilled, she disappears as inconspicuously from the biblical scene as she first entered it. Yet it is precisely her inconspicuousness, her voiceless passivity that is most captivating to those who study her, for it leaves us with some troubling questions. What is it about Dinah that caused this tragedy to happen to her? What is her role in the narrative and what became of her? To understand the answers to these questions from the rabbinic tradition, one should attempt to understand the text in all its complexities and in particular seek out its ambiguities, for it is these that the ancient rabbis attempted to

---

1 Alice Bach (ed.), 1999, *Women in the Hebrew Bible*, New York: Routledge, p. xiii–xiv.

answer. The picture that emerges from such a study is, though at times disconcerting, often astonishingly astute and psychologically deeply moving.

Dinah, the only daughter of Jacob and Leah, entered her biblical existence in such an unobtrusive, and matter-of-fact way that it stands out in its simplicity. Her birth, briefly mentioned in Genesis 30.21, seems only to be added into Jacob's complicated genealogy to indicate that she is Leah's seventh and last child. Her birth, contrary to that of her many brothers and half-brothers, does not lead to strife and envy between Jacob's wives and because of that happy fact, the text seems to deem it unnecessary to add any etymological explanation to her name as is the case with all her brothers. The text simply states: 'and afterwards she bore a daughter and called her name Dinah.' To the midrash and the traditional exegetes, the very unobtrusiveness of her birth is most conspicuous. The medieval commentator Radak, otherwise known as Rabbi David Kimchi (1160–1235), wondered why the text omits the usual formula 'and she conceived' but simply states that 'afterwards she bore a daughter'. He concluded that Dinah had to be Zebulon's twin sister, understanding 'afterwards' as meaning *immediately* after the birth of Zebulon in Genesis 30.20. According to the Babylonian Talmud, however, 'afterwards' does not refer to the birth of Zebulon but to the missing etymology of Dinah's name:

> What is meant by 'afterwards'? Rav said:[2] After Leah had passed judgement on herself, saying, 'Twelve tribes are destined to issue from Jacob. Six have issued from me and four from the handmaids, making ten. If this child will be male, my sister Rachel will not be equal to one of the handmaids'. Forthwith the child was turned to a girl, as it says, and she called her name Dinah.[3]

Both 'afterwards' and 'and' refer, according to the Talmud, to a moment outside the text; the missing etymology explaining why Leah called her daughter Dinah meaning 'judgement' from the Hebrew root *dyn*, to judge. That moment was the moment on which Leah *danna din* (passed judgement) regarding the gender of her child and when the child was born and appeared to be a girl she called her name Dinah. The Talmud affords us a glimpse of the rabbinic interpretation of Dinah's function in the text. It shows us a perplexing understanding of Dinah's role as an unwanted

---

2 A third-century CE Babylonian rabbi.
3 Babylonian Talmud *B'rachot* 60a.

child whose identity is violated and compromised while still in her mother's womb. There her identity as a boy is compromised for the benefit of Rachel and passed on to her half-brother Joseph. Within a moment of her mother's judgement Dinah's fate turned from being the potential forebear of a tribe to a practical nonentity. Dinah should not have been and therefore she hardly exists in Scripture. There is, however, an even more sinister side to her name that sealed her tragic fate. Her name does not just confirm the past but, as is so often the case in Scripture, also has a prophetic quality to it, for it predicts her tragic future. The real tragedy of Dinah is, as understood by the rabbis, that her narrative function is to be an instrument of judgement to others. Through her, judgement will be passed on to others. Her function within the narrative is to be the catalyst of these judgements and the price she has to pay for that function is being compromised and violated.

The rabbinic interpretation of Dinah's rape, the greatest form of human violation, follows this understanding of her literary function as an instrument of judgement. This context of judgement, however, is far from easy to discern, for chapter 34, which describes the rape and its aftermath, stands in splendid isolation from the rest of the Jacob narrative. Dinah's tragedy breaks the apparent tranquillity of Jacob's life after the emotional reconciliation with his brother Esau. Dinah's rape itself is no more mentioned or alluded to until Jacob's deathbed blessing in Genesis 49.5–6 in which he condemns Simeon and Levi for their acts of outrage in response to the incident. Dinah, however, is neither blessed nor condemned; her name is mentioned only once again among Leah's children in Jacob's genealogy in Genesis 46.15. So, what is the context of this episode? To the modern biblical commentator Gunther Plaut, the context and its function are to be found in the only time that the incident is mentioned again, namely Genesis 49.5–6. According to Plaut the episode might have functioned as a 'moral explanation for certain geographical realities of later centuries'.[4] Jacob's blessing (or rather condemnation) in Genesis 49.5–6 explains the future reality of the landless status of the two tribes of Simeon and Levi,[5] while chapter 34 provides the context for the blessing itself.

---

4 W. Gunther Plaut, 1967, *The Torah*, New York: Union of American Hebrew Congregations, p. 229.

5 The tribe of Levi became the hereditary Temple servants without territory of their own (Num. 18.20), while a portion of the tribe of Simeon eventually intermingled with Judah and the Canaanites.

The matter could be compared to the seemingly *en passant* mention of Reuben's fornication with his father's concubine Bilhah in Genesis 35.22, which functioned as moral explanation for the fact that the birthright passed on to Judah.[6] The writers of the midrash, however, preferred to seek the context of Dinah's tragedy in the past rather than future geographical reality. The midrash is, as we know, profoundly aware of the gaps in the text and such a gap can be found in Genesis 32.23 where Dinah's name is conspicuously absent:

> And he [Jacob] rose up that night, and took his two wives, and his two maidservants and his eleven children [sons] and crossed over the river Jabbok.

The medieval exegete Rashi (Rabbi Solomon ben Isaac, 1040–1105), following *Midrash Genesis Rabbah*, was confused by this verse because Jacob already had 12 children including Dinah (only Benjamin had not been born yet) by the time he crossed over the river Jabbok.

> And Dinah? Where was she? He [Jacob] placed her in a box and locked it, so that Esau should not lay eyes on her. For this, Jacob was punished, for withholding her from his brother – perhaps she would have redeemed him? – and she fell into the hands of Shechem.[7]

The absence of Dinah's name in Genesis 32.23 was once more understood by the midrash as a compromise to her existence, which it seems to have identified as the root of the tragedy that led to the rape. This midrashic understanding of the incident accentuated even more the tragedy of Dinah's character, for the violation of her freedom was neither punished nor redeemed; on the contrary she became the instrument of punishment by being violated even more. The truth of the matter is that the midrash did not deem Dinah's capture in a chest as the punishable act, but Jacob's refusal to let Esau see and marry Dinah, for Dinah could have redeemed Esau from being the evil man he was. Jacob's failure to show kindness and love to his brother Esau expressed itself in putting Dinah in a box and keeping her locked up.

---

6 Although Reuben was Jacob's eldest son, he had forfeited his birthright with the fornication with his father's handmaid, as did Simeon and Levi with their acts of outrage in Shechem. Judah, who was the fourth son, was next in line to receive the birthright.

7 *Genesis Rabbah* 76.9.

He said: This man has presumptuous eyes – let him not look at her and take her from me ... God said to him: 'The one who fails kindness is due from his friend' (Job 6.14). 'You have withheld kindness from your brother' ... You would not give her in marriage to one who is circumcised [Esau]; she will marry one who is uncircumcised. You would not give her in legitimate wedlock; she will be taken in illegitimate fashion.[8]

The perceptive understanding of the text of our midrash underlines the irony and the continuous repetition of a troubled family history imbedded in it. Jacob's inability to accept his brother without judgement and the possible future that was in store for his daughter resulted in a scenario worse than that which he sought to prevent. Jacob extended his inability to love to his daughter, so she found her love, albeit a subverted kind of love, with Shechem. From the male-orientated point of view of the midrash, Dinah's role is purely and only instrumental. It does not question the moral acceptability of its assumption that Dinah's rape is an act of divine punishment for Jacob's wrongdoing. This seems to affirm the assumption made by Judith Wegner in her book *Chattel or Person?* that in *mishnaic* and *midrashic* times an underage daughter would be sexually and biologically 'owned' by her father.[9] Thus Jacob could do as he sought fit to keep his daughter's sexual purity and he likewise could be punished through the defilement of his daughter.

The theme of the box seems to be archetypal to the midrash, which can be found also in the Abraham saga in which Abraham hides Sarah in a box to save her from the presumed sexual licentiousness of the Egyptians.[10] Although the midrash does not heed the moral issues regarding Dinah's role as an initiator, it does show an astute understanding of the ironical subversions in the text and the paradoxical connection between Dinah's absence (which it interprets as being concealed) in Genesis 32 and her going out (being seen) in chapter 34. Yet as soon as she ceased to be hidden we read in chapter 34, 'And Dinah went out to see the daughters of the land.' As soon as Dinah is present in the text, as soon as she is free, she goes out to see, she is seen and is raped:

---

8 *Genesis Rabbah* 76.9.

9 Judith R. Wegner, 1988, *Chattel or Person? The Status of Women in the Mishnah*, Oxford: Oxford University Press, p. 170.

10 *Genesis Rabbah* 40.5.

And Dinah, the daughter of Leah, whom she bore to Jacob, went out to see the daughters of the land.

Yet there is something about Dinah that brings about her own tragedy. What was there for her to see if she was a chaste woman? She should have stayed inside just as *Midrash Tanchumah* explains: Dinah takes on the role of her wicked uncle Esau who went out to hunt in the fields while her father Jacob stayed at home with his mother (Rebecca).[11] It is very interesting that here both Dinah and Jacob cross the traditional boundaries and gender roles. Like Esau, Dinah went out and that was her crime. According to the midrash, some of the men stayed inside to study Torah. Obviously Dinah was not expected to study Torah with her brothers, but maybe there was something of the boy in her – the boy she should have been had it not been for Leah's prayer. It was her female going-outness that brought the tragedy upon her. It was this very 'going-outness' that Jacob tried to control by hiding her in a chest from his evil brother Esau who was also a 'going-out' man. Yet Dinah could have saved Esau. She could have redeemed him and because of Jacob's lack of brotherly love he was punished.

But through this story Dinah becomes entirely bound up with her mother Leah. She is Leah's daughter because only through Leah she has become a daughter. The medieval exegete Moses Nachmanides (or Ramban) explained that Dinah is called here 'the daughter of Leah' not in order to identify her explicitly as Leah's daughter rather than Jacob's, but rather to identify her as a full sister of her mother's sons Simeon and Levi. Nachmanides touches on the subservient position of the two women Leah and Dinah, who were both wronged in their lives through men. Thus Shimon's and Levi's action was not as much an act of vengeance against Shechem who had wronged their sister but also a token of vengeance for their mother whom they recognized as maltreated by their father. Their outrage was even more an act of vengeance against their father's silence because of their father's silence and ineptitude in dealing with the internal strife between the wives.[12] They felt compromised by his incompetence in the face of Dinah's situation.

The fact that Dinah is in some ways more Leah's daughter than Leah's and Jacob's daughter, as would be expected, is made explicit in the

---

11 Gen. 25.27–28.
12 Gen. 34.5.

midrash which picks up on the verse *va-tetze Dinah bat Leah*, 'and Dinah the daughter of Leah went out' (Gen. 34.1). Yet as the midrash picks up, one would expect to read 'daughter of Jacob'. Both *Midrash Rabbah* and the Jerusalem Talmud remark that Dinah is called this because she took after her mother, for Dinah was a girl that *va-tetze*, 'went out' just like her mother.[13] Her mother 'went out' to tell her husband Jacob that he should spend the night with her instead of Rachel.[14] The underlying criticism of Dinah within this midrashic tradition is that Dinah was a 'gadabout'. Just like her mother, she was of rather loose morals. Their inherent going-out-ness generated criticism of both women in subsequent exegesis. The midrash *Bereshit Rabbah* put Dinah's 'getting about' in the context of the men studying. Yet Dinah went out. The Jerusalem Talmud poses the right question: what else could she do? Yet the matter is not that she went out, but the problem is that women are up to no good when they get out: 'women like to show themselves in the street'. Rather than the midrashic interpretation of *bat Leah* that Dinah was as morally unrestricted as her mother, women should be controlled and not left to go out on their own devices. Women are uncontrollable and have no self-control and therefore according to the rabbinic tradition both Dinah's and Leah's going out was dangerous and brought disaster to the family. Leah precipitated Dinah's misfortunes and Dinah brought shame on herself and her family. They feared, according to the exegete Rashi, that Dinah's self-afflicted misfortune would reflect badly on their mother. *Bat Leah* would mean that people would judge the mother according to the daughter; like mother like daughter. And just as Dinah acted as a *zonah* (prostitute) so would their mother be judged as a *zonah*.

Of course this notion was a misogynist misconception of the text to readily accept that Jacob could be punished by God through 'his' women. Of course we cannot today accept that God would act in such an unethical way. On a personal level, I can read the text, study it and give a sermon about it with the understanding that we have a different ethic today. We can study the rape of Dinah and understand it in its historical context. Most importantly, we ought to learn from this and, through our protest, ensure that it will not happen again. We can also ensure that Dinah's story is not explained away in the same way as it has been in the past. It is a posi-

---

13 *Bereshit Rabbah* 80 and *Talmud Jerushalmi* 2.6.
14 Gen. 30.16.

tive step forward that I as a woman can say this. Studying these difficult texts is necessary. Engaging with the problems that they pose is equally important even if there is no immediate and obvious answer. Through our dialogue, we, as Jewish and Christian women, can make sense of our inherited traditions and construct new ways of interpreting the stories that have marginalized or 'written out' women's history. In this respect, we are making progress which would have been unthinkable just a couple of generations ago.

II Studying Difficult Texts: The Rape of Dinah

Helen P. Fry

The rape of Dinah is one of the many difficult stories which our holy texts present to us. As Kathleen has suggested, not only is it outrageous in its treatment of Dinah but it also leaves the unanswered question of what the story is doing there at all. What do we do with such a text? This story is not necessarily difficult for us in terms of Jewish-Christian relations *per se*. It is not a text that lends itself to Christological interpretation in the way that many of the prophetic books do; nor is it part of the Christian history of anti-Judaism and therefore on one level poses no problem for Jewish-Christian dialogue. However, we are approaching Genesis 34 as Jews and Christians *and* as women and it is a text that does pose a problem for us as women. What difference does that make? What do our voices contribute to hermeneutics and tradition? In reading it together, we as women can voice our outrage not only at the patriarchal nature of the story but also what our traditions have made of it. In my response, I will not repeat all the points of Kathleen's study but will pick up on some of the central themes in her text. I will retain the phrases 'Old Testament' and 'New Testament' for Christian Scriptures and Torah or Hebrew Bible for the Jewish Scriptures, partly because it is clearer to the reader to which Scriptures I am referring, but also as Lynne has indicated, although we may share a basic common text, the content is different and the books are in a different order.

Historically, Christian tradition has interpreted Genesis 34 as rape and denied Dinah a voice of her own. Not only was she silenced in Christian exegesis but she was also blamed for the sexual act itself. The Church Fathers clearly understood that although Shechem had violated Dinah, Dinah herself was to blame because of her own curiosity in going out into the neighbourhood. In that sense, Christian exegesis paralleled many rabbinic commentaries which suggested that she was 'up to no good in going out'. Moreover, Dinah was often portrayed as a weak woman, particularly in medieval Christian exegesis. The sixteenth-century theologian Martin Luther took a slightly different angle by focusing on Jacob's anguish as a father over the rape of his daughter, which is interesting given Jacob's silence in the text. In the nineteenth century, Christian commentaries on the rape of Dinah paralleled forensic medical text-books in Germany at that time, which did not recognize the act of rape.[15] Christian commentaries during this period failed to recognize that Dinah had been raped or violated at all. Other biblical scholars, all male and in a position of power, marginalized the act of rape by blaming Dinah for what had happened. Again, these commentaries paralleled forensic medical textbooks in claiming that a woman's account of rape was not to be trusted and was probably fabricated. In the twenty-first century, the traditional readings of the text are unacceptable and have been challenged by feminist writers.[16]

Turning to the text itself, Dinah is mentioned in three places in the book of Genesis – 30.21; 34; 46.15. She is also mentioned in the Apocryphal book of Judith 9.2–4. The book of Judith refers to the rape of Dinah in the context of a lengthy prayer of lament in which Judith beseeches God to intervene to defeat those Gentiles who are threatening to defile the Jerusalem Temple. Here, Judith's request is paralleled with Simeon and Levi's act of slaying the Shechemites who 'defiled' Dinah. Judith prays for vengeance on Israel's enemies in a manner that shadows Simeon's vengeance for the 'rape' of Dinah. In the biblical story, as Kathleen has said, Dinah was unusually named as the daughter of Leah rather than the customary daughter of Jacob, but she was of course also the daughter of Jacob. It was Leah who named her after having already produced six sons (34.21). Dinah

---

15 This has been highlighted by Susanna Scholz. See Susanna Scholz, 1998, 'Through Whose Eyes? A Right Reading of Genesis 34', in Athalya Brenner (ed.), *Genesis: A Feminist Companion to the Bible*, Sheffield: Sheffield Academic Press.

16 A number of feminist scholars are doing just that. See for example the work of Ita Sheres, 1990, *Dinah's Rebellion: A Biblical Parable for our Time*, New York: Crossroad; Sharon Pace Jeansonne, 1990, *The Women of Genesis: From Sarah to Potiphar's Wife*, Minneapolis: Fortress Press; and Lynn M. Bechtel, 1994, 'What if Dinah is Not Raped?', in *The Journal for the Study of the Old Testament*, 62, p. 19–36.

was not the only daughter of Jacob, although she was the only one to be specifically named in the text (46.15). In the very first verse of Genesis 34, we read that Dinah 'went out'. The text states that she was going out to visit 'the women in the region', women who were not Israelites. She was quite comfortable with going out and meeting those women in the region who were outside the boundaries of her own social setting. Throughout Genesis 34 those who were outside the boundaries of Dinah's society were represented by Shechem, Hamor and the Shechemites. It was while she was out in the neighbourhood that Shechem, the Hivite Prince, saw her and 'seized her and lay with her and humbled her'. In so doing, he had taken control of events by his actions and Dinah herself was not from that moment in charge of her own destiny. As the feminist scholar Tikva Frymer-Kensky points out: 'patriarchy is about control. The man in power can determine the destiny of those under his rule.'[17] Dinah was the subject of patriarchal control; first from Shechem's actions and second from her brothers who acted against the Shechemites without consulting her.

Kathleen has highlighted how traditional Jewish exegesis of Genesis 34 has deemed the sexual act with Shechem as rape. Traditionally, Christian exegesis has understood the action in the same way. The book of Judith in the Apocrypha also assumes the interpretation of the story as rape; however, a re-reading of the biblical text raises questions over the rape allegation.[18] Was Dinah raped? Susanne Scholz argues quite firmly 'yes' by focusing on verse 2 where she translates the Hebrew as: 'and he took her, then he laid her, and he raped her.'[19] She argues that it does not say: 'he laid with her', which would indicate mutual consent. There is one aspect which remains puzzling for me – if Dinah was raped, then the text is surprisingly silent about her resistance and protestation. There was no cry for help as one might have expected, neither were there any obvious signs of a forcible act. Given this silence and the lack of protest over her 'defilement', the story can be read in an alternative way; namely, against the background of mutual consent to pre-marital sex rather than rape. Maybe Shechem did seduce Dinah, but then surely she had consented to lie with him? Not only were there no protestations from Dinah over the alleged

---

17 Tikva Frymer-Kensky, 2002, *Reading the Women of the Bible: A New Interpretation of Their Stories*, New York: Schocken Books.

18 For a fuller argument see Lynn M. Bechtel, 1994, 'What if Dinah is Not Raped?', p. 19–36.

19 Susanna Scholz, 1998, 'Through Whose Eyes?', p. 166.

rape, but her father Jacob was also surprisingly silent. Jacob's silence is both striking and outrageous if indeed Dinah was raped. Immediately after the sexual act, Hamor (Shechem's father) tried to arrange the marriage between his son and Dinah because Shechem 'loved her and spoke tenderly to her'. It was a gesture that could have secured peace in the region. Dinah's own brothers believed that Dinah had been defiled but they did not ask her for her version of the story. Throughout all of this, Dinah uttered not a single word. Her voice had been silenced. She was also silent while her brothers (primarily), and Jacob as a bystander, negotiated the terms of her marriage to Shechem – negotiations that were indicative of the patriarchal structures which governed women in the Ancient Near East at that time. They made her marriage conditional upon all the Shechemites conforming to Israelite identity by becoming circumcised. No circumcision of *all* Shechemite males, no marriage to Dinah. As we hear later from verse 24 onwards, Dinah's brothers went back on their word and killed the Shechemite males in spite of the fact that they had all been circumcised. Even now we do not hear Dinah's reaction to her brothers' acts of violence. Sacred text and tradition have silenced her. Maybe she wanted to marry Shechem, maybe she loved him too, but her feelings were of no consequence and were not taken into account. She had to conform to her brothers' expectations and the patriarchal norms of the day. Simeon and Levi, along with Jacob's other sons, were angry at the proposed liaison between Dinah and Shechem and opposed any notion of inter-marriage between the two groups, hence their violent hostility which resulted in them exacting their revenge by slaughtering the Shechemite men, plundering their cities and forcibly taking their wives and children. It was ultimately Simeon and Levi who had their way and jeopardized any chance of peaceful co-existence in the region.

There is an interesting response from Dinah's brothers at the end of the story in verse 31 after Jacob has reprimanded them over their slaying of the Shechemites. They justify their actions by saying: 'Should he [Shechem] treat our sister as a harlot?' They do not mention rape or defilement in this context. This comment is taken up by the biblical scholar Lynn Bechtel who has argued that prostitution is carried out with mutual consent for money with no obligations or permanent attachment. Shechem wanted to secure his obligation and attachment to Dinah by marrying her and therefore was not treating her like a 'prostitute'. Bechtel argues that, therefore, neither rape nor prostitution accurately describes

[116]

what happened to Dinah. Bechtel also comments that by using the word 'harlot' Simeon and Levi understood that the sexual act with Shechem could not lead to permanent bonding. She writes:

> By saying that Dinah has become like a prostitute (harlot), Simeon and Levi might be suggesting that, from their perspective, Dinah and Shechem's intercourse could never lead to bonding and obligation. They are not suggesting that she was raped.[20]

As Bechtel suggests, such emotions and desire for marriage are not usually displayed by someone who has just raped their victim. The use of the words 'shame' and 'defilement' in the earlier part of the story refer to an act of pre-marital sex which was deemed shameful in the Ancient Near East at that time. Ironically, it was Simeon and Levi who 'raped' the Shechemite people by their plundering and slaughtering. Lynn Bechtel's exegesis offers new hope in bringing to life a silenced Dinah. Although her interpretation may not bring consolation to those who wish to express outrage at the rape, she has raised important questions which challenge our inherited readings of the text. Maybe, on closer study, there are enough clues hidden within the text to enable us to recover Dinah's voice. I am aware that if we deny the rape allegation, we may be denying Dinah her voice once again and thereby paralleling and resurrecting nineteenth-century Christian commentators. By so doing, am I disempowering Dinah once again? These are legitimate concerns; however, I am not denying the act of rape itself for some women, but in Dinah's case I am raising with Lynn Bechtel the possibility that it may not be a right reading of Genesis 34.

Kathleen has asked: 'how can I as a woman face these texts as part of my religious heritage?' When I first studied this text, I asked myself the same question. How can I make sense of this story? Not by blaming Judaism for patriarchy, but by standing with my Jewish counterparts and voicing outrage at Dinah's treatment as a non-person and the subject of a male-dominated society. The story of Dinah quite rightly belongs to that collection of texts which Phyllis Trible calls 'texts of terror'.[21] We have seen how Dinah's story is not told in her words and her voice is not heard. Nowhere

---

20 See Lynn Bechtel, 2000, 'Dinah', in Carol Meyers, Toni Craven and Ross Kraemer Ross (eds), *Women in Scripture*, Grand Rapids: Eerdmans, p. 70.

21 Phyllis Trible, 1984, *Texts of Terror*, Philadelphia: Fortress Press.

do we hear her side of the story;[22] however, we can break the patriarchal mould that has defined and silenced Dinah for centuries by asking searching questions. Was she raped as tradition suggests? Did she accept those outside her social boundaries as the act of pre-marital intercourse with Shechem demonstrates? I wish to suggest that 'rape' was the preferred interpretation because of the fear by subsequent generations that Dinah's story could be used to endorse mixed marriages and assimilation. This was something that was not only an issue for Israelite society in Dinah's day or later at the time of Ezra and Nehemiah, but in our own contemporary society with the fear that assimilation and mixed marriages threaten Jewish identity and the very future of the Jewish faith itself. This re-reading of the text ties in with Dinah's name 'judgement'. Her story passes judgement on those men within her own family who failed to accept the *outsider* into their own tribal boundaries. Although she does not speak a word, her very name pronounces judgement on her brothers' actions of conquest, slaughter and submission. The relationship between the Israelites and their neighbours is one of the main themes running through Genesis 34. The story provides an insight into the struggles within Israelite society over whether inter-marriage with outsiders was permitted. Shechem, the Hivite prince, was clearly an outsider. Through sexual intercourse with him, Dinah had provided the ultimate acceptance of the outsider. She was prepared to cross the boundaries of tribal separatism and exclusivism through her meeting with the women of the region in the first instance and then through her subsequent liaison with Shechem. Within the Torah, there is this double-edge which on the one hand allows for the conquest and occupation of Canaan by the Israelites and on the other, through Dinah, delivers one of the most powerful judgements on the massacre and oppression because in the end the sons are denied Jacob's blessing.[23]

In contemporary times, as religious people, we look to our sacred Scriptures to provide a message for our own society. Dinah's story is one example that at the heart of each of our traditions is an ethic that is underpinned by an acceptance and inclusion of the stranger, or the outsider, in our midst. Perhaps that is the central message of relevance to us as Jews

---

22 Of course Anita Diamant's novel *The Red Tent* (New York: Picador, 1997) does give voice to Dinah.

23 Michael Prior has raised the issue of how biblical texts such as these have been used to justify oppression and genocide. See for example Michael Prior, 2002, 'Ethnic Cleansing and the Bible: A Moral Critique', in *Holy Land Studies*, vol. 1, no. 1, p. 37–59.

and Christians in contemporary society. It is a message that we, as women, have drawn from the text and can take into the wider Jewish-Christian dialogue to underpin our ethical world-view in our multi-cultural society.

There are wider implications for us in reading difficult texts together, not just as women but as Jews and Christians. The rape of Dinah is part of the Torah and therefore is read each year in the synagogue when it comes to that particular weekly portion. In Christianity, the situation is different. It is a text that is not part of the liturgical cycle and one that I have not heard read in church or preached about. On one level, we may suggest that it has no relevance whatsoever to the Christian life and therefore not worth reading, and such thoughts may be part of the reason why it is not in Christian liturgy. However, it is part of our sacred Scriptures and if we do not read such texts in our community or with our Jewish dialogue partners, then a valuable opportunity to deal with the story in a constructive way passes us by. But, there is more to it than that because it underlines a more fundamental problem for Christian exegesis – what do we as Christians do with difficult Old Testament texts like the rape of Dinah or passages in the book of Leviticus for example? Here I am thinking of passages in Leviticus that are largely ignored within Christianity unless they talk about sexuality, and in particular homosexuality. Is it enough for us to say that these have no relevance to our faith and can be passed over? What happens when we as Jews and Christians study such passages together? We cannot remain unchanged by exposure to Jewish interpretations of the text. When we read and interpret our texts in the presence of 'the other', it affects how we hear our own traditions and exegesis and sometimes forces us to change those interpretations. A similar analogy can be made with feminist biblical scholarship where the feminist voices on biblical texts have challenged our patriarchal heritage, whether as Jews or Christians, and we cannot ignore those new developments. I speak more about hearing our traditions in the presence of 'the other' in Chapter 9, but for Christians, Dinah's story raises a note of caution over the tendency to contrast this as a product of a patriarchal misogynist society, equated with the Old Testament and Jewish faith, with the liberating and loving society inaugurated by Jesus, equated with Christian faith.

While much work has been done in New Testament studies in understanding the Jewish roots of Christian faith, we, as Christians, have not yet made the same advances in Old Testament exegesis in the light of the new Jewish-Christian relationship. Here, I am not referring to scholarly research or advances in understanding the historical background to the Old Testament, rather I am referring to the acceptance of parallel interpretations of the text which are valid for Jews as well as Christians. Here, I am reinforcing the point made by Lynne in Chapter 5. Can Christians now take a major step forward and accept that Jewish interpretations of the Hebrew Bible are valid even if we disagree with those interpretations? This would parallel Jewish midrash where there are multiple possible interpretations of any one text. I wish to suggest that this is one of the most important advances that can be made towards reconciliation and acceptance. From the Jewish side, could there be an acceptance that Christian readings of the biblical texts are valid even if Jews radically disagree with those interpretations? Why is this move so important? Because from the Christian side it would remove some of the last bastions of supersessionist theology which claims Christian superiority over Judaism. It would signal an acceptance that Jewish interpretations have not been made obsolete by the Christ event. From the Jewish side, it would affirm an acceptance of Christian identity as not merely an errant form of Judaism. Such a move is especially difficult for Jews given the painful history of Christian anti-Judaism, but one which is necessary for the future of Jewish-Christian relations, especially for building a Jewish theology of Christianity which has yet to take shape, although the document *Dabru Emet* is an excellent start (see the Introduction to Part 1 for comments on this).

This chapter has underlined, through a study of the story of Dinah, that Jewish and Christian women have much to talk about in reclaiming their history from the traditional male-only perspective. We have shown that women can bring a new awareness to the text which confronts our inherited patriarchal traditions and exegesis. In that sense we have much to share with each other and can find mutual solidarity as women. In spite of the differing ways in which we approach our Scriptures, we are finding new levels of interpretative agreement across our faith traditions and our voices speak out against the marginalization of women, whether in the Hebrew Bible, the Old Testament or the New Testament. While the story of Dinah is different in many ways from that of other women, like Mary Magdalene in the New Testament (discussed in the next chapter), one was a rape victim and the other was labelled a prostitute, both texts deal with women and sexuality and have their parallels in the way in which our traditions have silenced them *as women.* So far, their voices have been silenced by those who have passed down their story to subsequent generations. Together, Jewish and Christian women can reclaim the stories of women like Dinah and restore their voices to the chain of tradition which will be handed on to future generations.

Further Reading

See the Bibliography section for full details on these titles.

Lynn M. Bechtel, 'Dinah', in Carol Meyers, Toni Craven and Ross Kraemer (eds), *Women in Scripture.*
Anita Diamant, *The Red Tent.*
Tikva Frymer-Kensky, *Reading the Women of the Bible: A New Interpretation of Their Stories.*
Susanna Scholz, 'Through Whose Eyes? A Right Reading of Genesis 34', in Athalya Brenner (ed.), *Genesis: A Feminist Companion to the Bible.*
Ita Sheres, *Dinah's Rebellion: A Biblical Parable for our Time.*
Avivah Gottlieb Zornberg, *Genesis: The Beginning of Desire.*

7 Mary Magdalene

Mary Magdalene and the other women ministered to them out of their resources.

Luke 8.3

I Apostle to the Apostles

Lynne Scholefield

I see Mary Magdalene as the most important woman in the New Testament because of her leadership role both before and after the death and resurrection of Jesus. She is the 'apostle to the apostles',[1] the one who, after a lengthy conversation with the risen Jesus, announces the resurrection to the other disciples. Yet, despite all this she is known in Christian tradition mainly as a reformed prostitute; one who represents sexual temptation and the need for repentance. In this section, I set out the evidence in the Gospels for Mary's important role and then discuss the way in which this came to be distorted. I also consider the claims of some contemporary women scholars for a leadership role in the Church for Mary, based on non-canonical material; namely in those writings that did not become part of the New Testament as we know it.

The third-century Roman presbyter, Hippolytus, praised Mary Magdalene because she clung to Jesus' feet with the intention of going with him to heaven. He sees her as a symbol of the synagogue which wants to join the church.[2] It is interesting that when Philippe Auguste expelled the Jews from Paris in the 1180s, their synagogue was then consecrated as a church by the bishop, Maurice de Sully, and dedicated to Mary Magdalene. This

---

1 Or 'of the apostles'. These are generally accepted titles for Mary Magdalene used for example by Bernard of Clairvaux and Thomas Aquinas. See Margaret Hebblethwaite, 1994, *Six New Gospels*, London: Geoffrey Chapman, p. 149.

2 E. de Boer, 1996, *Mary Magdalene: Beyond the Myth*, London: SCM Press, p. 62.

idea of Mary Magdalene being the synagogue who became church may have been widespread in the Middle Ages, but the same bishop was responsible for beginning the work on the Cathedral of Notre Dame where on its western front there are two female figures of *ekklesia* and *synagoga*, church and synagogue. As in many medieval sculptures *synagoga* is shown blindfolded with a broken staff whereas *ekklesia* is shown triumphant and majestic. In this section, I will develop a reading of Mary Magdalene as a Jewish woman of the first century who becomes a disciple and an apostle of Jesus and who offers an example of Christian faith and practice that is relevant today.

Mary Magdalene appears in each of the four Gospels. When Matthew, Mark and Luke name the group of women disciples who accompanied Jesus, Mary Magdalene's name comes first (Luke 8.1–3; 24.10; Matt. 27.55–56; Mark 15.40–41). The Gospel of John names her last but with Jesus' close family; his mother and her sister (John 19.25). Luke 8.1–3 is an interesting text and worth close attention despite the fact that it has received little exegetical attention until recently.[3] Verse 3 reads that: 'Mary Magdalene and the other women "ministered" to them out of their resources.' The Greek verb used here is *diakonein* which has a range of meanings from serving at table in a private setting to serving as a deacon in a public role in the early Church. I am not suggesting that these women were deacons in that sense during Jesus' lifetime but that the word used to describe their role in the original text has this echo and may reflect Mary's role in the post-resurrection community. There is another significant aspect to this verse and that is the reference to these women providing resources for Jesus which made it possible for his ministry to function.[4] For them to do so, they must have been of independent means, possibly widows, although the text gives no indication of that. Even so, these were powerful women with disposable income which they could use to enable Jesus to continue his work as an itinerant preacher and healer. However much their story and witness may have eventually been marginalized, we have a glimpse here in the text itself of independent women in strong leadership roles and the Gospels do not think that there is anything unusual or wrong with this.

---

3 C. Ricci, 1994, *Mary Magdalene and Many Others*, Minneapolis: Fortress Press, p. 29.

4 Another similar example is in the story of Mary and Martha who provide food for Jesus at their home.

To raise the issue of the role of these women in a different way, we can ask whether we should count Mary and the other women as disciples of Jesus. Luke 8.2 refers to 'women who had been cured of evil spirits and infirmities', and this suggests how the women first came to be connected with Jesus. There is no account of women being called to be disciples in the same way as the male disciples were in Mark 1.16–20,[5] but they must have been encouraged by Jesus to join his group; and it is worth noting that many of the men who were cured of evil spirits and infirmities by Jesus were sent away.[6] These women travelled with Jesus, shared in his life and suffering, served him and received his teaching, and were told to proclaim the good news of the resurrection. Even if they are not always specifically mentioned in the text, we can assume that they were present for the special teaching which Jesus gave the disciples. In the very next story of the Parable of the Sower in Luke 8.4–18, Jesus gave this special teaching to the disciples saying, 'To you it has been given to know the secrets of the kingdom of God' (v. 10) and there is no reason to think that the women did not hear Jesus explain the meaning of the parable. Surely, also, they were there at the Last Supper despite the way this scene has been traditionally depicted in art, including by Leonardo da Vinci? If this meal had been a *seder* meal, and that is not wholly clear, then women would certainly have been present as they would be for any Jewish meal. The scholar Esther de Boer goes as far as to argue that the 'beloved disciple' of John's Gospel is none other than Mary Magdalene.[7] At the beginning of the book of Acts the women are explicitly mentioned as present with the male disciples in Acts 1.14. At Pentecost in Acts 2.1 when 'they were all together in one place', they were all filled with the Holy Spirit (v. 4) and this included the women present. It seems entirely reasonable to say that these women were disciples of Jesus.

The text in Luke 8.1–3 also raises sharply the question of what was the role of Jewish women in the first century CE. There seems to be a prevailing anti-Jewish stereotype of a restricted and oppressive role for Jewish women. Here is one example from the New Testament scholar Ben Witherington III: '... the family was almost the exclusive sphere of the

---

5 Parallel Matt. 4.18–22, Luke 5.1–11.

6 A very clear example of this can be seen in Luke 8.38–39. The man from whom the demons had gone begged Jesus that he might be with him 'but Jesus sent him away'.

7 E. de Boer, 2000, 'Mary Magdalene and the Disciple Jesus Loved', in *Lectio Difficilior – European Electronic Journal for Feminist Exegesis*.

influence for Jewish women in the first century AD. For a Jewish woman to leave home and travel with a rabbi was not only unheard of, it was scandalous.'[8] Jesus is often presented in contemporary Christian preaching, and in early feminist writings, as the one who frees women from this restrictive role.[9] There is no suggestion in the New Testament that men and women were separated during congregational worship for example – something which might well have needed comment if that had been the practice in the synagogue. Certainly the Gospels present Jesus as attaching little importance to family roles, see for example Luke 8.20–21, but this is not the same as suggesting that women needed to be freed from Judaism. There still seems to be little real knowledge about the role of women within the diversity of the Judaisms of the first century, however, as Safrai argues, there was no separation of the sexes in synagogues and women could be counted as part of the required minimum number for public congregational prayer.[10] Perhaps, as some evidence seems to suggest, mainly archaeological evidence from inscriptions, women had leadership roles in both the synagogue and the early Church.[11] Rodney Stark has provided some compelling evidence that Christian women within the Christian subculture enjoyed considerably higher status than women in what he calls the pagan world. 'This was especially marked vis-à-vis gender relations within the family, but women also filled leadership positions within the Church.'[12]

Regarding the early Christian community, the New Testament mentions the following women who had some kind of leadership role: Phoebe who was a deacon (Rom. 16.1); Prisca who was a fellow worker of Paul and who risked her life for him (Rom. 16.3); Junia, eminent among the apostles (Rom. 16.7); Julia and Nereus' sister (Rom. 16.15); Mary and Persis who worked so hard (Rom. 16.6, 12); Euodia and Syntyche who

---

8 Ben Witherington quoted by Margaret Hebblethwaite, 1994, *Six New Gospels*, p. 128.

9 See for example Katharina von Kellenbach, 1994, *Anti-Judaism in Feminist Religious Writings*, Atlanta: Scholars Press.

10 S. Safrai, 'The Place of Women in the First-century Synagogues', at www.jerusalemperspective.com/articles/DisplayArticle.

11 Bernadette Brooten has done some excellent work in this respect. See *Women Leaders in the Ancient Synagogue*, Brown Judaic Studies, 36, 1982, Atlanta: Scholars Press.

12 Rodney Stark, 1995, 'Reconstructing the Rise of Christianity: The Role of Women', in *Sociology of Religion*, vol. 56, no. 3. p. 229–44 (242).

shared Paul's struggles in the cause of the gospel and who were his 'fellow-workers' (Phil. 4.2–3); Apphia 'our sister' (Philem. 2); Prisca mentioned again – the church met in her house (1 Cor. 16.19); Lydia who, once her household had all become Christians, insisted that Paul and others stay in her house (Acts 16.15);[13] Nympha – the church met in her house (Col. 4.15); and women praying and prophesying during worship (1 Cor. 11.5).[14] These are traces of leadership roles for women and, in the light of Mary Magdalene's role in the Gospels, it seems strange to find no further trace of her in the New Testament.[15]

So let's return to examining Mary's leading role in the Gospels. She was a witness of the crucifixion (Mark 15.40), she saw where the body was laid (15.47), she brought spices to anoint Jesus' body (16.1) and she was the first witness of the resurrection. All the Gospels refer to her in this role but in John's Gospel (20.1–18), Jesus appeared to Mary and they talk. She not only tells the disciples about the empty tomb but, as the text says: 'Mary Magdalene went and announced to the disciples, "I have seen the Lord" and she told them that he had said these things to her' (20.18). It is interesting to note that in 1 Corinthians 15.5–7, Paul lists all the people that the resurrected Jesus had appeared to but he does not mention Mary Magdalene. So who was this woman with a special place in relation to Jesus and what was her role? Unlike the other women in the Gospels Mary is not named in relation to a father, husband or son. Perhaps this indicates a person with full status in her own right and also the importance of her relationship with Jesus. Luke 8.2 says that Mary Magdalene was the one from whom seven demons had come out and different commentators give different accounts of what 'possession' means. Perhaps we could say that since she was freed from possession this too suggests that she was now her own person. However, nowhere in the Gospels does it suggest that she was

13 This is a very interesting story. Paul and others are at Philippi, 'Here we stayed for some days, and on the Sabbath we went outside the city gate by the riverside, where we thought there would be a place of prayer; we sat down and talked to the *women* who had gathered there' (Acts 16.12–13, my emphasis).

14 According to 1 Cor. 11.1–14 women must cover their heads when praying and prophesying, while men must not cover their heads.

15 The Pauline Epistles are earlier in date than the Gospels so this does not mean that later Christians tried to remove evidence of Mary Magdalene as a leader. Perhaps Paul was part of a group of Christians who rejected her leadership. This is, of course, merely speculation but certainly Acts 15 suggests that there were real differences of opinion in the early church.

a prostitute. So how did that powerful tradition and assumption come about?[16] This seems to be the reasoning: the woman who anointed Jesus in Luke 7.36–50 was a 'sinner' and this may imply a prostitute, although Luke uses a different word for 'prostitute' in 15.30. The woman who anointed Jesus in John's Gospel was Mary of Bethany (John 12.1–8); therefore Mary of Bethany was a prostitute, or, to put it another way, the prostitute was called Mary. Luke's story of the anointing is immediately followed by the information that Mary Magdalene was one of Jesus' followers from whom seven demons had come out, so Mary was obviously a very great sinner, despite the fact that exorcism was usually related to infirmity not sin. So, Mary Magdalene may be the sinner of the previous chapter, despite the fact that the text makes no link, but remember the prostitute was called Mary, therefore Mary Magdalene was a prostitute. Jerome was the first to start this conflation of three different women, when he wrote that: 'Mary Magdalene was that woman from whom he had driven out seven demons, in order that where sin had been abundant, grace might be more abundant.'[17] This started a tradition that would lead to Mary being seen as one in great need of repentance and forgiveness rather than as a leading figure among the disciples and in the early Church. This is an image found in western art which often portrays her as a scarlet women with red hair, seen in need of forgiveness rather than as a leader among the disciples of Jesus.

The story in John 20.1–18 portrays an intimate meeting between Jesus and Mary and also his commission to her to take the good news of the resurrection and ascension to the other disciples. Her presence at the crucifixion with Jesus' family also suggests their close relationship but it is in the non-canonical writings that this is made more fully explicit. For example, the Gospel of Philip says that Jesus loved Mary more than any other disciple and used to kiss her often, while the Gospel of Mary presents her as a leader to whom Jesus gave private teaching.[18] These texts did not become part of mainstream Christian literature but they are an indication of a strand of tradition where Mary Magdalene was a significant leader. In the non-canonical Gospel of Thomas, to remain a disciple Mary had to

---

16 I recently had an argument with my 15-year-old godson who was quite vehement that Mary was a prostitute – because his RE teacher had told him so.

17 Jerome quoted in Margaret Hebblethwaite, 1994, *Six New Gospels*, p. 119.

18 K. L. King, no date, 'Women in Ancient Christianity: The New Discoveries', page 4 at: www.pbs.org/wgbh/pages/frontline/shows/religion/first/women.html.

become 'male'. This seems to have been a widespread notion about women who wanted to aspire to holiness in that period. I have discussed more about this aspect in the work of the Jewish scholar Daniel Boyarin in Chapter 2.[19] There is also a legend that she extended her preaching to Provence and there is a thirteenth-century stained-glass window in the church in Semur in Burgundy showing her as a preacher. The novelist Michele Roberts drew on this tradition for her novel called *The Wild Girl* as well as weaving in elements about Mary of Bethany and the sinful woman who anointed Jesus. In the novel Mary, in Provence, is writing what is to become another long-lost Gospel.[20] The novel also uses the legend that Mary Magdalene gave birth to Jesus' child, a daughter. There were powerful heretical traditions of a bloodline of Jesus (the sangraal), especially in France; but I am less interested in these myths and legends about Mary Magdalene than I am in the Gospel material.

In the Gospels, I have argued, Mary Magdalene was both a disciple and an apostle and this suggests that, maybe, during Jesus' ministry and in some parts of the very early Church, women did have a full and equal role with men. That, to me, is a very encouraging thought. It also interests me, especially in the context of dialogue, that Mary Magdalene as a Jewish woman, along with other women in the New Testament, might throw unexpected light on the world of Jewish women in the first century.

II Mary Magdalene: A Jewish Response

Rachel Montagu

I enjoyed learning from Lynne's paper how significant a figure Mary Magdalene was among Jesus' disciples – more than later tradition allowed her to be. In response I will consider how male biblical commentators look at women who were prostitutes, the assumptions made about women of this era and, reading the New Testament as a Jew, what seems to me to be the significance of Mary Magdalene's role.

---

19 Daniel Boyarin, 1998, 'Gender', in Mark. C. Taylor (ed.), *Critical Terms for Religious Studies*, Chicago: University of Chicago Press, p. 125.

20 See for example M. Starbird, 1999, 'Mary Magdalene: The Beloved' at: www.magdalene.org/belovedessay.htm.

First, I wish to explain some difficulties in reading the New Testament for me as a Jewish reader. Even to open the New Testament, I have to over-come an instinctive recoil, a sense that this should be a closed book to Jews. I am surprised that after years of shared Jewish and Christian New Testament study, much of it with members of this discussion group, I still feel that way, but if I'm honest I do. My head knows and approves that the New Testament is now used as a source of information about Jewish life in the period between the Bible and the Mishnah (the first rabbinic code, from 200 CE), when there are no contemporary Jewish sources. My heart is still uncertain whether this means I want to read it myself.

Perhaps this is because there is a sense that I am entering a 'through the looking-glass' world where some of my normal points of reference are turned upside down and where at any moment I may come across a derogatory statement about Jews and/or Judaism. When I read on from Mary Magdalene witnessing the resurrection and reached, 'the doors of the house where the disciples had met were locked for fear of the Jews'[21] I didn't know what to think. For fear of people like me? For fear of them-selves? Even without looking at all the differences of scholarly opinion about responsibility for Jesus' death, this is an uncomfortable verse. Then there are all the comments about the Pharisees. When studying Jewish sources, the Pharisees are my heroes. They are the ones who found a way of taking Judaism forward after the horror of the destruction of the Temple and Roman persecution and gave the Jewish people a way to con-tinue serving God – by prayer rather than sacrifice – while hoping for future redemption. They were creative religious thinkers, who tacitly dropped biblical commandments of which they did not approve like the trial by ordeal for the wife suspected of adultery and thought of ways to preserve the spirit of the biblical commandments even if this meant alter-ing the prescribed procedure, as when Hillel created a legal fiction to enable the poor to borrow money at all times during the seven-year cycle.[22] They also have a sense of humour and the wisdom to laugh at themselves.[23] What then am I to make of the New Testament image of the Pharisees? The people who in their own literature say: 'the man who lets a woman drown because it would be immodest to look at her and save her

---

21 John 20.19.

22 Mishnah *Sheviith* 10.3–7.

23 Hyam Maccoby, 1978, *The Day God Laughed: Sayings, Fables and Entertainments of the Jewish Sages*, London: Robson Books.

[129]

is a pious fool'[24] are collectively accused in the New Testament of precisely that kind of idiocy. Even allowing for the fact that the beauty of a religion's teaching may not always be reflected by the beauty of all its adherents' behaviour, the description of the Pharisees bewilders me. The Gospels were written down at the time when Church and Synagogue were becoming ever more separate. Nowadays, one would not look to right-wing political propaganda for an accurate picture of the virtues of socialism but it is problematic when that same type of destructive polemic against another is included in sacred texts. Perhaps as well as a quest for the historical Jesus we need a quest for the historical Pharisee. At the same time, I admire the way some Christians have for years now tried to find a Christianity that does not depend on the 'Christianity good, Judaism bad' mantra, even if it means looking at their most sacred texts in a wholly new way. And as well as the strange sayings, the New Testament contains some phrases that directly reflect my own religious life – for instance naming Friday as 'Day of Preparation'[25] – and a style of story-telling to make moral points that is familiar from Jewish literature.

Also I am aware that I have no expertise in the New Testament. Texts which puzzle me when I read them in the New Testament, I have learnt from my Christian partners in dialogue to be easily understood in the context of centuries of traditional Christian exegesis about which I still have much to learn.

I am interested by what Lynne says about the readiness of the early Church to identify Mary Magdalene as a prostitute, without any supporting evidence. Mel Gibson went further; in his film *The Passion of The Christ*, he portrayed her as the woman taken in adultery.[26] It appears that whether a woman was described as a prostitute or not by post-biblical commentators owed more to their feelings about her than it did to her activities, professional or otherwise. For instance, in the book of Joshua, Rahab, who helped the Children of Israel conquer the Promised Land, is described as a *zonah*, a prostitute. Rashi, the medieval biblical commentator, does not accept that the normal etymology of the word can apply to a woman like Rahab whose bravery saved the Jewish people and asserts that *zonah* means that she sold provisions (*m'zonot* in Hebrew) rather than

---

24 Babylonian Talmud *Sotah* 21b.

25 Mark 15.42.

26 John 8.3. My thanks to Jane Clements for pointing this out and for a helpful discussion on Mary Magdalene's significance.

herself.[27] Similarly, in Genesis 38, Tamar, a childless widow whose in-laws kept her in her father's house, dressed up as a prostitute to intercept her father-in-law Judah. She asked for his seal and staff as an assurance that he would pay the agreed price for her sexual services and showed these tokens when she was accused of immorality once the resulting pregnancy was obvious. Judah responded '*Tsadkah mimeni*' which can mean either 'She is more righteous than I', or 'She is righteous: it [the pregnancy] is from me.'[28] The medieval Jewish commentators praise Tamar for her extreme modesty. In contrast, Mary Magdalene, on far less evidence than Rahab and Tamar, is held to be a prostitute. This made an opportunity for artists to paint her scantily dressed or covered only by her long red hair.[29] Regularly seeing pictures of her more or less naked, so different from other more respectably dressed women saints, may well have diminished her credibility for churchmen. She is a key witness to the resurrection; she is described as 'the apostle to the apostles', so is it her sexually charged image that ensures that she is not always seen as a role model by contemporary Christian women and does not have the status within the Church that one might expect? Lynne says that Mary Magdalene 'represents sexual temptation and the need for repentance'. In this role she proves that repentance from however sinful a past is always possible. But if she is a reformed prostitute, then why is her past as a prostitute the most conspicuous thing about her? This seems to represent an odd and inconsistent attitude to repentance and forgiveness. Her sins are forgiven but not for a moment forgotten; they remain her most significant identity. The suggestion that she is a positive example of repentance would be more convincing if it were not for the way in which, as Carol Osiek says, 'Onto her was projected the male fascination with the repristinated sex object in spite of a total lack of evidence [that she was] ... a reformed prostitute.'[30] If a little girl said to her Christian parents that she wanted to be like Mary Magdalene when she grew up, what would be the image that sprang to their minds? Preacher of the Resurrection? Maybe.

---

27 Joshua 2.1, Rashi ad loc.

28 Tikva Frymer Kensky, 2000, 'Mary Magdalene', in Carol Meyers, Toni Craven and Ross Kraemer (eds), *Women in Scripture*, Grand Rapids: Eerdmans, p. 162.

29 Susan Haskins, 1993, *Mary Magdalen: Myth and Metaphor*, London: Harper Collins. See also www.Google.co.uk/Images/Mary Magdalene.

30 Carolyn Osiek in Carol Meyers, Toni Craven and Ross Kraemer (eds), 2000, *Women in Scripture*, p. 122.

Lynne also talks about using Mary Magdalene to find out more about the lives of first-century Jewish women. The problem with finding out anything about the lives of first-century Jewish women is that the information we have is so limited that complex structures of interpretation are sometimes built on slender or non-existent foundations. In Chapter 1 Helen cites a letter in a local newspaper saying that any women of Jesus' time who joined an itinerant band of preachers would be stoned. In the Hebrew Bible stoning is the punishment for serious crimes like blasphemy, witchcraft and desecrating the sabbath.[31] In fact, in the rabbinic period the death penalty seems hardly ever to have been carried out although it remained on the statute book; a Sanhedrin that imposed the death penalty once in 70 years was said to be a murderous Sanhedrin and Akiba and Tarphon, two authoritative early rabbis, said the death penalty should never be carried out at all. Yet Rabbi Akiba was quoted in discussions on the use of capital punishment; this proves how theoretical such discussions sometimes were.[32] The rabbis preferred to make it impossible to carry out the death penalty for sins for which it was prescribed in the Bible rather than explicitly to alter the biblical commandment. Joining an itinerant band of preachers is certainly not considered a capital crime in the Bible for men or women.

As I say later in Chapter 11, issues of purity often generate excessive Christian negativity about woman's role in Judaism. Another example of misplaced confidence in interpretation is the New Testament scholar Ben Witherington III who says that, 'since [women] could not be depended upon to be ritually clean they were not even eligible to participate in those ordinances of the Law which were periodic [sic] in nature, such as certain feasts, daily appearances in the synagogue to make a quorum, periodic [sic] prayer.'[33] In fact nobody, man or woman, could be depended upon to be ritually clean in Temple times; the most serious source of impurity was a human corpse and nobody could guarantee against contact with one. That is why the Mishnah says there was a reserve high priest on standby before the Day of Atonement in case anything should happen to render the first one unfit to officiate.[34] Menstrual impurity was trivial by

---

31 Lev. 20.27, Lev. 24.23, Num. 15.36.

32 Mishnah *Makkot* 1.10 and *Sanhedrin* 9.6.

33 Ben Witherington III, 1990, *Women and the Genesis of Christianity*, Cambridge: Cambridge University Press, p. 9.

34 Mishnah *Yoma* 1.1.

comparison and, as I argue in Chapter 11, never a bar to prayer, something that Jewish women were and are commanded to do every day, irrespective of menstrual status.

Bonnie Thurston says 'any money [a wife] earned belonged to her husband.'[35] There is a risk of over-simplification here. Men were supposed to support their wives, and the extent of the appropriate support is specified in some detail:[36] women were supposed to contribute their earnings to the family budget, although any money brought to the marriage remained their own. If we look at the woman of Proverbs 31.10–31, she was obviously capable of generating a considerable income and there is no suggestion that she consulted her husband in either the making or the spending of it. Just as nowadays couples with a joint bank account may discuss the allocation of some funds and each spend some as they choose, so knowing that women's earnings were part of the household income does not imply the financial powerlessness some commentators suggest. As now, women in the more moneyed classes would have far more financial choices than poorer women. Widows and divorcees were financially autonomous, which as Lynne says may explain their ability to support Jesus from their resources, but wealthy married women may also have had this option. It is certainly not reasonable to assume that the financial situation of women in first-century Palestine means that the 'expensive ointment' must have been derived from immoral earnings. Both the New Testament and early Jewish literature are so limited in the context offered to many statements that it is hard to be sure exactly what they are telling us, but that does not excuse fantasy and speculation presented as fact; when these fantasies are devoted to 'proving' negative ideas about Judaism, I ask myself why they are so important to their authors.

Helen has discussed in Chapter 3 whether Jesus can be the messiah of Jewish expectation. Messiah means anointed one; if Jesus was proved to the Jewish community of his day to be the messiah, then as a Jewish reader I would expect him to be ceremonially anointed with oil, as Samuel anointed David as king and as Moses anointed Aaron and his sons as priests.[37] His baptism by John marks the beginning of his public ministry;

---

35 Bonnie Thurston, 1998, *Women in the New Testament: Questions and Commentary*, New York: Crossroad Publishing Company, p. 14.

36 See Judith R. Wegner, 1988, *Chattel or Person? The Status of Women in the Mishnah*, Oxford: Oxford University Press.

37 Lev. 8.30 and 1 Sam. 16.13.

Judaism does use immersion to mark new beginnings, as Marcia explains in Chapter 10, but immersion does not carry the theological meaning in Judaism that baptism does in Christianity. The nearest thing to an anointing Jesus has in the New Testament is the anointing, although with costly perfume rather than with oil, by the woman who although she is not named as Mary in the Synoptic Gospels, is assumed to be Mary Magdalene.[38] This could be merely an anointing as part of cleaning: this was a contemporary routine and was one of the physical pleasures abstained from on the Day of Atonement.[39] In Psalm 23, anointing implies simply comfort and well-being. But it could be a symbolic anointing as Messiah. This would mean that Mary Magdalene is not only the first witness to his resurrection, she is also the one who has the authority to anoint Jesus and thus inaugurate his messianic mission. Therefore I wonder about the protests with which the disciples greet the anointing. Are they really protesting about the cost of the perfume? Are they objecting to the use of perfumed oil rather than olive oil for the anointing of a leader? Is this a debate about issues of authority and whether it is appropriate for Mary Magdalene to be the one who anoints? The word nard is used only in two contexts in the Bible, in the story of the anointing with perfume given in the Gospels, and in the Song of Songs where the scent of nard is one of the elements in the sensuous delight the lovers take in each other.[40] The Song of Songs can be read as the story of two human lovers or as a metaphorical poem about the love between God and Israel or on both these levels simultaneously, with added interest from the dual significance. This double layer of meaning may be a factor too in Mary anointing Jesus with nard, signifying either the love between Jesus and Mary or the love Jesus inspired in all his disciples then and since in the life of the Church, or both simultaneously.

Mary Magdalene was the first witness to the resurrection but her status as a witness who is a Jewish woman has been used against Judaism by Christian commentators. Christine Schenk says, 'Women were not accepted as witnesses in Jewish law.'[41] In fact, women can be accepted as witnesses in rabbinic courts; indeed whereas usually two witnesses were

---

38 Matt. 26.7–9, Mark 14.3–5, Luke 7.37–8, John 12.3–7.
39 Mishnah *Yoma* 8.1.
40 Song of Songs 1.14 and 4.13–14, Mark 14.3, John 12.3.
41 Christine Schenk, 'A Call for National Dialogue on Women in Church Leadership', at: www.cta-usa.org/wicl/4Jesusand women.html.

the norm, one woman can testify about the death of a missing man and the court accepts her testimony. There are many other occasions when Jewish literature specifies that a woman's testimony can be accepted.[42] The fact that women were not summoned to court in civil cases nowhere implies that they were unreliable or untruthful. In Luke 24.11 it is not because they are Jewish *women* that the male disciples do not believe Mary Magdalene, Joanna and Mary but because what they said they had seen seemed so unlikely.

Was it possible to see women as leaders in the early Church and in the contemporary synagogue? Surely the main issue here is what we *see* as significant. We can only see what our culture allows us to see. A friend told me that when his wife organized a surprise champagne breakfast, complete with waitress service, for his birthday, he completely overlooked the waitress standing ready to pour his breakfast champagne as she was too unlikely a vision in their home's early morning routine. Were women leaders rendered invisible because they were as improbable as a uniformed waitress at a family breakfast table? I suspect that while women could fulfil leadership functions – teach, be a disciple, be a synagogue leader, even be a queen or an apostle – somehow this was always, each and every time, both seen and not seen in the Jewish and Christian world. Various women are quoted in Jewish literature as teaching others but still the perception that women did not teach appears in the works of some authors. It is assumed that the reason women were not called to the court as witnesses is that women had no public role, and this assumption persists despite numerous references to women appearing in public; the theory that they could not or should not prevails over the evidence that they sometimes could and did. It is only recently that Jewish literature was read by those who, because they did not regard women as incidental, paid serious attention to all the references there to women and also considered the archaeological evidence and so a more nuanced picture is emerging.

The book of Genesis is full of stories of sibling rivalry. The tension of sibling rivalry can be profound – to the point where I have suggested elsewhere it can be a model for competitiveness between religions, each faith wishing to believe that it is God's favourite child.[43] With Mary Magdalene

---

42 For a discussion of the issues surrounding women and testimony, see Judith Hauptman, 1998, *Rereading the Rabbis: A Woman's Voice*, Colorado: Westview Press.

43 Rachel Montagu, 1987, 'With God-like Struggles I have Wrestled with My Sister and Prevailed', *European Judaism* 87:1, p. 23f.

and the other apostles, the issue seems to be disciple rivalry. The Gospel of Mary says:

> Peter: 'Did he really speak privately to a woman, not openly to us? Are we to turn about and all listen to her? Did he prefer her to us?' Distressed at his rage, Mary replies, 'My brother Peter, what do you think? Do you think that I thought this up myself in my heart or that I am lying about the Saviour?' Levi breaks in at this point to mediate the dispute: 'Peter, you have always been hot-tempered. Now I see you contending against the woman like the adversaries. But if the Saviour made her worthy, who are you, indeed, to reject her? Surely the Lord knew her very well. That is why he loved her more than us.'[44]

Is the key 'Did he prefer her to us?', or how one resolves contradictions in a teaching when some have heard one version and others another? Is Mary's testimony downgraded because of suspicions about the nature of her relationship with Jesus? Either way, the pain and anger are obvious. These days religions are learning to think less in terms of themselves as the favourite child and their sibling faiths as barely legitimate, never mind loved, and are realizing that God can love all human beings and that God can be manifest in all religions. As Jonathan Sacks says, 'We will make peace only when we learn that God loves difference and so, at last, must we.'[45] Perhaps too men and women can realize that each gender can have different perceptions and approaches to the faith to which they both belong that do not delegitimize that of the other but together make a more diverse and interesting unity.

A recent competition in the *Church Times* for a caption to a picture of Mary and Jesus in the garden elicited the entry, 'I'm ordaining you bishop but don't tell anyone for several centuries.' Is Mary Magdalene, who anoints Jesus and witnesses his resurrection, who was apostle and leader in the early Church, a potential role-model within today's Church whose image has yet to reach its full development? I trust we will soon reach a time when Mary Magdalene can be seen for what she was, as women and men see more clearly what women can be and do in Judaism and Christianity.

---

44 Gospel of Mary 17.17–18.15.

45 Jonathan Sacks, 2002, *The Dignity of Difference: How to Avoid the Clash of Civilisations*, London: Continuum, p. 23.

Further Reading

See the Bibliography section for full details on these titles.

Richard Bauckham, *Gospel Women: Studies of the Named Women in the Gospels.*
E. de Boer, *Mary Magdalene: Beyond the Myth.*
Mary Ann Getty-Sullivan, *Women in the New Testament.*
Ross Kraemer and Mary Rose D'Angelo (eds), *Women and Christian Origins.*
Amy-Jill Levine (ed.), *Women Like This: New Perspectives on Jewish Women in the Greco-Roman World.*
C. Ricci, *Mary Magdalene and Many Others.*
M. Roberts, *The Wild Girl.*

8 Women Prophets

Before I formed you in the womb I knew you, and before you were born
I consecrated you; I appointed you a prophet to the nations.

Jeremiah 1.5

I Prophetesses in the Hebrew Bible

Rachel Montagu

What is it prophets do and is it a job for a nice biblical girl? And if it is a job
for a nice biblical girl, how do the nice post-biblical boys who interpreted
the biblical text for us feel about that? This chapter looks first at women
called 'prophet' in the Hebrew Bible, then at the women described as
prophet by the rabbis of the Talmud. In English 'prophecy' is synonymous
with 'telling the future'. In biblical thought prophets are messengers who
bring God's word to the people; a prophet's message from God may indeed
describe future events, but foretelling the future is not the essence of
prophecy; to prophesy is to proclaim God's word, whether that word is a
call to righteous behaviour or a warning of the consequences of idolatry.
Any reader of the Bible can see that it describes women's relationships with
God and that women, including women prophets, are able to hear God
speaking to them. What about conveying God's message to the people?
While only a minority of the biblical prophets are women, those who are
prophets conveyed God's message like any other prophet. Post-biblical
Jewish tradition has a more ambivalent attitude to women prophets
because of the unwillingness experienced in Judaism, as in Christianity
and other traditions, during some eras to recognize women as public
figures.

Interestingly, the women described as 'prophet' in the Bible are some-
what different from the list of women prophets given in the Talmud, the

[138]

early medieval compendium of rabbinic law and lore to which all later Jewish codes refer. Women named as prophets in the biblical text include Miriam, Deborah, Huldah, Noadiah (of whom nothing other than her name is known)[1] and the wife of Isaiah whose own name, as distinct from her husband's, is not given.[2] It is unclear from the context whether Isaiah's wife was a prophet in her own right or whether 'prophetess' means that as Isaiah's wife she is 'Mrs Prophet' similar to the way in German 'Frau Doktor' used to mean a doctor's wife.[3]

Miriam is the first woman to be called prophet in the Bible. We first meet her watching over her baby brother Moses lying in his basket in the Nile. When he was found by Pharaoh's daughter, Miriam offered to find a wet nurse for him, thus ensuring he was still cared for in the bosom of his family. After the Exodus when the Children of Israel cross the Sea of Reeds dry-shod, we read that: 'then the prophet Miriam, Aaron's sister, took a tambourine in her hand; and all the women went out after her with tambourines and with dancing. And Miriam sang to them: "Sing to the Eternal, who has triumphed gloriously; throwing horse and rider into the sea."'[4] The Bible gives only this one verse of her song yet Moses' song lasts a whole chapter. Although she is described here as a prophet we do not hear any of her prophecies. The rabbinic interpreters, keen as always to fill in any gaps in the biblical text, ascribed a prophecy to her that restricts her to the role of God's messenger to the family:

'And there went a man of the house of Levi.'[5] Where did he go? Rabbi Judah son of Zebina said that he went in the counsel of his daughter. A *Tanna* [rabbi from before 200 CE] taught: Amram, Miriam's father, was the greatest man of his generation; when he saw that the wicked Pharaoh had decreed 'Every son that is born you shall cast into the river', he said: In vain do we labour. He arose and divorced his wife. All [the Israelites] thereupon arose and divorced their wives. His daughter

---

1 Neh. 6.14.

2 Isa. 8.3.

3 'Frau Doktor' is now used by women who are doctors. Rabbi Regina Jonas, the first woman rabbi, used to have to make it explicit to those she visited in hospital that she was a rabbi herself rather than the wife of a rabbi. Elizabeth Sarah, 1994, 'Rabbiner Regina Jonas 1902–1944: Missing link in a broken chain', in Sybil Sheridan (ed.), *Hear Our Voices: Women Rabbis Tell their Stories*, London: SCM Press, p. 6.

4 Exod. 15.20.

5 Exod. 2.1.

said to him, 'Father, your decree is more severe than Pharaoh's; because Pharaoh decreed only against the males whereas you have decreed against the males and females [by preventing all births]' ... He arose and took his wife back; and they all arose and took their wives back. 'And took to wife'[6] – it should have read 'and took back'! Rabbi Judah son of Zebina said: – He acted towards her as though it had been the first marriage; he seated her in a palanquin, Aaron and Miriam danced before her, and the Ministering Angels proclaimed, A joyful mother of children[7] ... 'And Miriam the prophetess, the sister of Aaron, took etc.' [Why does the Bible say]: 'the sister of Aaron' and not the sister of Moses? It teaches that she prophesied while she yet was the sister of Aaron only and said: 'My mother will bear a son who will be the saviour of Israel.' When Moses was born, the whole house was filled with light; and her father arose and kissed her upon her head, saying 'My daughter, your prophecy has been fulfilled.'[8]

The only occasion on which Miriam spoke out in public we see her frustration – Moses, despite his Cushite (non-Jewish) wife, was the leader and prototype rabbi, Aaron was the High Priest and what was her role? Her words are not accepted and she is punished with leprosy for uttering them. But we learn too that the people were loyal to her because they all, not just the women whom she led in song, refuse to move on without her.[9] 'Difficult' women may be easier to deal with after their death when their assertive demands for a voice need no longer be addressed. The commentators noticed that as soon as Miriam died the people were thirsty and said that they were rescued by water from 'Miriam's well'.[10] Later Jewish mystical tradition said it was Miriam's merit and her well that not only rescued the people from thirst in the wilderness but enabled all Jewish learning to take place:

Only by the merit of Miriam did the well reappear to them during their desert wanderings. But why was the well revealed in the name of Miriam? ... As a midwife in Egypt she had used her voice in her work ... With a voice as calming as the rippling of water, Miriam coaxed reluc-

6 Exod. 2.1.
7 Ps. 113.9.
8 Babylonian Talmud *Sotah* 12a.
9 Num. 12.1–15.
10 *Numbers Rabbah* 1.2 (a collection of exegesis on the book of Numbers).

tant new-borns out of the womb and into the world. After the Israelites had crossed the Red Sea, Miriam and the women took up instruments as they danced and sang the song of redemption ... It was believed that God gave the well in Miriam's name, since Moses could barely speak, let alone sing, while the voice of Aaron the priest was so loud that it frightened both children and animals ... But later when they entered the Promised Land, Miriam's well disappeared. It was thought that it had vanished because they were in their homeland once again and it was natural to drink from other wells. But some missed Miriam's well and never stopped their search for it. They were the students of the Torah who sought its sustenance in the wisdom of the sacred text ... One drink from its pure waters was said to alert the heart, mind and soul and make the meanings of the Torah become more clear.[11]

Deborah was one of the Judges who led the people for several generations between the death of Joshua, Moses' disciple, and the development of the next leaders of the people, the prophets and kings who provided spiritual and military leadership in tandem. Deborah is the only one of the judges who is also described as a prophet (although Moses and Samuel both included judging in their role). Male Judges, like Jepthah, both judged and led in war: Deborah had Barak to be her general. Yet he insisted that she accompany the campaign, which shows her importance to her generation: Saul did not insist on Samuel being present when he fought to defend Israel: the people had wished to appoint a king to lead them in battle and once he had been anointed king he did not need Samuel's support in that role.[12] Once the campaign is over, Deborah and Barak sang a song of triumph in which delight at having vanquished their enemy is tempered by awareness of the pain suffered by Sisera's mother when her son did not return home.[13] Deborah described herself in the song as a 'mother in Israel'. None of the judges or prophets is described as a 'father in Israel'. Perhaps this is an early example of combining motherhood and professional life – women in public life now who have children find their role as mother generates more comment than their male colleagues' role as father. Deborah's leadership was accepted in the Bible but seems to have

---

11 Penina Adelman, 1986, *Miriam's Well*, New York, Biblio Press, p. 63. Jewish post-biblical tradition identified the midwives who refused to kill the Hebrew baby boys with Miriam and her mother Jocheved.

12 1 Sam. 8.19–20.

13 Judg. 5.28.

worried the Talmudic sages. The palm tree under which she sat when giving judgement was, we are told, to prevent inappropriate seclusion with men since a palm tree's branches are all high up and do not screen anyone sitting under it.[14] Is this just a way of drawing a moral point? Did the rabbis really, truly think that Deborah, prophet, judge and mother in Israel[15] would have behaved immodestly with those who brought their cases before her if she had given judgement under the embracing branches of a willow tree?

Miriam was mystically mythologized and removed from centre stage but Deborah's public leadership as a judge was too explicit to be denied. Attempts have been made to explain it away – the medieval exegetes of the Talmud, the Tosafists, suggested in their commentary that she taught others rather than judging herself – which Joel Roth points out at least makes her teaching authoritative even if not her power to judge. More helpfully the Tosafists suggested that her authority may have derived from people's acceptance of her in this role.[16] Maimonides, the medieval codifier and philosopher, said that women may not take on public leadership roles: Deborah is frequently cited as a counter-argument in discussions of this claim,[17] whether on women's ordination or for women like Leah Shakdiel who broke new ground in 1988 by being elected to her local religious council in Israel.

In the book of Kings the prophet Huldah and her husband live in a *mishneh*, variously translated 'second quarter' and 'college'. It is possible that this means that Huldah combined the roles of prophet and scholar as Deborah combined prophecy and judgement. When a 'scroll of the teaching', assumed to be Deuteronomy was found, it was taken to Huldah to be verified. Huldah said it was indeed God's word and with delicate tact, encouraged Josiah to stay on the straight and narrow path of monotheism.[18] Although the Bible recognized Deborah and Huldah as prophets who convey God's word, it seems that their public role as prophet worried the rabbis of the Talmud who began the process of interpreting the Bible

---

14 Babylonian Talmud *Megillah* 14a: And she sat under a palm tree. Why just a palm tree? – R. Simeon b. Abishalom said: [To avoid] privacy.

15 Judg. 5.7.

16 See Joel Roth, 1988, in Simon Greenberg (ed.), *The Ordination of Women as Rabbis: Studies and Responsa*, New York: Jewish Theological Seminary of America, p. 164–5.

17 Maimonides (1135–1204), *Mishneh Torah* Laws of Kings 1.5.

18 2 Kings 22.8–20.

into a system of precedent by which the Jews of their generation could organize their lives. The Talmud said that Deborah and Huldah were 'a hornet and a weasel', a reference to the meaning of their names, and that they were 'haughty which does not befit women'.[19] Interpreting animal comparisons necessitates sensitivity to cultural implications; we regard dogs quite highly but in the Bible, where they were an object of contempt rather than humanity's best friend, any comparison to a dog is bound to be unfavourable. 'Hornet' is obviously uncomplimentary and what is more, a distorted translation: *devorah* means 'bee', a far more useful creature than a hornet; weasels are also unattractive. The Talmud cited verses to prove their haughtiness:

> Of the hornet it is written, 'And she sent and called Barak,' instead of going to him. Of the weasel it is written, 'Say to the man', instead of 'say to the king.'[20]

These interpretations prove the subjective nature of much biblical exegesis. The verses justify the comment, yet only a strong belief in the point being made leads to the verse being read in this way; we need to be aware when what we describe as exegesis (reading from the text) can be eisegesis (reading our own ideas into the text). This can be seen in the rest of the rabbinic discussion of Huldah. 'If she was a contemporary of Jeremiah's how could she have prophesied at the same time?' asked the Talmud. 'By his permission as she was a relative of his,' came the answer, which is certainly not sourced in the Bible.

The Babylonian Talmud refers five times to 'prophetess' and three times to 'prophetesses', with 267 references to prophet and 272 to prophets. The Talmud says, 'Our Rabbis taught: "Forty-eight prophets and seven prophetesses prophesied to Israel, and they neither took away from nor added aught to what is written in the Torah ... Seven prophetesses". Who were these? – Sarah, Miriam, Deborah, Hannah, Abigail, Huldah and Esther.'[21] We already know that the Bible described Miriam, Deborah and Huldah as prophets. We will now see how the Talmud added Sarah, Hannah, Abigail and Esther to the list.

A watchword of rabbinic literature on the sphere of women is 'All the glory of the king's daughter is within', which is interpreted to mean

---

19 Babylonian Talmud *Megillah* 14b.
20 Babylonian Talmud *Megillah* 14b.
21 Babylonian Talmud *Megillah* 14a.

'women cannot take on public religious roles'.[22] This is given as a general rule, although it has not prevented Jewish woman from becoming queen, prophet, judge or teacher. In accordance with this governing principle, the rabbis of the Talmud seem more comfortable with some of the women to whom they, not the Bible, ascribe a prophetic role but one which took place within the family and, as we have seen, they can be ambivalent about those women in the Bible who prophesied in public.

The Talmud says that it is God's words, 'In all that Sarah says to you, listen to her voice',[23] which entitle her to be called prophet. These words are cited by ultra-Orthodox Jews to prove that their wives' lack of a public role does not mean that they lack status since their husbands must listen to them and obey, following Abraham's example. This prophetic authority complements the spiritual authority Sarah is given in the interpretation of the rather odd phrase in the Bible 'the seventy souls which they made in Haran', which Rashi explained as follows: 'The souls which he had brought beneath the wings of the *Shechinah*, God's presence. Abraham converted the men and Sarah converted the women and Scripture accounts it to them as if they had made them.' However, the literal sense of the text is 'the slaves and maids which they acquired'.[24] This is a domestic kind of prophetess, a wife working together with her husband to spread awareness of God and conveying God's word to her husband. It is, however, difficult for the modern reader to be happy that Sarah's prophetic authority is derived even in part from her command to her husband – 'send away the handmaid and her son',[25] because of her jealousy at the idea of Ishmael inheriting with Isaac. Sarah's emotions about Hagar, who behaved so insensitively to her mistress once she had achieved the pregnancy for which Sarah longed in vain, and about Ishmael once she has a child of her own are understandable and the reader sympathizes. But ordering a woman and her son out into the desert, perhaps to suffer, perhaps to die, does not seem to be the behaviour of someone who conveys

---

22 Ps. 45.15. Here, as on many occasions in rabbinic literature and in the New Testament, the meaning ascribed to the verse when it is used as a source in Jewish law ignores other words in the verse and is not the only possible interpretation.

23 Gen. 21.12.

24 Gen. 12.5. Rashi is the acronym for Rabbi Solomon Ben Isaac (1040–1105), commentary ad loc. Rashi's commentary which combines earlier interpretations with his own attempt to look at the literal meaning of the biblical and talmudic text is the starting point for all subsequent Jewish exegesis.

25 The word used here is the word used for divorce.

God's message to her audience rather than her own wishes. Even knowing that Abraham received a reassuring promise from God that Ishmael too would have a blessing from God even if not the covenant blessing promised to Isaac, and that blessing presupposes his survival, one wonders at the harshness of Sarah's decree.[26]

The rabbis of the Talmud justified including Hannah on their list of woman prophets, inferring from her prayer a reference foretelling Samuel's anointing of David as King.[27] They included Esther by using an interpretative analogy to suggest she was clothed in God's spirit.[28] Both Hannah as an exemplar of women who pray and Esther who has the courage to risk death by speaking to Ahasuerus to try to rescue her people might be thought to be valued already yet the Talmudic rabbis added status to them by calling them 'prophet'. We seem to have an odd balance between discomfort with woman who prophesied to kings or the whole community and promotion of 'safe' women who spoke to God or their husbands.

The Talmud's description of Abigail also shows this uncertainty about women's prophecy – the rabbis reassure us that Deborah's palm tree ensures modesty in public judgement while ascribing to Abigail the prophetic value of a quick flash of thigh. Their version of the arguments Abigail used to rescue her uncouth husband Nabal from being punished by David included a veiled reference to David's future relationship with Bathsheba and says,[29] 'she bared her thigh and he went three parasangs by its light', which might kindly be interpreted as a reference to her and David's future marriage but conveys a very different image to the biblical account where Abigail convinces David by the soundness of her arguments and not by the brightness of her thighs.[30] The Talmudic rabbis both give and take away. They give her status as a prophet by the reference to Bathsheba and they take away from her dignity by unclothing her.[31] Blessed be the rabbis of the Talmud.

---

26 Gen. 17.20.

27 Babylonian Talmud *Megillah* 14a and 1 Sam. 2.

28 Babylonian Talmud *Megillah* 14b, Esther 5.1 and 1 Chron. 12.18, 19.

29 Babylonian Talmud *Megillah* 14a–b.

30 1 Sam. 25.20–36.

31 Even if Bathsheva is not mentioned here in the biblical text there is a certain irony in Abigail's words in vv. 30–1: '(when the Eternal) has appointed you prince over Israel, my lord shall have no cause of grief, or pangs of conscience, for having shed blood without cause or for having saved himself.'

The attitudes of post-Talmudic exegetes show the mores of their generation but still recognize the importance of women's prophetic voice. Louis Ginzberg in his magnificent anthology of rabbinic biblical exegesis named Rebeccah and indeed all the matriarchs as prophetesses.[32] Ginzberg was a great scholar who came from Europe to teach at the Jewish Theological Seminary in 1899.[33] It may be questioned whether he liked powerful women in his personal life and when he cited stories found in the traditional collections of *midrash*,[34] rabbinic moral stories derived from the biblical text, he had no shame about interpolating critical generalizations about women. In his notes on the story of Rachel he cited his sources (where the midrash he quoted is given with no hostile overtones) and added the rider 'Women are of a jealous disposition, and Rachel shared this weakness with her sex' and he described Deborah as 'subject to the frailties of her sex'.[35] Yet he felt no ambivalence about ascribing prophetic talents to women whom the Bible does not name as prophets. Weak and jealous, alas yes. Incapable of prophecy – no, he was too good a scholar of the Bible and Jewish tradition for that.

'What manner of man is the prophet?' asked Abraham Joshua Heschel, the twentieth-century Jewish thinker, at the beginning of his book, *The Prophets*, thus making regrettably clear his stance on gender and prophecy.[36] In his otherwise comprehensive analysis of the prophetical books of the Bible he refrained from mentioning any women prophets. Even using an equivalent of the term 'lady doctor' or 'lady rabbi', endured in

---

32 Louis Ginzberg, 1909, *The Legends of the Jews*, Philadelphia: Jewish Publication Society of America, seven volumes, vol. 1, p. 341.

33 Joan Dash, 1979, *Summoned to Jerusalem: The life of Henrietta Szold*, New York: Harper & Row, p. 50.

34 *The Legends of the Jews* was translated into English by Henrietta Szold, the executive secretary of the Jewish Publication Society and one of the most Jewishly learned woman of her generation. She translated other material for Ginzberg, spent many hours helping him with his English and many of the seminary faculty expected they would marry although Miss Szold was 13 years Ginzberg's senior. In 1908 Ginzberg caused astonishment by returning from a summer in Europe engaged to a woman far younger than himself and not a scholar though known for her happy temperament (Joan Dash, 1979, *Summoned to Jerusalem*, p. 71). Seventy years later in 1979 when I took summer courses at the Jewish Theological Seminary the professor who introduced me to Adele Ginzberg, then a widow, hissed as he took me across to her, 'She's the one Ginzberg married instead of Henrietta Szold you know': a long time for such a scandal to be remembered.

35 Ginzberg, *The Legends of the Jews*, vol. 5, p. 296 and vol. 4, p. 36.

36 Abraham J. Heschel, 1962, *The Prophets*, Philadelphia: Jewish Publication Society of America, p. 3.

recent years to imply not the real thing but a hopeful though ladylike imitation, did not make Deborah or Huldah worthy of his attention. The Talmudic rabbis in their exegesis of the Bible had far less difficulty than Heschel with the idea of women hearing God's voice; their difficulty lay in envisaging how she could offer her prophecies to society at large, rather than just voicing them in the home.

In the Bible women can be prophets. The Bible describes a world where women do have a public role, so it is not surprising that in the following section Clare finds women in the New Testament in positions of leadership. In the Talmud women can be prophets, although there is more emphasis on their private prophetic capacity rather than on their public voice. Ginzberg, living at the beginning of the twentieth century, before the revolution in women's rights and education, was more inclined to make patronizing remarks about women, yet in his writings he could not deny their status as prophets. Heschel's daughter, Susannah, says: 'my father ... believed strongly in women's equality.' She describes how saying *kaddish* for her father was not always accepted in the synagogues she attended but says that ideas have changed in our generation and that no woman now would endure the difficulties she did: 'The *kaddish* I recited was not only for the death of my father but also for the death of Judaism's exclusion of women.'[37] We live in a world where women's opportunities in both religious and secular life have been transformed within a couple of generations; we can appreciate with whole-hearted enthusiasm the biblical precedents for women taking on leadership roles in the Jewish community.

II Women Prophets in the New Testament

Clare Jardine

Rachel has discussed women who were named as prophets or prophetesses in the Hebrew Bible. I will look at those women in the New Testament who were called prophetesses or who had a prophetic role. Prophetic activity is

---

37 Susannah Heschel, 2003, 'Judaism', in Arvind Sharma and Katherine K. Young (eds), *Her Voice Her Faith: Women Speak on World Religions*, Colorado: Westview Press, p. 147 and p. 167.

not limited to biblical times because modern-day women and men such as Emmeline Pankhurst and Martin Luther King are also counted in Christianity among those who have exercised a prophetic ministry. But what about the women in the New Testament? Do they play a prophetic role?

In the past the positive contribution of the women in the Gospels and early Church was overlooked, with the exception of Mary,[38] the mother of Jesus who has always been held in high regard especially in Roman Catholic circles. However, recent scholarship particularly in feminist circles has highlighted the place of women in the early centuries of the Common Era.[39] Before discussing women who exercised prophetic ministries in the Church, I will look at two women who could be thought of as prophets in a wider sense, Elizabeth the mother of John the Baptist, and the woman with a haemorrhage.

Elizabeth is one of the first women we meet in the Gospel of Luke (1.5–80). Elizabeth and her husband Zechariah are elderly and childless and Elizabeth is described as barren, associating her childlessness with divine punishment. Socially, as Vasiliki Limberis points out, failure to bear children had grave consequences for women: disfavour with the husband and his family, possible occasion for divorce, embarrassment to the woman's father, contempt, shame, humiliation, and on the barren woman's part, envy.[40] As so often happens in the Bible, divine intervention results in a positive ending to this potentially disastrous situation and Elizabeth conceives a child. Three months later her cousin Mary is told by an angel that she too is to conceive and bear a son in miraculous circumstances and Mary, knowing that Elizabeth is pregnant, decides to go and see her.

The meeting between the two women has been a favourite subject of icons and paintings as a symbol of mutual support, and love. It can also be seen as a prophetic symbol in that it communicates an attitude of reciprocal receptivity. While Mary is selfless in her desire to help her cousin,

---

38 As so much is written on the role of Mary in the Gospels and in the early Church we will not be dealing with her in this chapter.

39 See for example Elisabeth Schüssler Fiorenza (ed.), 1993, *Searching the Scriptures, Vol. 1: A Feminist Introduction*, New York: Crossroad. See also A. Brenner and C. Fontaine, 1997, *Reading the Bible: Approaches, Methods and Strategies*, Sheffield: Sheffield Academic Press; and Sandra Schneiders, 1991, *The Revelatory Text: Interpreting the New Testament as Sacred Scripture*, San Francisco: Harper San Francisco.

40 'Elizabeth', 2000, in Carol Meyers, Toni Craven and Ross Kraemer (eds), *Women in Scripture*, Grand Rapids: Eerdmans, p. 73.

Elizabeth does not draw attention towards her own locus of God's action but to God's presence in Mary. In her loud blessing she proclaims that Mary is the mother of Elizabeth's Lord. In his book *The Woman Among her People,* Carlo-Maria Martini says that Elizabeth has not received a revelation concerning this but has simply let herself become involved in Mary's greeting and has understood her.[41] Elizabeth the prophet shows the reader the importance of relationship and of tuning in to the presence of God in 'the other', whatever form that 'other' may take.

My particular interest as a Christian woman engaged in the Christian-Jewish relationship, draws me to listen to the voice of the Jewish woman. Barbara H. Geller Nathanson stresses the point that the study of women in the New Testament should not be separated from the study of Jewish women's history; rather, she says, it is an important component of such study. Taking into account the Jewish background of a character helps us to understand her milieu and prevents us from falling into the trap of attributing Christian subordination of women largely to Christianity's Jewish roots.[42] So it is important to acknowledge that Elizabeth is of priestly descent from the lineage of Aaron and also married to a priest. Their marriage was ideal and through heredity and character they would have been considered: 'righteous before God, living blamelessly according to all the commandments and regulations of the Lord'.[43] Elizabeth's background adds to the picture of her as a prophet. She is a woman of high standing in the community, brought to shame through barrenness but still able to recognize God's action in 'the other', her cousin. The result of her perceptiveness was that, as Limberis rightly says, the first Christological confession of the Gospel is in a woman's voice.[44] A further factor to take into account is that the hermeneutic for understanding the story of Elizabeth and Zechariah is the Abraham and Sarah tradition of Genesis 17–21. Abraham and Sarah are also old and childless and give birth to a child, who, like Elizabeth's son John the Baptist, would ensure that God's promise would be fulfilled.

Another woman who showed prophetic qualities was the woman in Mark 5.25–34 suffering from severe bleeding who touched the hem of

---

41 Carlo-Maria Martini, 1989, *The Woman Among her People: A Spiritual Journey into the Planet Woman,* London: St Paul's.

42 In Elisabeth Schüssler Fiorenza (ed.), 1993, *Searching the Scriptures,* p. 273.

43 Vasiliki Limberis, 2000, 'Elizabeth', p. 73.

44 Vasiliki Limberis, 2000, 'Elizabeth', p. 74.

Jesus' garment in order to be healed by the power emanating from him. Lieve Troch has an interesting analysis of this passage.[45] She says that the classical way of working with this text focuses on the appraisal of Jesus who ignores the laws of the outcast to which this woman belongs because of her loss of blood. In touching Jesus she comes to life and is no longer limited by her illness, which was related to her being a woman. Troch says that this interpretation draws attention away from the woman and her possible position in the theological design of the first Jesus communities. In a closer reading of the text, women focus on the action, courage and endurance of the woman herself: she initiates; it is she who touches him, believing that her touch will be adequate. She breaks through the stigmatization of being an outcast, which leads her to full presence in the community. But it is not just her strength that is the key feature but the fact that 'she told him the whole truth'. Troch identifies the woman's truth as different from the truth according to which she had to live. Her vision of life, society, the political, social, and religious position of women must have been different from what was allowed to her in the context of a patriarchal design.

This unnamed woman was a woman of faith who was able to call forth the power of God into her body. She was a prophet with integrity who was able to recognize the truth within herself and to impart that truth to another. The ability to communicate one's own truth to someone is especially valuable in situations of dialogue when each person exposes herself to 'the other' in faith and trust that her truth will be accepted even if it is different.

The writings of Paul indicate that within the early Church prophecy was a gift of the spirit freely given to believers and to be used for the sake of the whole community. It was clearly a gift given to both men and women as the four daughters of the apostle Philip had each received the gift (Acts 21.9). Paula Clifford maintains that it was not unknown for spiritual gifts to pass from one generation of a family to the next and perhaps these four young women had developed their gifts in the atmosphere of their home.[46]

An excellent analysis of women prophets in the early Church by Karen Jo Torjesen describes how they performed functions similar to those per-

---

45 In Elisabeth Schüssler Fiorenza (ed.), *Searching the Scriptures*, p. 361f.
46 Paula Clifford, 2001, *Women Doing Excellently: Biblical Women and their Successors*, Norwich: Canterbury Press, p. 113f.

[150]

formed by women in Greek and Roman religions.[47] Prophecy permeated every aspect of Graeco-Roman life and professional prophets provided guidance for governments on different area of public life and counsel for individuals on personal matters. In all these arenas, Torjesen says, prophets were interpreters of a divine will because they spoke under the influence, inspiration or possession of a divine spirit.

In the first Christian community at Corinth prophets and especially women prophets provided inspired leadership in personal and communal matters. Torjesen cites the work of Antoinette Clark Wire who has reconstructed a profile of women prophets through a meticulous analysis of Paul's rhetoric in his letter to the Corinthians. Although they entered the community possessing little social status, their new identity as Christian prophets gave them wisdom, power and rank, and their self-understanding as new creations made in God's image clothed them with honour and authority.

Priscilla, or Prisca, is mentioned six times in the New Testament, twice in Paul's letters, several times in Acts 18, and once in 2 Timothy. She is always mentioned with her husband Aquila who is described in Acts as a Jew who came from Pontus (Acts 18.2). The couple were forced to leave Rome because an edict of the emperor Claudius had expelled all the Jews, including those who believed in Jesus as the Christ. According to Acts, Paul met Priscilla and Aquila in Corinth, then they accompanied him to Antioch and Ephesus. After Paul had left Ephesus Priscilla and Aquila stayed on as leaders in the church community which met in their house (1 Cor. 16.19). There were many similar house churches in early Christianity (see also Rom. 16.5; Col. 4.15 and Philem. 2). Jouette Bassler points out that the head of the house naturally assumed leadership of the group, and the fact that in four of the six instances the New Testament sources mention Priscilla before her husband (inverting the usual Graeco-Roman custom) probably points to her more active role in the life of the Church.[48] On their return to Rome, Priscilla and Aquila used their home again for a house church. Paul greets them in his letter to the Romans (16.3–5) describing them as co-workers, a term Paul uses for associates actively engaged with him in missionary work.[49] They evidently instructed Apollos

---

47 In Elisabeth Schüssler Fiorenza (ed.), *Searching the Scriptures*, p. 297ff.

48 Jouette Bassler, 2000, 'Prisca/Priscilla', in Carol Meyers, Toni Craven and Ross Kraemer (eds.), *Women in Scripture*, p. 136.

49 Jouette Bassler, 2000, 'Prisca/Priscilla', p. 137.

in the Christian faith or 'the Way' (Acts 18.26). Bassler notes that these references to Priscilla reflect an enduring memory in the early Church that she was an authoritative teacher who not only performed missionary work herself but also helped to train others.

Priscilla could rightly be counted as a prophet. She was a woman who displayed qualities as a leader and teacher. She was an innovator within a new movement and her vision and strength of character enabled her to go into previously unexplored mission territory in the face of possible adversity. Paul records in Romans 16 that she even risked her life for him. While we have no record of Priscilla's words, her actions are eloquent and she uses all her financial and material resources for the sake of the local Christian community. There are parallels here with Mary Magdalene and the other women, discussed by Lynne in Chapter 7, who used their financial resources to support Jesus' ministry.

As women of dialogue our vision takes us into new territory, not to proselytize but to reach out to someone of another faith in friendship. Dialogue is relatively unexplored territory and practitioners can find themselves at risk even with their own community.

Phoebe is another woman mentioned by Paul. He commends her to the Christians in Rome at the end of his letter to them (Rom. 16.12). The mention is brief but, as Bassler indicates, it offers a tantalizing glimpse of the leadership of women in early Christianity.[50] Phoebe is described as 'our sister'. This suggests that she is a co-worker and may have been sent ahead by Paul to begin the complex arrangements for his mission to Spain.[51] She probably carried the letter of recommendation with her from Cenchreae, the eastern port of Corinth where she was *diakonos*. Bassler points out that although this title is sometimes translated as servant or deaconess and sometimes defined in terms of informal service or limited service to women or to the sick, it is the same title that Paul applies to himself and to others engaged in a ministry of preaching and teaching (1 Cor. 3.5; 2 Cor. 6.4; Phil. 1.1). Bassler concludes that the word clearly points to a leadership role over the whole Church and not just part of it. Phoebe is in fact a church official, a minister of the church in Cenchreae.

Phoebe is also described as *prostatis*, the feminine form of a noun that can denote a position as leader, president, presiding officer, guardian or

---

50 Jouette Bassler, 2000, 'Phoebe', in Carol Meyers, Toni Craven and Ross Kraemer (eds), *Women in Scripture*, p. 135.

51 Timothy is introduced in the same way to the Thessalonians in 1 Thess. 3.2.

patron. Because Paul presented her as *prostatis*, 'of many and of myself as well' (Rom. 16.2), Bassler concludes that the emphasis is probably on her role as patron or benefactor as well as reinforcing the concept of authority conveyed by her position as deacon. Phoebe probably provided funds for the local church and supported people in other ways. Paul certainly seems to be indebted to her as he includes himself among the people she has helped.

Even though Phoebe is not identified as a prophet she can be included as a prophet in the sense that she is a leader to whom people turn in the community for help and probably advice. She contributed in many ways to the building up of the early Christian community in Corinth and travelled to Rome, perhaps to exercise her leadership qualities there too. She was obviously a woman upon whom Paul depended and held in high regard and he clearly wants the Roman Christians to help her 'with anything she needs' (16.2). Phoebe is an example of a woman leader accepted within her Christian community. A manual on church organization, *Statutes of the Apostles*, shows that by the second century the functions of woman prophets were institutionalized as a church office.[52] The role of teacher, however, was never institutionalized in the same way. Sadly, as Torjesen points out, while women's leadership in early Christian churches had much in common with women's religious leadership in Greek and Roman societies, there is one striking difference – women's leadership in some Christian circles was bitterly contested.[53] Ross Kraemer's study in *Maenads* concludes that 'only among Christians is women's religious leadership an issue. Only Christians both attempt, sometimes successfully, to exclude women from religious office and community authority and argue about it.'[54] Here she is referring to Christian women in Graeco-Roman society.

We can conclude from this examination of the four women – Elizabeth, the unnamed woman with a haemorrhage, Priscilla and Phoebe – that there were indeed women who carried out a prophetic-style ministry in the first century. None of them is identified as such in the biblical text and they may not have regarded themselves as prophets, but they all display characteristics which were prophetic then and can be prophetic for us

---

52 Karen Jo Torjesen, 1993, 'Reconstruction of Women's Early Christian History', in Elisabeth Schüssler Fiorenza (ed.), *Searching the Scriptures*, p. 298.

53 Karen Jo Torjesen, 1993, 'Reconstruction'.

54 Quoted by Karen Jo Torjesen, 1993, 'Reconstruction', p. 301.

today. Elizabeth's attention to intimate relationship enables her to recognize God's action in 'the other'. The unnamed woman with a haemorrhage is able to communicate her own truth to another. Priscilla's vision and leadership qualities take her into new territory and Phoebe exercises a ministry as an accepted leader in her community. Prophecy not only concerns speaking out against the injustices of the day. It also involves new attitudes towards one another. Living in today's multi-cultural society demands that women and men alike can communicate with one another, can speak their truth and be listened to, can recognize the divine in someone maybe very different and that we acknowledge qualities of leadership in each other. Elizabeth and the unnamed woman can teach us today about the value of being prophetic quietly, even within our own homes. Priscilla and Phoebe challenge us to be active as well, to go out of our own milieu into the unknown and maybe even dangerous terrain.

Further Reading

See the Bibliography section for full details on these titles.

Paula Clifford, *Women Doing Excellently: Biblical Women and their Successors.*
Simon Greenberg (ed.), *The Ordination of Women as Rabbis: Studies and Responsa.*
Amy-Jill Levine with Marianne Blickenstaff (ed.), *A Feminist Companion to Matthew.*
Sybil Sheridan (ed.), *Hear Our Voice: Women Rabbis Tell their Stories.*

Part 3: Spiritual Journey

Introduction

Part 3 explores our spiritual journeys as women of faith and looks at our response to God and to each other. It is an area where little has been written within a Jewish-Christian context, except on the Jewish roots of Christian liturgy or prayer. Here we focus primarily on what happens to our own faith experience when we as Jews and Christians encounter the deep spirituality of 'the other'. What does that do to our own faith? We have been on a journey together as a group of women but also within our wider communities through our involvement in some aspect of Jewish-Christian relations. For many of the women in our group, this encounter is transformative on two levels: first, it affects how we hear the tradition of 'the other'; and second, profound changes emerge in the way in which we understand our own tradition in the presence of that 'other'. Such dialogue and encounter often challenge our exclusive understanding of truth and provide a catalyst for a non-missionary approach and this has been true for the women in our group. In this section, we are focusing on the encounter rather than writing new liturgies for women's life cycles and journeys. Work is already going on in this respect especially within the different Jewish traditions where prayers and services have been written to celebrate women's experiences of pregnancy, childbirth, loss of a child, and the menopause. Much less is being done among Christian women and this is one area where Jewish women's spirituality is increasingly influencing Christian women's faith. On an official level, there is nothing within either Christianity or Judaism to mark life-experiences particular to women and this is something where women are seeking to change their established traditions.

In Chapter 9 Helen argues through her own experience of attending liturgies connected to Jewish and Christian life cycles that in the presence of Jews and other Christians we can no longer listen to our own traditions in the same way because the very presence of 'the other' changes how we hear our liturgy and understand our difficult texts. Kathleen's response explores parallel examples where attending a life cycle event of another faith challenges how she can express her faith as a Jew, especially when attending a life cycle event for a non-Jewish relative. In Chapter 10 Clare explores the ways in which the traditional understandings of the Eucharist are challenged by the encounter with Jews as well as providing pointers about the Jewish roots of the Christian Eucharist. In Marcia's response, she explores the impact of attending Catholic Mass regularly as part of a programme of inter-faith encounter and understanding when she was studying to be a rabbi. She reflects on parallels between some Christian ways of understanding the Eucharist as a memorial to Jesus' Last Supper and Jewish ways of remembering the Exodus experience through the Passover meal. In the final part of her chapter she shares some insights into the transformative power of the *mikveh* for Jewish women and of the Eucharist for Christians.

Chapter 11 is on prayer and Clare provides a personal account of her prayer life as a Roman Catholic nun; a life that has been transformed as a result of her encounter with Judaism. She takes up the theme of Helen's chapter on life cycles where her faith and prayer life has been shaped and changed by the encounter with 'the other'. In her response, Rachel looks at a number of stereotypes and prejudices that can surface within the dialogue regarding Jewish women and prayer. She also explores the question of whether women and men respond differently to rituals and liturgy. Chapter 12 focuses on pilgrimage in which Beryl explores how leading Jewish-Christian study tours to Israel has impacted upon her understanding of pilgrimage. She focuses on the experiences of the fourth-century Spanish pilgrim and nun Egeria, and shows how in Egeria's life and that of some Jewish pilgrims, holy places have facilitated their search for God. In her response, Rachel asks what the status of Jerusalem as a place of pilgrimage does to the people who live there. She reflects upon the impact of Jerusalem on her own experience and whether pilgrimage is, as Beryl says, a journey towards holiness.

The concluding chapter of the book draws together the insights and conclusions from the dialogue and looks to the future. Suggestions are made about the ways forward for the future of the women's dialogue as well as some of the challenges that are, as yet, unfulfilled within the wider Jewish-Christian dialogue.

9 Life Cycles

My soul magnifies the Lord, and my spirit rejoices in God my saviour.
Luke 1.46–47

I Life Cycles: Hearing Our Traditions in the Presence of the Other

Helen P. Fry

In this chapter I wish to share some reflections from my own experience where various life cycle events have been part of my Christian encounter with Judaism. I will not, therefore, be explaining what Christians believe or practise because adequate material is available elsewhere; rather I will explore some of the dynamics of the shared encounter at our life cycle events. No longer is the experience of attending a major life cycle ceremony a matter of solely Jewish or Christian presence. Within Jewish-Christian relations today, because of the depth of friendship and trust, there are an increasing number of occasions when Jews and Christians share together those precious and painful moments of life: birth, marriage, *bar/bat mitzvah*, and death. Since our group has been meeting, four women have given birth; there has been one marriage and the deaths of parents and a grandparent. These are experiences which have often affected the dynamics of the group and the way in which we express our faith.

Life cycle events are sacred markers on our journey through life and provide important spaces of holiness in our lives; although they are not, of course, the only time when holiness touches us. The celebration of key events, often termed rites of passage, provides the opportunity to sanctify life with blessings and prayers. There are life cycle events which pertain only to women, such as birth, the menstrual cycle and the menopause and this is forming a fruitful and creative dynamic to the women's movement. In recent years a number of books have been written by Jewish and

Christian women on rituals and prayers, created especially by women to mark life-changing events, although they have yet to be incorporated into official liturgy. Participating in and being present at a major life cycle event of a faith other than our own, not solely attending a sabbath service or Roman Catholic Mass to learn about the other (although that is an important part of the encounter), raises particular challenges and questions. I am talking about situations when we actually participate together in a service to celebrate a birth or a marriage or to mourn a death. What can we do together without diluting or compromising our beliefs and traditions? When we join our Jewish or Christian friends in marking key life cycle events, we enter their story and make it part of our own. This does not imply that we give up our own distinctive traditions or convert to the faith of the other, or blend our traditions into a kind of 'religious soup'.

There seems to be a fundamental need within the human soul to create ritual to express our deepest spirituality. For me, this was the case after the birth of my sons when my husband and I created our own 'service of thanks' in our home with a blessing over our boys on the day that they came out of hospital. I found the experience of giving birth profoundly spiritual, not at the time of birth itself, but afterwards. Even though childbirth is very natural, the experience gives a sense of the awe and wonder of life and creation. One of the main feelings that I remember after the birth of my sons was the sense of wanting a service of thanksgiving to God for their lives and safe deliverance – something which, even in this technological age, is not to be taken for granted. When they were about five weeks old, we had a dedication service in the chapel where I had grown up and where my husband and I had met some 12 years earlier. This was a joyous occasion of thanks and one that was attended by many relatives and friends. We had asked one of our Jewish friends to say a Jewish blessing over the boys: with Jonathan he recited the priestly blessing over him in Hebrew and English: 'may the Lord bless you and keep you, may he make his face to shine upon you and grant you peace.' With our twin boys Edward and David, he sang in Hebrew the priestly blessing over one and a prayer over the other about being brought up to love of Bible, marriage, and good deeds, based on the blessing recited at a circumcision service. It was certainly the only time in the history of that chapel that a Jewish person had said a blessing in Hebrew at the dedication of a Christian child. It was done in such a way as not to compromise either faith; however, the difficulty for me came during the sermon. The minister knew of the Jewish presence in the congregation because he had graciously agreed to the Jewish blessings and had obviously made a conscious effort to say something about the Jewish roots of Christian faith. His motivations were well intentioned, but out came the age-long contrast between the God of wrath of the Old Testament and Judaism and the God of love reflected in the New Testament and life of Christ. I am convinced to this day that he did not realize the difficulty over his sermon; however, hearing those words in the presence of Jewish people, knowing that these stereotypes were inaccurate, brought shivers down my spine. In the presence of 'the other', we hear our sermons differently and with a heightened awareness of how Judaism is being portrayed.

The dedication services for our boys were moving occasions which bonded our faiths, without compromising our traditions. The boundaries of our distinctive faiths were respected and honoured, although the presence of the other can change the way in which we understand our own traditions. I believe that it is possible to share in and celebrate each other's life cycle events without blurring the boundaries of our distinct and separate communities and beliefs. Perhaps it is appropriate to clarify at this point that, in so saying, I am not making any subtle conversionary claims. I would always want Jews to practise their faith in their own particular way without becoming Christians or Jewish-Christians. I do believe that the painful history of Jewish-Christian encounter and antisemitism has taught us Christians that God intends the covenant with the Jewish people to remain for eternity.

In the hospital after Jonathan's birth, I became friendly with a Jewish woman who had given birth to twins, a girl and a boy. Some weeks later, we were invited to the girl's blessing and the boy's *brit* (circumcision ceremony). The women present were very emotional and could not look while the circumcision itself was being carried out. The mother commented that she would be glad when this part was over. I could empathize with her, thinking how difficult I would find it in her situation and could not help thinking how much easier it was for the baby girl. Several of the guests assumed that we were Jewish and asked whether Jonathan had had his *brit*. When we replied 'no, because we are not actually Jewish', one of the guests made a joke, saying, 'you had better keep his nappy on then.' We felt privileged to be at the ceremony at such a personal time in one's family life – to be there as participants and not as 'outsiders' learning 'how Jews do this'.

We had become participants without compromising our own identity. We had entered their story and made it part of our own.

The Jewish-Christian encounter affects how we hear our liturgies and sermons in the presence of the other and this was evident at a friend's funeral.[1] I had worked closely with this friend for a number of years in improving Jewish-Christian understanding in our area. We both found a number of new friends among the local Jewish community. When he died in 1995, his Roman Catholic funeral Mass took place in the local Anglican church because his own church was too small to hold all the mourners and it was attended by most of the local Jewish community. One of the most moving moments of the Mass was the singing of *in paradisum*, the chorus of which reads:

> May the choirs of angels come to greet you. May they speed you to paradise. May the Lord enfold you in his mercy, may you find eternal life.

The imagery evoked such beauty at a particularly difficult time when David had so courageously lost his fight for life at such a young age. The dynamics of that occasion raised some important questions for me about our shared experiences as Jews and Christians. I found myself united with the Anglicans and the Jews in not being able to take the elements of bread and wine because none of us was officially in communion with the Roman Catholic Church. One might easily assume that with the progress in ecumenical relations it would have been the Jews present who would be the only ones not participating in the Mass rather than other Christians also. On such an ecumenical occasion as this, the boundaries of who is in and who is not, are sharpened. There were several priests officiating on that occasion, but the main officiating priest invited anyone to come forward for a blessing if they wished. I went forward. Then something happened which again showed the blurring of who is in and who is not. The priest looked at me with horror and bewilderment. He did mutter something and moved on to the next person. It later transpired that he thought that I was Jewish and was not sure whether to give me a blessing. For that moment, at that time, it forced him to think about his tradition in relation

---

1 A helpful overview of the changes in Roman Catholic liturgy can be found in Eugene Fisher, 1986, 'The Roman Liturgy and Catholic-Jewish Relations since the Second Vatican Council', in Eugene Fisher, A. James Rudin and Marc H. Tanenbaum (eds), *Twenty Years of Jewish-Catholic Relations*, Mahweh: Paulist Press.

to Judaism even if for only a second. However, the most difficult part of the service came with the readings which were tied to the liturgy for that week, and this example highlights the difficulty of listening to our texts and tradition in the presence of the other. It was just after Easter week and the reading was from John's Gospel, the story of 'doubting Thomas'. I can vividly remember my shock when the words of the first verse resounded throughout this quiet parish Church, heard in the presence of most of the local Jewish community:

> On the evening of that day, the first day of the week, the doors being shut where the disciples were, for fear of the Jews, Jesus came and stood among them.[2]

'For fear of the Jews?' Which Jews? The Jews sitting behind me in the pew? The Jews of Jesus' day? Shortly after this, the president of the local synagogue gave the eulogy. Nothing was said, of course, but many Christians felt extremely uncomfortable and uneasy about the words. It has raised a number of questions for me, questions that are still part of the ongoing debate in Jewish-Christian relations and should continue to be part of our dialogue. Should we omit those parts of our traditions that are difficult? On the occasion of this funeral, should the words *for fear of the Jews* not have been read? Could the reading have started at the next verse instead? Do we omit the hard sayings of our traditions and choose another reading or do we confront the challenges which the text poses? Philip Cunningham has published an excellent volume with a preface to each of the biblical texts that are used in Sunday worship in the common lectionary.[3] Each of the texts can be prefaced with an explanation in the light of the new Jewish-Christian understanding. In the context of a funeral, it may not be appropriate to preface the reading with a commentary and so in these circumstances, the challenge of difficult texts remains. In my tradition, the United Reformed Church, the minister or preacher chooses the theme of the service for that week and therefore also chooses the reading.[4] The

---

2 John 20.19–29.

3 Philip A. Cunningham, 1995, *Proclaiming Shalom: Lectionary Introductions to Foster the Catholic and Jewish Relationship*, Collegeville: The Liturgical Press.

4 The readings would reflect parts of the Christian liturgical year, such as Easter, Christmas, Pentecost and so forth, but for some churches these readings are not necessarily fixed to particular weeks but a matter of choice.

[161]

opportunity is there not to preach on particular texts if the minister so chooses; however, this may be dangerous for Jewish-Christian relations because if we do not read some of our difficult texts in community, or in the presence of the other, the opportunity to deal with them in a constructive way passes us by.

Another example occurred from the Jewish side when a close friend invited me to attend the *shiva* for her father. The *shiva* is a period of seven days of mourning when special prayers are said in the home of the deceased. Although my friend is not Orthodox herself, the *shiva* was conducted according to the Orthodox tradition in her parents' home. It was an occasion when both she and I were uncomfortable with the tradition. In the front room of her parents' home, the rabbi deliberately made a physical separation between the men and women by asking the men to step forward and start the service. The women were excluded from taking part. They were not included in the *minyan* (the required number of ten men to say certain prayers) or in saying *kaddish* (the central mourner's prayer). My friend had asked the rabbi earlier if she could say *kaddish* and his reply was: 'only in your head'. This is not the case in all parts of the Orthodox tradition and much depends on the individual rabbi leading the service. The Chief Rabbi, Jonathan Sacks, commissioned a report during the 1990s on women in the community where women saying *kaddish* was one of the issues discussed.[5]

The dynamics of the presence of a non-Jew at a Jewish life cycle event highlighted something unexpected for me. It was bizarre to realize that I was excluded from the prayers and liturgy not because I am Christian but because I am a woman. In that sense, I could identify with the women's struggle within both Judaism and Christianity. This occasion affected how I 'heard' the Jewish tradition. I know from my friend's comments at the time that she was distinctly uncomfortable about the tradition and it affected how she heard it in my presence. On that occasion our stories as women had broken the boundaries of distinction between Jew and Christian and our experience spoke with the same voice. The occasion portrayed Orthodox tradition in a particularly bad light as seemingly heartless and insensitive in excluding the women mourners. But, I knew from other contacts with the Orthodox community that the whole Orthodox tradi-

---

5 See, 1994, *Women in the Jewish Community: Survey Report*, and, 1994, *Women in the Jewish Community: Review and Recommendations*, London: Office of the Chief Rabbi.

tion is not like this. There are parts which are compassionate and caring, and in saying the above comments, I am careful not to reinforce centuries of Christian stereotyping and mis-information which branded Judaism as a religion of the God of wrath and anger against a Christian God of love and compassion. It remains difficult for me as a Christian to criticize parts of Orthodox Jewish tradition given the painful history of Jewish-Christian relations. I am also aware that Christianity has not been the great liberator of women that is often claimed for it.

The occasion of the stone-setting, some eight months later, was a different experience again and one that seemed much more inclusive. It is customary for Jews to have a ceremony to mark the erection of a memorial stone for the deceased person. Prayers and psalms are said in the prayer hall at the cemetery and then the mourners walk to the tombstone itself for some prayers and the reading of the inscription on the stone. It is customary for people to put a small stone on the grave as they walk by. Afterwards, they usually return to the home of a relative for refreshments and an opportunity to reflect the life of the person who have died. On this occasion, the two daughters provided a moving tribute to their father's life and his particular relationship with them. The whole day was one of dignity and quiet respect. It was an appropriate way to honour that person's life and the contribution that he had made to this world. It was one of those rare moments of holiness when time seems to be timeless. Within Jewish tradition, it is one of the greatest *mitzvot* (commandments) to honour and respect the dead, particularly one's parents, and that was reflected in the service. I felt profoundly honoured to have shared this experience which initiated thoughts for me about how Christianity could improve some of its rituals for mourning. Those ways of sanctifying life and honouring the dead are things which we as Christians could incorporate more readily into our own tradition. Christians have their own ways of honouring the dead, but sometimes within the Reformed Churches and other Protestant churches, it is quite minimal. There are times when we, as non-conformist Christians, seem to have lost the structure of how to grieve and that is why the different stages of mourning in the Jewish tradition and the lengthy liturgy in the Roman Catholic Church provide a framework within which to express that grief. Again, it fulfils the deepest need within the human soul for ritual to mark major moments of life and death. After David's death, the lengthy Catholic Requiem Mass and the symbolism that accompanied it seemed the appropriate amount of space to grieve for someone whose life had been so cut short by such an aggressive illness. Anything less would not have been right for that moment in time. During our times of grief, through the liturgies, holiness momentarily touches our lives and we feel God's presence.

These incidents are just some examples where the encounter with 'the other' forces us to grapple with those parts of our tradition that have led to the isolation and hostility between Jews and Christians for two millennia. When we are present at each other's liturgies or hear the sermons, our faith is not the same thereafter because something changes within us and in our understanding of faith. The dynamics of the encounter has been the transformative power in Jewish-Christian relations and, as we have seen, one that is affecting how we understand each other's traditions as well as our own. Once we as Jewish and Christian women have shared these experiences, we are empowered to take that knowledge and understanding back to our communities and the dialogue-forum to effect a transformation from exclusion to inclusion.

II Women and Life Cycles: A Jewish Perspective

Kathleen de Magtige-Middleton

My brother and I were at Sinai.
He kept a journal of what he saw, of what he heard, of what it all
    meant to him.
I wish I had such a record of what happened to me there.
It seems that every time I want to write, I can't.
I'm always holding a baby, one of my own, or one for a friend,
always holding a baby, so my hands are never free to write things
    down.[6]

Having thought and written about Jewish life cycles for the past four years in my synagogue, this response to Helen's part seems particularly relevant to me at this moment of writing, two months after the birth of my first

---

6 Extract from Merle Feld's poem, 'We all stood Together' in Ellen M. Umansky and Dianne Ashton (eds), 1992, *Four Centuries of Jewish Women's Spirituality*, Boston: Beacon Press, p. 222–3.

child. Even more pertinent seems the extract quoted above from a poem by Merle Feld which is more than simply a personal acknowledgement of the difference being a mother makes to life. In Jewish life cycle events, there are many patriarchal remnants from traditional Rabbinic Judaism which has led to a prolific resurgence of new and creative life cycle ceremonies written by Jewish women for Jewish women. These patriarchal remnants have also, sadly and unfairly, generated a fair amount of anti-Jewish feelings in the international women's movement and among some Christian feminists.

Life cycle ceremonies are emotionally and religiously momentous markers on the continuum of life. They are single moments that form the demarcation lines on life's journey and define each person's ever changing and developing identity through life. Each one of these life cycle moments are emotionally volatile instances of transition, in which confusion, challenge, hope even despair are comingled. Because they are such complex, profound and emotionally challenging moments, we turn to our faith and tradition for support, holiness and blessing and for the comforting affirmation of our religious identity. Life cycle ceremonies also provide us with the reassuring knowledge that our tradition remains unchanged, and that our faith, as it connects us to past, present and future, will provide us with an anchor in life. As Debra Orenstein mentions in the introduction to the book *Lifecycles*:

> Traditional religious ritual was designed, and continues, to meet a variety of needs that relate to life passages: The need for the individual to be acknowledged by community, the need for the community/tribe to read itself into the passages of each member, the need for bonding, which serves both individual and community, the need to (re-)enact dramatically the great stories and messages of the tradition, for the sake of individuals and of the tradition. Through rituals, we create structures that provide an element of predictability and, therefore, safety, around times of insecurity, transition, and/or loss.[7]

Ancient ceremonies and prayers 'translate', through a particular and known set of traditions, symbols and allusions, the bewildering moments

---

7 Debra Orenstein (ed.), 1998, *Lifecycles: Jewish Women on Life Passages and Personal Milestones*, Woodstock: Jewish Lights, vol. 1, p. xx.

of change in our lives into the safe and comforting language of our faith so that we can incorporate them into our lives and our ever developing identities.[8] If faith and tradition provide as well as moments of holiness also a sense of safety in challenging times of life's transition, then to share these moments with friends or family members of another faith may challenge that sense of safety. On the other hand, sharing each other's life cycle events may add a much deeper dimension to inter-faith encounter, which may not be gained through dialogue alone, as dialogue often remains a purely cerebral activity. However, to experience the intensely religious and crucially identity-forming moments of life's transition with our dialogue partners – those moments that we share and yet translate in such different religious ceremonies – provides an opportunity to better understand the religious identity of the other; an opportunity to really understand the language of their faith. We dialogue best, and are challenged most, when we have an opportunity to understand each other's language. The most personal way in which we can do so is by experiencing each other's life cycle events as those markers that support, define, acknowledge and enhance our faith and religious identity.

I have not had the privilege to share many life cycle events with my non-Jewish friends in the same way that Helen has with her Jewish friends, but many of them do feel disillusioned with the Church or define themselves as humanists. However, in my capacity as a congregational rabbi who has taught 'The Jewish Life Cycle' to proselytes (converts to Judaism) for a number of years, I am often confronted with congregants' non-Jewish family who wish to participate in life cycle events. I am well aware of the challenges which participation or the presence of 'the other' pose at our life cycle events. I had a painful experience with the funeral of a Catholic member of my family, an adopted grandmother, which focused for me the profound effect that ritual language has on one's personal experience. Apart from the emotional upheaval of this unexpected bereavement, it was especially the discomfort of not possessing the right language as a Jew for mourning at a church ritual. My family and I found that we would not

---

8 With 'language' I do not necessarily mean the vocabulary itself whether English, Latin or Hebrew. Although the use of a specific language also impacts on the meaning and world of thought of the user, I also mean the entire construct of theology, tradition and history that is reflected in the 'language' of prayer and ritual, which all help to shape the frame of mind in which one forms one's personal faith, one's world-view, religious ideas and identity.

be able to mourn her death other than through Jewish tradition, with its own particular language and rituals and therefore felt very apprehensive about the upcoming funeral service. As it happened, the priest was aware of our family's situation and discussed the service beforehand to make sure that we would feel comfortable with the prayers and readings, and afterwards we buried her much according to the Jewish tradition and said the mourners' prayer, the *kaddish*, at her grave.

Yet it was the unexpected death of the father of an Orthodox Jewish friend of mine which made me painfully aware of how challenging a Jewish funeral could be in the presence of non-Jews. My experience of this funeral was not unlike the one Helen has described. This friend, her sisters and mother were the only mourners;[9] but because they were women my friend's fiancé said the burial *kaddish* as a proxy and filled the grave with earth. My friend and her family were excluded from these *mitzvoth* (commandments) according to Orthodox tradition and were kept separated from the men. My friend's mother was a convert to Judaism and her family who attended the funeral stood at a distance from the grave. Of course not all Orthodox authorities are so strict, and there are Orthodox rabbis who would permit women to say *kaddish*. However, in this instance the separation between men and women and between Jewish and non-Jewish mourners pained me; and it made me feel ashamed of this part of Jewish tradition in the presence of my friend's non-Jewish family. It was not just they who did not possess the 'tools' to mark this life cycle moment with ritual and prayer, but that they stood apart outside the tradition at this life cycle event just as the chief mourners stood apart within their tradition. Both the non-Jewish family and the mourning women were set apart from the most important ritual marking the life cycle of which they partook. As a Jewish woman I felt equalled to the non-Jews attending the funeral; attending, but not partaking, and as such I felt that we were equally debarred from properly expressing our grief or offering our support. The separation between men and women, and the exclusion of women from the mourning ritual seemed to set apart my friend's mother's non-Jewish family even more than their lack of knowledge of the ritual language itself.

Although Jewish women and non-Jews may feel the same sense of exclusion at many life cycle events, the reason for their exclusion is

---

9 Mourners according to Jewish law are the following category of people: parents, spouses, children or siblings.

different. For non-Jews to attend or even participate (if allowed) in Jewish life cycle events is challenging on two grounds: first, there is always the obstacle of the use of Hebrew and second, there is also a real difference in theological language. Words and rituals which may seem similar to Christian concepts often have a completely different meaning in Jewish tradition. To mention just one example: blessing over wine and bread has a completely different connotation in a Christian context. Perhaps even more challenging than participation in, or attendance at, Jewish life cycle events for non-Jews is the fact that the Jewish story is not always universalistic but often notably exclusivist and particularistic. The Jewish story, and therefore much of its language and symbolism, is a 'love story' between the Jewish people and the Eternal One. Our prayers and festival cycles concentrate on the covenantal relationship between God and the Jewish people. Most statutory Jewish prayers mention the two relational aspects of God: namely Creator and the One who brought us out of Egypt. Sylvia Rothschild has explained this very point in *Taking up the Timbrel*:

> In particular, Jewish prayer is built on the two places of our meeting with God – what one might call the state of Creation and the state of Exodus/Revelation. Creation encompasses God as universal Creator, master of the Universe, transcendent Being. Exodus/Revelation speaks to us as children of the Covenant in our particular relationship with God of mutual obligation and interdependence.[10]

Many of our life cycle celebrations also focus on the covenantal relationship between God and the Jewish people as well as on the individual as member of the community. This covenantal aspect is pertinent to the Jewish framework of faith and theology. Even God as Creator, reminds us of the fact that God created the world for a purpose and that we have a role to fulfil in God's creation. The inter-changeability between Creation and Exodus affirms a circular perception of time, which we also encounter in the personal life cycles. Although time may be perceived as a linear continuum leading from Creation through Exodus/Revelation towards Redemption, Redemption itself reverts back to the ideal conditions of Creation. Because the covenantal aspect of the Jewish relationship with

---

10 Sylvia Rothschild, 2000, 'Expanding the Borders of Prayer', in Sylvia Rothschild and Sybil Sheridan (eds), *Taking up the Timbrel: The Challenge of Creating Ritual for Jewish Women Today*, London: SCM Press, p. 14.

God is also overwhelmingly present in many life cycle rituals, they are therefore necessarily excluding those non-Jews who attend or share these important moments with their Jewish friends or family.

Jewish life cycles have often excluded non-Jews who attend for the reasons explained above, but also they have traditionally excluded women. The life cycle of the Jew appertains mostly only to the male Jew. Terms such as *brith milah* (circumcision), *pidyon ha-ben* (redemption of the first-born son) and *bar mitzvah* (religious coming of age for a boy) are universally known. They are all life cycle events for men, carried out by men. Even in an Orthodox marriage ceremony the groom actively weds his bride, while the bride is married to him.[11] Yet there are so many life cycle moments that pertain only to women, such as pregnancy, giving birth, miscarriage, menopause, just to mention a few, which have never been reflected by prayer or ritual, or if they did, they never became part of mainstream tradition. As a Progressive Jewish woman, this traditional exclusion of women has often enraged me even through I understand the historical and *halachic* processes by which this traditional patriarchalism came about. Helen has emphasized the very need for ritual expression for women in these 'forgotten' life cycle events. In recent times, through the women's movement, and especially among Jewish women, there has been a growth of new and creative rituals to mark those events in their lives which are life-changing. Strangely enough the recent experience of the birth of my daughter taught me that my need for ritual at such a profoundly spiritual, awe-inspiring and life-changing moment was hardly present. The birth itself was like a ritual, a physical process, which led to a profound sense of spirituality, even holiness. Apart from the sheer exhaustion from giving birth itself, for myself I just felt the need for private thanksgiving in the form of two very short traditional blessings. For my daughter, I felt a great need for a covenantal ceremony as close as possible to that which is given for boys as offered in our Liberal Jewish prayer book, but without the surgical act.[12] Why would only men be accepted in God's covenant with a ceremony like *brith milah*, when the women too were part of God's covenant on Mount Sinai? The Torah says that women as well as

---

11 In the Orthodox Jewish marriage ceremony the groom weds his bride, and this action is not a reciprocal one: the groom and his male witnesses sign the *k'tubbah* (marriage contract); he presents his bride with a ring, but does not receive one, and pronounces his bride as 'consecrated to me, according to the law of Moses and Israel'.

12 *Siddur Lev Chadash*, p. 585–7: Initiating a Girl into the Covenant.

men were part of God's covenant. What is more, according to rabbinic interpretation, the women were included first in the covenant. Leviticus 19.3–6 reads:

> And Moses went up unto God, and the Eternal One called unto him, out of the mountain, saying: 'Thus shall you say to the house of Jacob, and tell the children of Israel: You have seen what I did to the Egyptians, and how I bore you on eagles' wings, and brought you unto myself. Now therefore, if you hearken to my voice indeed, and keep my covenant, then you shall be my own treasure from among all peoples; for all the earth is mine; and you shall be to me a kingdom of priests, and a holy nation.'

The rabbis interpret this text as follows: 'Thus you shall say to the house of Jacob' actually refers to the women; and the phrase: 'and tell the children of Israel,' refers to the men.[13] And indeed why would I not wish for my daughter that she should grow up for Torah, marriage and good deeds, as we traditionally wish for boys at their *brith milah*?[14] After all I will bring her up to know Torah, as if she were a boy, she will become *bat mitzvah* (a ceremony for a girl coming of age) and when, God willing, she marries, I hope she will do so according to Progressive Jewish tradition as an equal partner to her husband.

As female dialogue partners we have found throughout our years of dialogue that it has been precisely our experiences as *women* that have brought us most together and not condemnation of the patriarchal remnants of our traditions. The universal experiences that we share as women, we carry through in our faiths and seek in our traditions.

---

13 *Mechilta* on Lev. 19.3.

14 At the circumcision ceremony the attendants recite: Even as he has entered into the covenant, so may he enter into Torah, into marriage and into good deeds. *The Authorised Daily Prayer Book*, 1998, p. 782.

Further Reading

See the Bibliography section for full details on these titles.

Tamar Frankiel, *The Voice of Sarah: Feminine Spirituality and Traditional Judaism*.

Rela Geffen (ed.), *Celebration and Renewal: Rites of Passage in Judaism*.

Debra Orenstein (ed.), *Lifecycles: Jewish Women on Life Passages and Personal Milestones*.

Debra Orenstein and Jane Litman (eds), *Lifecycles: Jewish Women on Biblical Themes in Contemporary Life*.

Sylvia Rothschild and Sybil Sheridan (eds), *Taking up the Timbrel: The Challenge of Creating Ritual for Jewish Women Today*.

'Spirituality and the Jewish-Christian Dialogue', *The Way Supplement*, 2000/97, London: Heythrop.

10 The Eucharist

As they were eating, he took bread and blessed and broke it and gave it to them, and said, 'Take; this is my body.' And he took a cup and when he had given thanks he gave it to them, and they all drank of it. And he said to them, 'this is my blood of the covenant which is poured out for many.'

Mark 14.22–24

I The Eucharist and Jewish-Christian Relations

Clare Jardine

The Eucharist, or liturgy of thanksgiving, has been the central act of worship in the Christian liturgy since the beginnings of the Church. The Acts of the Apostles tells how those who believed in Jesus as the Christ, or messiah, not only 'went as a body to the Temple every day but met in their houses for the breaking of bread'.[1] In this section, I will explore the origins and theology of the Eucharist and reflect on how it can be enhanced by an appreciation of Jewish practices of Passover and Jewish blessings over bread and wine on the sabbath. In so doing, I am not implying any supersessionist claim that the Eucharist has in any way replaced the Passover seder, as is often believed in conservative or fundamentalist Christian thought; rather by understanding the Jewish roots of our liturgy it may deepen our faith as well as provide an understanding of Jewish practice today. I am speaking from a Roman Catholic perspective and therefore some of what I say will differ from beliefs and practices in the Protestant churches.

Christians understand that the Eucharist has its origins in the Last Supper and is remembered by the Church on Holy Thursday (Maundy Thursday). It was the last meal that Jesus and his disciples celebrated just

---

1 Acts 2.46.

before his death. The Synoptic Gospels of Matthew, Mark and Luke put the Last Supper in the context of the Passover because their purpose was to show that Jesus had in some way transformed the memorial of that feast.[2] When Jesus' followers blessed bread and wine they were to remember not only the Exodus from Egypt but also Jesus' own life, subsequent death and resurrection. Jesus had become the symbol of a new Exodus, the liberation of humanity by God from the slavery of sin to the freedom of a new existence with God anticipated by Jesus' resurrection from the dead. John's Gospel, the fourth Gospel, is quite different, situating Jesus' death at the time of the sacrifice of the Passover lamb and therefore before the Passover meal begins.[3] Theologically, the fourth Gospel writer imputes to the Passover sacrificial lamb the expiatory qualities of the goat offered at the Day of Atonement. The New Testament scholar Raymond Brown concludes from his study of the timing of the Last Supper that, contrary to many scholars, the fourth Gospel account may in fact be the more accurate.[4] The writer of John's Gospel clearly wanted to identify Jesus with the Passover lamb, a theme echoed in the last book of the New Testament, the book of Revelation. The author of the Letter to the Hebrews develops the sacrificial aspect even further by presenting Jesus as the High Priest who has gone once and for all behind the veil to take away sins. The priesthood of Christ is the main emphasis of this letter and his priesthood is seen as eternal. It contrasts the High Priest of the Temple who had to go into the Holy of Holies every year with Christ who 'entered once for all into the sanctuary' and 'not with the blood of goats and calves, but with his own blood' (Heb. 9.11ff.).

The most explicit theology of the Eucharist is found in the apostle Paul's Letters to the Corinthians. There the Eucharist has several dimensions: the sharing of a spiritual meal as an act of unity of the community with Jesus Christ and with one another and as a memorial of the life, death and resurrection of Jesus. In the first Letter to the Corinthians, Paul describes the Eucharist as the 'Lord's Supper' (1 Cor. 11.20) when the new people of God eats its 'spiritual food' and consumes its 'spiritual drink' (1 Cor. 10.3–4). When the believing community engaged in this action it was manifesting itself as the community of the 'new covenant' (1 Cor.

---

2 Matt. 26.17–30; Mark 14.12–26; Luke 22.7–20.

3 John 13.1ff.; 18.28; 19.14.

4 Raymond Brown, 1966, *The Gospel According to John*, London: Geoffrey Chapman, p. 553f.

11.25) as it shared in the 'table of the Lord' (1 Cor. 10.21). The idea of a spiritual meal would not have been new to Paul who would have recalled Exodus 24.8 where Moses, Aaron and the elders of Israel shared in a spiritual meal to seal the covenant with God. The Passover meal itself was, and is today, a shared meal which bonds the Jewish community.

Since the early days of the nascent Church, the theology and practice of the Eucharist has developed. Some of the earlier celebrations did not contain an institution narrative, but added to thanksgiving and praise to God for the works of Christ, were petitions for the coming of the kingdom.[5] In today's form the structure of the eucharistic prayer in the Roman Catholic tradition comprises a praise of God for the creation of the world and the redemption of humanity through Christ, a re-enactment of salvation at the consecration and an acclamation proclaiming the expected return of the messiah. Another dimension to the celebration of the Eucharist is the aspect of memorial – through it we remember the life, death and resurrection of Jesus Christ. In 1 Corinthians 11.26, Paul tells us that Jesus asked his disciples to perform the same action as he had done as a memorial of the Last Supper he had with them. This aspect of the Eucharist as a memorial is a prominent focus in the Protestant churches; however, in Catholic theology, it is more than a memorial of the supper. It is a repetition of a ritual act in which the Lord's body and blood are made present to nourish his people and to make available to them the salvific effect of that death. This dimension of making a past event present is well known to Jews in the Passover meal when they make present the past event of the Exodus from Egypt and the redemption of the people of Israel. The eucharistic cup of the 'new covenant' taken from Jeremiah 31.31 is an allusion to Moses' sealing of the first covenant with the blood of sacrificed animals (Exod. 24.8). This allusion invests the shedding of Christ's blood with an efficacy analogous to that of the sacrifice sealing the covenant of Sinai.[6] In Christian terms this action is sacramental and the re-enactment of the sacrifice at each eucharistic celebration brings salvific effects to each participant. So when Christians celebrate the Eucharist they enter into that same transformative event by symbolically going with Jesus into his death and resurrection and experiencing freedom from slavery to sin. This act of liberation is similar to the Passover meal when every person at the

---

5 Sharon Burns, 1990, 'The Beginnings of Christian Liturgy in Judaism', in Eugene Fisher (ed.), *The Jewish Roots of Christian Liturgy,* New York: Paulist Press.

6 1 Cor. 10.14–21.

table actually goes through the liberating event of the Exodus. Both the Eucharist and the Passover meal are thus symbolic meals in which the effects of a past event are actually experienced today.

The term 'Eucharist' probably comes from the Greek rendering of the Hebrew *todah*, meaning thanksgiving praise of God.[7] The eucharistic prayers derive partly from Jewish table blessings and they echo the language of grace after meals. Blessed loaves were set out as a weekly offering in the Temple. The Eucharist contains many prayers and actions which echo Jewish table blessings, thus recalling how Jesus on various occasions took bread, blessed and broke it. The New Testament scholar Joachim Jeremias states that in Judaism the term 'breaking of bread' never refers to a whole meal but to the action of tearing bread and to the rite preceding a meal.[8] In Christianity, the term 'breaking bread' became a technical term for the celebration of the Eucharist. The actions of the followers of Jesus were in direct response to Jesus' command – 'Do this in memory of me' – during the last supper he ate with his disciples.[9] In Judaism, wine and bread are used to mark the beginning of the sabbath after the candles have been lit on a Friday night. Blessings are said over the wine and then over the bread but this is not understood in any sacramental way. The Synoptic Gospels suggest that Jesus was celebrating a Passover meal just before his death rather than a sabbath meal; but it is important to understand that bread and wine have a meaning and use in the Jewish tradition that differs from the way they are used in Christianity. The use of unleavened wafers in the Mass in the Roman Catholic Church is a reminder of the unleavened bread used in Judaism during Passover.[10] The point at which 'theology' of the Passover and the Eucharist would differ is that the Passover food eaten and the wine drunk are not thought of as spiritual food and drink even though words of blessing are said over them. It is interesting for Christians to experience *kiddush* after the synagogue service on Shabbat morning and hear the same blessings over wine and bread as are said during the Offertory at a Catholic Eucharist.

---

7 See John F. Baldovin, 1991, 'Christian Worship to the Reformation', in Paul F. Bradshaw and Lawrence A. Hoffman (eds), *The Making of Jewish and Christian Worship*, Indiana: University of Notre Dame Press, p. 161.

8 Joachim Jeremias, 1966, *The Eucharistic Words of Jesus*, London: SCM Press.

9 Luke 22.19; 1 Cor. 11.23–7.

10 There is a history of debate within Christianity over whether or not the bread should be leavened or unleavened. In the Protestant churches and Orthodox Christian traditions it is usually leavened; but in the Roman Catholic Church it is unleavened.

As well as the putative link with the Passover, there are common features between the Eucharist and every meal. The scholar Louis Bouyer maintains that the connection between the Passover and the Eucharist is solely what the Passover meal has in common with every meal, that is the breaking of bread at the beginning and the rite of thanksgiving over the cup of wine mixed with water at the end.[11] This is what made it possible for the Christian Eucharist to be celebrated as often as one wished and not only once a year. However interesting the significance of the paschal lamb may be for an understanding of Christ's death, we must not look to the rite of the eating of the lamb and even less to the secondary rites like the unleavened bread or the bitter herbs for the source of the Christian eucharistic prayer. For an understanding of this prayer our starting point is with the broken bread at the beginning of the meal, the shared cup at the end and the blessings which were traditionally connected with them.

While the sharing of a common meal has resonance for Jews, the Christian belief that through the Eucharist, there is a union between the believing community and Jesus as well as with one another, may be difficult to understand. The apostle Paul explicitly identifies the sanctified bread and wine with the body and blood of Jesus in his account of the institution of the Eucharist (1 Cor. 11.23–5). In Christian theology, most especially Roman Catholic theology, this presence is real but the substances do not change. In other words, the bread and wine remain as they were as regards their physical elements but their reality has changed. This reality entirely depends on a person's faith because it does not stand up to any scientific probing; but for one who does not believe in it, it must be very puzzling. Of course the problem is not so acute in those Christian traditions where the emphasis is placed on table fellowship or on a simple recalling the memory of Jesus' actions.[12]

Even more incomprehensible must be the fact that these elements, believed to be the body and blood of Christ, are actually consumed by the participants in the 'meal'. For Christians, this moment of reception is an intense moment of communion with Jesus Christ and with the whole community gathered for the celebration. For Jews attending a Eucharist, it can

---

11 Louis Bouyer, 1968, *Eucharist*, Notre Dame: Notre Dame Press, p. 79.

12 In some of the Protestant traditions, the bread which is left over after the Eucharist service is thrown outside for the birds to eat. This would be unthinkable in the Roman Catholic or Anglican churches because of the way the bread (or 'host') is understood to be the body of Christ.

be a shocking experience to hear the words of consecration, 'This is my body', said over the bread, and 'This is my blood', said over the wine, and then to see Christians consuming bread and drinking wine that they believe to be the body and blood of Jesus. Perhaps that shock which Jews experience can help Christians to think about what they are doing and to learn to articulate their beliefs. Christians are so used to this sacred meal that its radical nature often passes them by. At the annual Christian-Jewish textual study weekend at the Ammerdown Centre near Bath in Somerset, the Christian and Jewish participants of the weekend gather together for the Sunday worship which is usually celebrated according to the Roman Catholic rite. I am conscious of the Jews present during the service and in a sense this heightens my awareness of potentially difficult areas in the service, in much the same way as Helen spoke about in the previous chapter; however, in my experience, there are usually no shock reactions from the Jews who attend. Everyone is very respectful because appreciation of the tradition of 'the other' is very much part of our time together.

I have often thought that it must be strange for Jews now to hear the sacrificial language of the Eucharist with the reference to the blood of the covenant. Many of the allusions to sacrificial blood are taken from the Hebrew Scriptures, but Temple sacrifice ended in 70 CE and contemporary Judaism has no priesthood.[13] When Christians celebrate the Eucharist, are they also thinking of the sacrificial powers of the event and of Jesus the great High Priest? I would think that for many Christians as well as for many Jews today, the idea of sacrifice is not an attractive one. The concept brings to mind the idea of placating the deity or pleading with the gods. Since the Second Vatican Council of 1962–5 the theological emphasis of the Eucharist has shifted from dwelling entirely on the sacrificial aspect of a community sharing of a meal.[14] It has shifted away from the idea of Christ as the High Priest to the common priesthood of all the baptized. When the Eucharist is celebrated today, the priest no longer has his back to the people offering a sacrifice on their behalf but turns to face them. Theologically, the sacrificial aspect is still there but the emphasis is on the common sharing of a meal. After the Second Vatican Council many groups and families have invited a priest to celebrate the Eucharist at their home round a coffee table. I can still remember the thrill of being so close

---

13 Rabbinic Judaism transferred key elements to the home and synagogue.

14 The reforming Ecumenical Council in the Catholic Church which took place between 1962 and 1965.

to the table at such a Eucharist with a real sense of engagement in the action. Sadly, these occasions are not a regular occurrence today. Perhaps, if women were to be accepted to the priesthood in the Catholic Church, small intimate gatherings could be developed as part of a variety of expressions of worship in the community. It is deeply regrettable that women are excluded from this ministry but we should take comfort from the great strides made by women in the Anglican Communion in the last decade and be encouraged by women who continue the debate.[15]

The Eucharist then is a communal thanksgiving meal at which wine is blessed and bread broken and shared. At this meal participants undergo a transformation that empowers them to go out and spread the love they have received with others. Recent developments have helped Catholics to understand the communal aspects of the Eucharist by playing down the sacrificial aspect of the liturgy. Knowledge and experience of the blessings said at Jewish meals as well as an experience of Passover can also be very beneficial to all Christians who are trying to deepen their understanding and develop their practice of the Eucharist. However, knowledge of the Jewish background to the liturgical practices of the Church is limited to a minority. Now is the time for more efforts to be made in this regard to make people more aware of the Jewish roots of our liturgy. I suggest that women who could bring the gifts of 'spiritual nourishment, communication and creative involvement', which Esther Gordon calls for, can take a lead in this respect.[16]

II A Jewish Woman Reflects on the Eucharist

Marcia Plumb

While a rabbinic student at a Roman Catholic seminary, and as the former associate director of a programme that brought seminary students from different faiths together to study at each other's seminaries and pray together, I have attended many Masses. After getting over my initial resist-

15 Dorothea McEwan and Myra Poole, 2003, *Making All Things New: Women's Ordination, A Catalyst for Change in the Catholic Church*, London: Canterbury Press.
16 Esther Gordon, 2003, *The Mass Then and Now*, London: St Paul's.

ance to the exclusivity of the rite of the Eucharist or Mass, I began to appreciate the power of the ritual. In this part of the chapter I will reflect on the impact that attending these liturgies has had on me as a Jewish woman, partly as my response to Clare but also as a response to Lynne's searching question in Chapter 1: 'is your understanding of being a Jew transformed in any way by dialogue with us Christians?' In my answer, it will become clear that I have been affected by attending and listening to Christian liturgy, mainly at a Eucharist service but also that my prayer life has been directly influenced by Christian practice. In the second part of my response here, I also contribute insights into the Eucharist and memorial by looking at Judaism and the role of memorial for Jews.

Watching Christians in prayer and praying with them has had a deep impact on my own faith and prayer practices. Jewish liturgy is generally quite fixed. We recite the same certain prayers three times a day and on Shabbat (the sabbath). The fixed prayers act like a river, gently moving us along, closer and closer to God. The only problem is that, as in a boat being pulled by a current, it is often hard to stop and reflect with your own thoughts. Protestant Christian prayer, however, is often not fixed. There is enormous scope for the leader of the prayers and for the congregants to pray from their own hearts using their own words. The minister is able to react spontaneously to the needs of the congregation or of the wider world. From this openness and flexibility, I have learned to be more spontaneous as a leader of prayer myself. I now often stop in the service and insert special prayers or blessings that I feel, within my soul, would be helpful to others. I have also gained a love of silence. While studying at Howard Divinity School, which is an African-American Protestant seminary in Washington, DC, I loved to sit in the 'listening room'. The room, set up by the founder of the seminary, Howard Thurman, was small with large leather chairs. One went into the room simply to listen. It was up to you and God to determine what you would hear. Judaism blends the physical with the spiritual easily and powerfully. When Jews pray, we bend, bow and rock back and forth with regularity. When praying in a Eucharist setting, however, Christians often pray with open hands and this has added a new meaningful way to use my body to pray. I borrowed the custom of placing one's palms open to receive God's grace. I still regularly open my hands in this way when I pray as a physical way of opening my soul to God and bringing in and welcoming God's presence.

Being present at a Eucharist service has also had an impact on me.

When I attended Mass, I watched in awe as believers waited for their turn at the altar of bread and wine. They would look so 'normal', as they waited in the queue, but after the experience, and that is what I saw happen, an experience, I would be moved and in awe. Their faces looked different – they were transformed. Something mysterious had happened to them through the act of taking the bread and wine. I knew that God had not physically entered their bodies, but something physical happened to these believers. Clare spoke of this experience, saying that the 'moment of reception is an intense moment of communion with Jesus' and maybe that was what I saw reflected in the faces of those people. As a Jew, I have often wondered, what does it mean to eat the body of Christ and drink his blood? When Christians take in their mouth the body of Christ and take a sip from the chalice of his blood, is it slightly cannibalistic or is it mysteriously transforming for the believer? Does the Eucharist serve as a reminder of Jesus' sacrifice or does the sacrifice and the one who did the sacrifice actually somehow become part of the individual through the physical nature of the Mass? Is the Eucharist a memorial or a present-day reality?

Judaism is full of sacred memorials, mainly expressed through festivals and days of mourning. We remember the destruction of the Second Temple and other tragic events in our history and we dedicate a day for mourning the victims of the Holocaust. At each of these sacred days of remembrance we reflect on the role of these historical events for our lives today. According to the Jewish scholar Lawrence Hoffman, these memorial days act as pointers to Jews to remind us of God's role in history and of those who died in the name of Judaism.[17] These days, however, and the liturgy that accompanies them, are also meant to attract God's attention to us. In our liturgy, we ask God to remember events and people and then to bless us because of their memory. In Judaism, remembrance is often linked to salvation and redemption. During the High Holy Days, the time when we ask God to forgive us our sins, we read the story of the Binding of Isaac (the *Akedah*) as a way of reminding God of our faith. By remembering the story, we encourage God to forgive us. Hoffman also points out that the act of remembering leads to forgiveness and salvation.[18] In

17 See Lawrence Hoffman, 2001, 'Does God Remember? A Liturgical Theology of Memory', in Michael Signer (ed.), *Memory and History in Christianity and Judaism*, Indiana: University of Notre Dame Press, p. 41–72.

18 Lawrence Hoffman, 2001, 'Does God Remember?', p. 61–2.

remembering our sacred story, the story of the Exodus, however, we are told to re-live the experience, not just remember it. We are to 'see ourselves as we ourselves came out of Egypt'.[19] We tell the story during the Passover seder, but we are meant to reflect on our own experience of enslavement, whether through active oppression, or being emotionally stuck (or bound) in personal situations. We give to charities, in particular ones connected with poverty or hunger, as a way of fulfilling the command to 'let all who are hungry at this season come and eat'. The story of the Exodus motivates us to try to relieve our own personal difficulties and the suffering of others. During the ritual of the Passover seder night, we read from the *Haggadah*, our liturgy for the evening. In the *Haggadah*, we find that the past becomes the present and also blends with the future. The past, present and future collapse into one. We re-live the past in the present moment while at the same time we look towards the future messianic time of world peace and harmony. By re-living the past during the seder night, we also welcome in the future when we open the door during the evening to Elijah, the prophet who represents the messianic age.

Linked to our sacred story of the Exodus is a prayer in our daily service called the *Mi Kamocha* that reminds us that God is the saviour and the one who redeemed us from Egypt. We recall the moment when the Israelites crossed the Red Sea and 'Moses, Miriam and all Israel together sang to you this song: Who is like you O God, Who is like you doing wonders.' Through this prayer we remember what God did for us and how God redeemed us. It is common to read this prayer as a remembrance prayer which simply recalls a historical event, but when I lead this prayer in a service I like to stop and ask people to make this prayer present and relevant for them in their own lives today. I invite them to bring that experience of thanksgiving forward and transform it from a memory into a moment of thanksgiving and redemption that happened to us today or in the past week. I ask congregants, and myself, to compare ourselves to the Israelites and the way we with God's help overcame obstacles, fears, and challenges in the past week. What were our achievements and accomplishments this week? For what are we grateful? I want the *Mi Kamocha* prayer to be our song of gratitude and blessing. I want it to be meaningful for us today rather than simply a prayer that recalls a miracle. In this way, we can feel redeemed today as in ancient times. Do people feel redeemed

---

19 The *Haggadah*.

at the moment of the Eucharist or is it a pointer to the past? The Anglican-Roman Catholic Agreed Statement says:

> The notion of memorial as understood in the Passover celebration at the time of Christ – i.e. the making effective in the present of an event in the past – has opened the way to a clearer understanding of the relationship between Christ's sacrifice and the Eucharist. The Eucharistic memorial is no mere calling to mind of a past event or of its significance but the Church's effectual proclamation of God's mighty acts. As often as the death of the Lord is proclaimed at the Lord's supper ... God is reminded of the unfulfilled climax of the work of salvation ... The disciples represent the initiated salvation work before God and they pray for its consummation.[20]

But the World Council of Churches' document *Baptism, Eucharist and Ministry* similarly claims that, 'the Eucharist is the memorial of the crucified and risen Christ, i.e. the living and effective sign of his sacrifice, accomplished once and for all on the cross and still operative on behalf of all humankind. The biblical idea of memorial as applied to the Eucharist refers to this present efficacy of God's work when it is celebrated by God's people in a liturgy.'[21] So, for both Christianity and Judaism, memory can lead to salvation and forgiveness. It can enable us to feel God's presence in our world and in our personal lives.

As a Jewish woman, there is one more Jewish ritual that reminds me of the healing powers of the Eucharist and the transformative effect that it can have on believers, and that is the *mikveh*. The *mikveh* is the precursor to the baptism. The *mikveh* is a small pool of water that looks similar to a Jacuzzi. Some of the water in the *mikveh* must be '*mayim hayyim*', or 'living water', which usually means rainwater. In Judaism, there are many times that people go to the *mikveh*, but for the sake of this chapter, I will focus on three times that the *mikveh* can be seen as transformative. Converts to Judaism go to the *mikveh* as part of the their conversion process, individuals go before their wedding, and finally Jews go to the *mikveh* before the High Holy Days of *Rosh Hashanah* and *Yom Kippur*. In each case the act of immersing oneself in the waters which symbolize the

---

20 Michael Signer (ed.), 2001, *Memory and History in Christianity and Judaism*, p. 79.
21 *Faith and Order Paper No. III*, 1982, Geneva: World Council of Churches, Section 5.

waters of Creation spiritually cleanses one of one's past sins. One is reborn through the act of going to the *mikveh*. In the case of the convert, one symbolically washes away one's past beliefs and, in a certain way, separates from the way the person saw the world in the past and faces the future as a newly born Jew. One is commanded to go to the *mikveh* before one's wedding as a way of letting go of one's sins in the past life and one emerges from the *mikveh* as a new soul ready to enter a new life as a married person. Finally, at Rosh Hashanah, we feel as if God washes us clean of all our sins, faults and transgressions. The *mikveh* acts as the birth waters of salvation and we emerge with clean, fresh souls.[22]

When I go to the *mikveh*, I wonder if I appear changed from the moment I went in to when I come out. I certainly feel changed. I feel as if I have been inside the womb of God and have been reborn through the cleansing birth waters of Eden. I feel forgiven by God and by myself. I feel at peace. Perhaps the Eucharist experience is similar. Perhaps one stands in line waiting for one's turn, then approaches the altar, and by taking the bread and wine enters God's presence as if entering the Holy of Holies, then exits, redeemed, forgiven and at peace. No wonder I always wanted to try it.

Further Reading

See the Bibliography section for full details on these titles.

Paul F. Bradshaw and Lawrence A. Hoffman (eds), *The Making of Jewish and Christian Worship*.

Philip A. Cunningham, *Proclaiming Shalom: Lectionary Introductions to Foster the Catholic and Jewish Relationship*.

Eugene Fisher (ed), *The Jewish Roots of Christian Liturgy*.

Lawrence A. Hoffman, *Beyond the Text: A Holistic Approach to Liturgy*.

Clark M. Williamson, *When Jews and Christians Meet: A Guide for Christian Preaching and Teaching*.

---

22 There is a tradition that women go to the *mikveh* monthly after menstruation, but I did not include this aspect in the discussion.

11 Prayer

'I have been pouring out my heart to God.'

1 Samuel 1.15

I The Renewal of Prayer: A Christian Woman Reflects

Clare Jardine

As a Sister of Sion, I am living my Christian faith and life of prayer in a very particular way and since my community is dedicated to a better understanding in the life of the Church between Catholics and Jews, my starting point is all the more unique. In the context of women's dialogue, this particularity is important and valuable. Like members of other faith traditions, my prayer has been challenged and changed by the circumstances of my life.

As a younger person prayer consisted in repeating formulae learned at home, church or at school. My faith was unshakable although it had never been tested like the local martyrs of Padley who had died for their faith.[1] My identity as a Catholic was strong; the 'other' at that time was the Protestant or any non-Catholic, not a person of another faith and my certainty that all others should become members of the one, true Church reflected pre-Conciliar ecclesiology that there is no salvation outside the Church.[2] On the whole my prayer was directed to the Father and prayers usually ended with the formula 'through Jesus Christ, Our Lord'. But my image of God was that of a strict father of whom I was rather frightened. I did not give much thought to the content of my prayers; the mere act of praying seemed to be sufficient to keep myself on the right side of God.

---

1 The site of the martyrdom of several English Catholics, near Grindleford, Derbyshire.

2 The theology of *nulla sallus extra ecclesiam* (outside the Church no salvation) prevailed until the Vatican Council Declaration on Other Faiths, 1965.

I rather liked devotional prayer with all the rituals – candles, incense, hymn singing. Unlike many young Catholic women and girls I did not find Mary a very satisfactory intercessor because for me she was not a real person, only a sort of plaster-cast statue.

The greatest influence on my prayer life since those early days has been my life as a religious sister. The call to religious life came, as these things usually do, rather unexpectedly. I had felt drawn to go on pilgrimage to Israel and walk in the footsteps of Jesus and met two evangelical Christian women on the same tour. At first I found them rather overwhelming in their religious fervour but came to realize that they had something which I did not – personal conviction and commitment to Jesus Christ. I suddenly started to see a yawning gap I had experienced in my life in spiritual terms. Perhaps God could provide the missing element. It was surprisingly in the Holy Land that I made my commitment and vowed to deepen my relationship with God and Jesus. Then I realized that God might be calling me to religious life and I was even more astounded. I had never wanted to become a nun and had never been attracted to, or inspired by, any of the nuns I had known, mainly at school. Somehow, however, I felt drawn to the religious life and the pull like a magnet could not be resisted.

Prayer for me now is a deepening of my relationship with God, and rather than simply repeat prayer formulae at set times, my prayer is an integral part of my life. It emerges from my life as I reflect on my day-to-day involvements; prayer affects my life as I bring to it my meditation. God is no longer the stern father figure but a loving and merciful father-and-mother with whom I can have a deep and lasting relationship. Like many other Christians my spirituality is Ignatian which means, among other things, that I use imagination to engage with a Gospel passage. This way of praying is based in the '18th Annotation' of St Ignatius of Loyola, the founder of the Jesuit order. It is a process whereby a person enters into the life, death and resurrection of Jesus through a series of meditations and thereby seeks to discern the will of God. This is a technique which enables the one praying to enter into the Gospel story in a personal way, identifying with the scene and one of the characters. Through this method my whole being is relating to the action or the words. All my senses are brought into play infusing me with God's light. This light does not always bring me consolation; often I experience desolation or what John of the Cross, the sixteenth-century Carmelite mystic, describes as 'the dark night of the soul'. I used to think that men might have more difficulties than women in using imaginative prayer to develop their relationship with Jesus but men have told me that they can relate to Jesus just as easily as women since the relationship is not sexual in nature but one based on real friendship.

Years ago religious sisters were encouraged to think of themselves as brides of Christ, and like Mary pure and virginal. Virginity was seen as a positive and compelling ideal. Set apart from the world behind an enclosure, her purity intact, the virginal nun was a bride destined for higher consummation. These notions had persisted since the time of the Late Middle Ages but today such ideas are not popular. Recently Sandra Schneiders, a North American religious woman, has tried to recover the bridal image as a valid one for today.[3] She argues that the essential element of the commitment of a religious woman today is still her relationship with the person of Christ and the bridal image emphasizes the sole commitment. Although I agree with the exclusiveness of the relationship I prefer to think of it in terms of a deep friendship with Jesus rather than as his bride.

When it comes to thinking about myself as a Christian woman, my mind immediately turns to the treatment of women in the Roman Catholic Church. Women have always been acceptable as mothers, nuns, teachers, catechists and parish workers but, on the whole, have never had a real voice. For example, as a religious sister I can take vows and contribute to the life of the Church but I cannot take part in any real decision making. I am not exactly silenced but I am not heard. I therefore associate with organizations that are pro-active in promoting a fuller role for women, including ordination. The 'Catholic Women's Network' and 'We are Church' are just two examples of groups springing up in the Church empowering and encouraging lay people, particularly women. Their journals reflect the fact that feelings of alienation are not restricted to women. Many men want to stand alongside women because they understand that the way women are treated is a reflection of the attitude of all human beings in an organization. Recent difficulties with the shortage of priests, and a general movement in society towards women playing a more significant role in business and other professions, has made a little difference in the Church's attitude towards women but there is still a long way to go before there is any meaningful equality and appreciation of women's gifts.

---

3 Sandra Schneiders, 2001, in *Selling All: Commitment, Consecrated Celibacy and Community in Catholic Religious Life*, New Jersey: Paulist Press.

As a Christian, the celebration of the Eucharist is central to my life; through it my life is taken up and transformed. Sadly, as a woman in the Roman Catholic tradition I am barred from ordination and therefore not allowed to preside at the eucharistic liturgy even if I felt called to this ministry. Even the order of deacon is closed to Catholic women when theologically there seems, to me at least, to be no reason why this should be so. By excluding women, the Church is depriving itself of the giftedness of at least half its members. I have frequently felt excluded especially at gatherings when several priests are concelebrating standing round the altar. Many have no concept of what it feels like to be a woman (sometimes one of the few not concelebrating) in these circumstances. Our own weekends as Sisters of Sion usually end with a Eucharist and we have to 'import' a priest to preside. We often find it difficult to bring the priest into the movement of the weekend although some are extremely sensitive and adaptable. Pope John Paul II has declared that there should be no further discussion on the ordination of women, so Catholics have in effect been silenced on this subject.[4]

Since Mary has never been a role-model for me, I often ask myself which women inspire me from tradition. I do admire women of deep prayer like Teresa of Avila, another sixteenth-century Carmelite mystic, but they are not the ones who attract me and whose lives I want to imitate. I am much more attracted to social reformers and people who work for justice; for example Dorothy Day, who died in 1980 aged 83, was a committed pacifist who started the journal *The Catholic Worker* and opened a house for the poor in the slums of New York. Another inspiration for me is Helen Prejean, the American sister who befriended a man on death row and is now immortalized in the film *Dead Man Walking*. Of course, there is no real dichotomy between prayer and action but I think for me it is the action which is the starting point for my prayer, feeding into it and getting nourishment from it.

Has becoming a Sister of Sion altered my identity? I am still a Christian woman in the Roman Catholic tradition but my thinking on prayer and my life of prayer has changed enormously. How has this happened? First, living and praying in community. Praying together as a group of women

---

4 See *Ordinatio Sacerdotalis* (On Reserving Priestly Ordination to Men Alone), 1994. Pope John Paul II says, 'I declare that the Church has no authority whatsoever to confer priestly ordination on women and that this judgement is to be definitively held by all the Church's faithful.'

all dedicated to the same end is an extremely enriching experience and one which nourishes and challenges my life. Our prayer consists of readings from the Bible, reflection on the reading, sharing our thoughts and personal prayers. The Roman Catholic Church has an enormous range of resources for prayer, contained in the monastic offices. There is a daily, weekly and yearly structure of regular liturgy. That liturgy draws on the Psalms, texts taken from the whole of the Bible (and are often read consecutively), Church history and Christian writers from all the centuries. The liturgy relates to the yearly life cycle of the Church, structured around waiting for the birth of Jesus (Advent), his death, resurrection and ascension (Easter) and waiting for the Second Coming of Christ.

Most communities do not strictly follow the prayer of the Church but try to create a liturgy which is meaningful for the situation of the community members. I am most stimulated by the community reflection which touches on theological and scholarly issues. The personal sharing between community members can be very deep, often allowing others into the most intimate areas of life, an exercise which is probably much easier for women than for men.

The second reason for the development of my prayer life is the studies I have undertaken in theology and Judaism. Having an understanding of the background to the Bible, learning the languages of the Bible and studying theology have all contributed to a deeper consciousness of my faith and of my understanding of God. I realize that these studies were much more available to me as a religious sister than to many other women. As a Sister of Sion, Jewish studies were within my reach and I was especially fortunate to spend a year in Jerusalem. Because I belong to an international congregation, I have opportunities to visit other countries, exchange with people from other cultures and traditions all of which is life-enhancing, opening my mind to other possibilities of thought and expression.

Third, my particular ministry within the congregation brings me into contact with people from other faith traditions, primarily Judaism. My main work is to promote a better understanding of the relationship of the Church to the Jewish people. This ministry is not yet at the forefront of the life of the Church, resulting in marginalization of those involved in it. There is a certain amount of pain attached to this ministry – pain for the treatment of the Jewish people by Christians, and pain that the ministry is still so little understood. All this pain goes with me into my prayer as well

[188]

as the depth of knowledge that my encounters inevitably bring. All my experiences of contact with Jews and Judaism, my studies of theology and Judaism and being a Sister of Sion have graced me with a different view of God than I previously held. The Jewish belief in the oneness of God has increased my own awareness and has helped me put my beliefs in Christ in perspective without diminishing my faith in him. I pray to God now without necessarily thinking of God as Father. I have many other images – lover, friend, rock, mother, some biblical and others relational. I am now much more aware of the Jewishness of Jesus, Mary and all the early followers of Jesus. Reading the Gospels I picture Jesus being taken to the Temple to be presented, discussing with the rabbis and praying the *Shema*, the central prayer in Judaism. Instead of the plaster-cast statue, Mary has become a Jewish woman keeping the dietary laws and running a Jewish home. As an ordinary person she can even be a role-model for me now.

As I engage in dialogue I listen to Jews speak about their own beliefs and practices. I sometimes find myself praying in their company and am much more aware of the way we pray as Christians. Being with Jews has helped me to become less absolute in my convictions, more open to 'the other', now much more likely to be a person from another faith tradition rather than the vague non-Catholic of my youth. I have had the privilege of being present at a Passover meal and appreciate it as part of the Jewish tradition which provides some insights into the roots of the Christian Eucharist. However, many Christians use the Passover meal to illustrate the background of the Last Supper and Eucharist and unwittingly transmit the idea that the Passover has been superseded by the Christian practice. Some Holy Week liturgies in Church are often conducted without any sensitivity towards Jews and Judaism particularly when the Passion account is dramatized with the congregation taking the part of the crowd shouting, 'Crucify him, crucify him!' These incidents make me realize just how much work needs to be done in sensitizing others.

My prayer as a Christian woman has changed and developed over the years and there are a number of factors that have influenced it. The call to religious life and becoming a member of a religious community has brought many spiritual blessings which would have been beyond my reach as a lay woman in the Church. As a member of my particular Congregation, I have become more deeply conscious of the spiritual traditions of the Jewish people, the joys of which enlivens and at the same time quickens my prayer.

II Women and Prayer in Judaism

Rachel Montagu

Clare has explored the influence that the Jewish-Christian encounter has had on her understanding and practice of prayer. In this part, I will look at women and prayer in Judaism because it is an area that is often mis-understood and a number of stereotypes and prejudices can surface with-in Christian theology.

The main prayer in Judaism, the *Amidah*, which consists of 18 para-graphs on weekdays and seven on the sabbath and is said standing and facing Jerusalem, is supposed to imitate Hannah: 'standing and silently pouring out her soul before the Eternal' and praying for a child.[5] Another biblical source for Jewish prayer is also a woman's example: Rebeccah going *lidrosh et hashem*, to enquire from the Eternal just what was the meaning of the extraordinary sensations she was feeling as her twin sons began a lifetime of struggle while still within her womb.[6] So if women's prayer is important in Judaism and is indeed the biblical role model for prayer for all Jews, why is it that women's role in prayer in Judaism throughout history has not been an equal one?

The rabbis were aware of women's spiritual needs, they permitted them to take part in sacrifices in the Temple[7] and there are several sources with-in the Talmud which suggest great respect for women's piety and spiritu-ality.[8] However, three pieces of rabbinic legislation had the effect of

---

5 1 Sam. 1.10–16. The medieval book of biblical exegesis *Yalkut Shmoni*, 80 says: 'And Hannah prayed' (1 Sam. 2.1). From this we learn that women are required to pray, for Hannah was reciting *Shemonah Esreh* (the *Amidah*, the daily liturgy).

6 Gen. 25.22.

7 Babylonian Talmud *Hagiga* 16b: 'The daughters of Israel do not lay on the hands. The daughters of Israel lay on the hands optionally. Rabbi Jose said Abba Eleazer told me, Once we had a calf which was a peace-sacrifice, and we brought it to the women's court and the women laid the hands on it, not that the laying on of the hands has to be done by women, but to gratify the women.' *Mishnah Nazir* 6.11 describes Miriam of Tarmod bringing the offerings made at the end of the period for which one took the Nazirite vows of abstinence, being interrupted by her daughter's death and then com-pleting the offerings. This is particularly noteworthy as it is one of the few references to women in the *Mishnah*. Miriam of Tarmod was a woman of considerable property and married to a priest so it is possible that slightly different rules applied to her.

8 Babylonian Talmud *Ta'anit* 23a–b.

restricting the religious life of Jewish women. Some parts of Jewish liturgy Orthodox Jews say only in the presence of a *minyan*, quorum of ten adult (i.e. aged over 13) Jewish men. This generates two problems for women in prayer. It is not encouraging to hear someone checking whether there is a *minyan* present say 'there are only nine people here', when there are actually ten or more in the room. Maybe only nine of them have penises, but penis and person are not synonymous. It is unbelievable how often I have heard this 'only nine people' phrase used in the presence of a larger mixed group and it is extremely offensive. Admittedly on one such occasion, the prayer leader did come over later to my mother and me and say, 'I'm sure that in God's eyes, there was a *minyan* already when we counted.' An unusually literal demonstration of 1 Samuel 16.7: 'God does not see as men see.' (I should say too that my parents' congregation treated my family with incredible loving-kindness when my mother died and part of that loving-kindness was the flexibility people with differing principles about *minyan* showed as part of their support to us as mourners. It was taken for granted that my sister and I said *kaddish*, an experience completely at variance to that described by Helen and Kathleen in Chapter 9.) To be told that your presence in a room is insignificant is infuriating but the traditional definition of *minyan* has worse consequences for women. If one is expected to join one's friends at 4 p.m. for a service, it may be inconvenient, but one schedules one's afternoon round that fixed moment. If one is not expected to turn up at synagogue to pray and can pray any time in the afternoon, but the phone rings, the children need attention, the errands need doing, it is very easy to find that the afternoon has slipped by and the prayers have never been said. Many observant Jewish men say that knowing that their friends require them to go to synagogue to help make up the *minyan* helps them find that specific time and so one of the main supports for men in regular daily prayer does not exist for women. This is one of the reasons why there are many traditional families in which the men pray regularly during the week and the women do not. It should be borne in mind that their lack of participation in public synagogue prayer does not mean that traditional women do not pray. In some very traditional families where sex roles are most distinct, a lot of status is given to women's personal private prayer. Shoshana Gelerenter-Liebowitz, an ultra-Orthodox woman, has described how her parents encouraged her to pray. She grew up within the Lubavitch movement which believes in strictly separate roles for the sexes but which also believes in the spiritual importance of women's prayer. Also, while women in conventional families often live an intense religious life in which the synagogue does not figure much, there is a tradition among Sephardi widows who, being free now of any family responsibilities, attend synagogue regularly, Shabbat and weekday alike.[9] Conversely, there are many Progressive Jewish women whose synagogues permit them to participate on an equal basis who choose not to do so, perhaps because daily prayer is less emphasized in the Liberal and Reform movements.

Another problem is the concept of *mitsvot aseh b'zman geramah*, positive time-bound commandments.[10] Women are exempted from those positive observances which are linked to a specific time, like wearing tefillin, although they must keep those positive commandments which are not linked to a specific time, for instance giving to charity. They are given no exemption from the negative commandments like 'you shall not murder'. The problem with this general principle is that it simply does not work. The Talmudic discussion on the Mishnah makes it clear that even the rabbis of the following generations had problems with this formulation. No reason is given in the Mishnah; the normal assumption is that women are exempted because of their responsibility for child-bearing and child-rearing. There is a certain logic in this, as shown by the beautiful poem by Merle Feld that Kathleen quotes in Chapter 9. But many of the commandments women do keep are positive and time-bound, for instance lighting Shabbat candles, the time for which is specified to the minute, and the observance of specific customs associated with the festivals. Also, while child-rearing does take time, and a crying baby needs attention now this minute, no woman has child-care responsibilities throughout her life and many never have them at all. We have agreed that 'penis' and 'person' are not synonymous; neither are 'woman' and 'mother'. Furthermore, while children may require instant attention, the *halachic* source does not cite a woman's role with respect to children but her role with respect to her husband.[11] This shows that while the rabbis

---

9 Shoshana Gelerenter-Liebowitz, 1992, 'Growing Up Lubavitch', in Susan Grossman and Rivka Haut (eds), *Daughters of the King, Women and the Synagogue*, Philadelphia: The Jewish Publication Society. And Susan Starr Sered, 1992, 'The Synagogue as Sacred Space for Elderly Oriental Women in Jerusalem', in Susan Grossman and Rivka Haut (eds), *Daughters of the King*.

10 *Mishnah Kiddushin* 1.7.

11 Abudarham (fourteenth century), Section II, Blessings before the Mitzvot, cited in Getzel Ellinson, 1986, *HaIshah vHaMitzvot, Woman and the commandments*, vol. 1,

were kind to women,[12] they did not regard them as their equals but only as adjuncts to and supports for themselves. This is one of the areas where there has been a radical shift in perception over the last generation: contemporary Jewish husbands would be as alarmed by this view of marriage as their wives.

It was suggested in the 1970s by an American Jewish scholar David Bleich that a more effective organizing principle for understanding where women are and are not included would be public and private. Women are included in the private – lighting the *shabbat* candles in the home to usher in the sabbath being a woman's responsibility suddenly makes perfect sense, likewise women hearing shofar on *Rosh HaShanah* and sitting in the *succah* on Tabernacles. Similarly that would explain why women are not normally called to the courts as witnesses and in the rabbinic period (as distinct from the time of Deborah in the Bible) do not act as judges, without there being any slur on their truthfulness or reliability – the court is a public domain, and so is the synagogue. There are still problems: the rabbis were not stupid, far from it, and their organizing categories usually make good sense, so why this exception? There were also many women whose appearances in the public domain are quoted in the rabbinic literature so we seem to have an inherent gap between theory and practice.

An example of the positive time-bound prayer-related observance from which women are exempt is the wearing of *tefillin* (phylacteries) and *tallit* (prayer-shawl for prayer). Despite the assurance within the Talmud that where women are exempt, they may take on the observance if they wish, women are excluded from *tallit* and *tefillin* in virtually all contemporary

---

Jerusalem: World Zionist Organization, p. 40: 'Woman is exempt from Positive Precepts dependent on a set time because she is bound to her husband, to attend to his needs. Were a woman obliged to perform such mitzvot, her husband might bid her do something at the precise moment she is fulfilling one of these mitzvot. Should she fulfil the bidding of her Creator and neglect her husband's demands, she faces her husband's wrath. On the other hand, should she fulfil her huband's demands and neglect the bidding of her Creator, she faces the wrath of her Creator. Consequently, the Creator exempted her for these obligations in order to promote harmony between husband and wife.'

12 There are a number of commandments in the Bible which are unfavourable to women and which the rabbis discuss but do not implement as written, for instance the trial by ordeal of the woman suspected of adultery (Num. 5.11–31) and the power of a man to send away his wife if she does something displeasing to him; the rabbis insisted that he provide for her financially (Deut. 24.1). While there are few figures in rabbinic literature which compare for strength with the matriarchs or other significant biblical women, women were far more socially protected in the rabbinic era.

Orthodox synagogues; it is only in the last 20 years that women have worn them in Reform and Liberal synagogues which have claimed to promote the equality of men and women for the last century. There is no reason why a woman cannot do this: there are historical precedents for women doing so. The granddaughters of Rashi the great French Bible commentator are said to have worn the *tallit* and Michal, the daughter of Saul, is said in the Talmud to have worn *tefillin* – although given the nature of Michal's and David's relationship, I think it is possible that this phrase does not refer to Michal's religious observances but is the rabbinic equivalent of the English expression 'she wears the trousers in that marriage'. Rabbi Fred Morgan commented in a pamphlet on women and *tallit* produced by the Reform Synagogues of Great Britain that women thinking seriously about wearing *tallit* might prompt men to think more deeply about an observance which has become routine for them.

I was delighted when I first noticed that David Bleich's distinction between public and private for women's observance also solves the puzzling question of women's exemption from saying *Shema*.[13] The Mishnah specifically exempts women from saying *Shema*[14] although they must say the *Amidah*. It can be argued that they are equally time-bound,[15] and certainly saying the *Amidah*, like the Grace after Meals, takes much more of that precious child-care and husband-cherishing time than saying *Shema*.[16] If, however, we say that the *Shema* is a communal declaration in which the community remind each other of God's existence,[17] then the

---

13 Deut. 6.4–9.

14 *Mishnah Berachot* 3.3: 'Women, slaves and minors are exempt from reciting the *Shema* and from wearing *tefillin*, but they are obliged to say the *Amidah*, to place a *mezuzah* on their door and to say Grace After Meals. The Talmud on *Berachot* says that when several women eat together they are obliged to form a *mezuman* (the formal invitation and response which introduces Grace After Meals), so we are obviously dealing here not with any question of the time taken by the observance, but whether women can form a group, as men do, for the purpose of carrying out the commandments.'

15 The classic explanation is that the *Shema* is a positive biblical commandment and the *Amidah* a positive rabbinic commandment, and it is positive biblical commandments from which women are exempt. Another explanation cited is that the *Amidah* is a plea for mercy and both men and women are in need of God's mercy, so no exemptions apply.

16 *Mishnah Berachot* 2.4.

17 It is the custom of some Jewish renewal groups to say the *Shema* round the room, each person inserting the name of their neighbour: 'Hear, (e.g.) Sarah, the Eternal is Our God, the Eternal is One.' Similarly, my Israeli nephew on a recent visit to London, said that if at home he says '*Shema Yisrael*', surely in England it should be '*Shema Anglia*'!

Mishnah's exemption of women from *Shema* makes sense. Most of the *Amidah* can be said as a private prayer and so women are obliged to say it individually at home, whereas the *Shema* is an essentially communal prayer and so the rabbis did not make it part of women's prayer regime.[18] However, women can count as public persons. Jewish law says that in times of persecution if you are told in private to break a minor commandment or die, for instance 'eat this pork', you may eat it and live to keep the commandments in future, but if this happens in public, where your pork eating can be used to bring shame on the Jewish community, then you must choose to be martyred instead. What constitutes 'in public'? In the presence of ten Jews, gender unspecified, so one might think that what is right for martyrdom applies also to the liturgy.

The third piece of traditional Jewish law that can be problematic for women is *mechitzah*. In Orthodox synagogues it is customary for men and women to be physically separated during the statutory service. There is no reliable evidence for the separation of men and women in the Temple except during one festival of the year, the *Simchat Beit HaShoevah*, an occasion of great rejoicing when it was implied that participants might rejoice to an improper extent; a special gallery was built each year and taken down again. The earliest sources for *mechitzah* are medieval and its observance has become far stricter in the last century, perhaps an Orthodox response to Progressive Jews promoting their synagogues by saying that a family can all sit together there.[19] *Mechitzah* is a difficult issue because it is very much a matter of personal taste; some women like the separation,[20] others dislike it intensely and quote it as a reason for not

---

18 Although I think it is clear that saying the *Shema* is a communal theological declaration or act of study rather than an individual prayer, it should perhaps be said that in most traditional synagogues now the manner of reciting it emphasizes the obligation to concentrate on the words rather than the need to remind one's neighbour of God's unity. It is said in a quiet voice with a hand covering the eyes to remove surrounding distractions.

19 For a fuller discussion see Sylvia Rothschild, 1994, 'Undermining the Pillars of the Women's Gallery', in Sybil Sheridan (ed.), *Hear Our Voice: Women Rabbis Tell Their Stories*, London: SCM Press. The interpretation of Jewish law is often subjective; many of the texts used in Baruch Litvin, 1987, *The Sanctity of the Synagogue, the Case for Mechitzah: Separation between Men and Women in the Synagogue*, New York: Ktav, are the same as those cited more credibly by Rabbi Rothschild to prove how little historical evidence there is for *mechitzah*.

20 For instance Norma Baumel Joseph in *Half the Kingdom: Jewish Feminists Speak*, a TV documentary on the position of women in Judaism broadcast on Channel 4.

coming to synagogue. At its best, the women's gallery provides an autonomous space for women;[21] at its worst, it means that women can neither hear nor see the service and therefore feel excluded from it.[22] It can be an additional problem for Orthodox women wishing to join the daily services, which are often held in a small room with no separate area for women, sometimes forcing those women who wish to take on the observance of daily prayer or of saying *kaddish* for a parent to stand outside the door or behind a make-shift barrier.

Despite the extent to which the rabbinic enactments make it hard for women to observe the commandments of regular prayer, the rabbis themselves did not intend this or indeed approve it; a nineteenth-century code of Jewish law exclaims: 'It is difficult to justify the practice of women in contemporary society; they are not meticulous in reciting the three daily services.'[23]

Another frequent contention of Jewish women in our day is that while Judaism has rituals for all stages of the life cycle, this applies only to the life cycle of men and there are many significant stages of a woman's life which go unmarked.[24] Unmarked in the standard prayer books, that is. There has recently been an explosion of new liturgical writing for events such as miscarriage, birth, weaning, divorce.[25] For instance a new prayer creatively adapts the traditional blessing said after going to the lavatory and the problematic blessing said by women in the morning service and recasts them to celebrate the fact that birth means both the arrival of a new baby and a profound change of status for the new mother:

---

21 See Emily Taitz, 1992, 'Women's Voices, Women's Prayers: The European Synagogues of the Middle Ages', in Susan Grossman and Rivka Haut (eds), *Daughters of the King*, in which she describes women who acted as prayer leaders for the women sitting together in the gallery.

22 See Esther Broner in *Half the Kingdom*.

23 Arukh HaShulchan, *Orach Hayyim* 106.7.

24 Blu Greenberg, 1981, *On Women and Judaism*, Philadelphia: Jewish Publication Society.

25 Here is a modern form for the weaning ceremony mentioned in Gen. 21.6–8 of which we had no contemporary version. 'From the Weaning Ceremony', in Elizabeth Resnick Levine (ed.), 1991, *A Ceremonies Sampler: New Rites, Celebrations and Observances of Jewish Women*, San Diego: Woman's Institute for Continuing Jewish Education, p. 39. (After reading Gen. 21.6–8) Parents: Today we present to Artemis her own Kiddush cup, to symbolize her increasing ability to drink from other sources. We make Kiddush with white wine to symbolize mother's milk. Mother: He drew out for me because he delighted in me. (Ps. 18.20) Rabbi Jochanan explained the verse as follows: God drew out her breast to give me Torah. (Then follows Psalm 131.2 and *Havdalah*.)

Blessed are You, *Shechinah,* who in wisdom formed women's bodies and created in us unique openings, passages, organs and glands. These are known and revealed to You. If one of these opens when it should close or closes when it should open, it is impossible for us to live and sustain ourselves or to create and sustain our children. Blessed are You *Shechinah,* Healer of all flesh Who creates and sustains our bodies in wondrous ways. Blessed are You, *Shechinah,* Who has made me a woman.[26]

Traditional *tekhinot* (women's prayers written in Yiddish which were never included in the standard liturgy) are being translated and made available. One collection includes a Pregnant Woman's Prayer:

I pray unto You, Lord God of Israel, that you consider my prayer as You did that of mother Channa, the prophetess who prayed for a son the prophet Shmuel (Samuel). May her merit stand me in good stead. May I, Your maidservant, who am with child (Your creation!), carry full term and give birth to a healthy child who will become a pious Jew and serve you heart and soul; one who will love Torah and be God-fearing according to Your holy will, a beautiful plant in the Jewish vineyard for the beauty of Israel. Omayn.[27]

The anthology also includes a 'Prayer to be Said on the First Visit to Synagogue After Giving Birth' and a 'Prayer on the Appearance of a Child's First Tooth', as well as *tekhinot* not related to specifically maternal events but which are personal meditations to be said on occasions which do figure in the official prayer book such as visiting the Wailing Wall and on the various festivals. In the *tekhinot,* God is invoked as God of the matriarchs rather than God of the patriarchs, or as the God of other significant biblical women such as Deborah and Huldah:

This the woman says when she puts the Sabbath loaf into the oven: Lord of all the world, in your hand is all blessing. I come now to revere your holiness, and pray to you to bestow your blessing on the baked goods. Send an angel to guard the baking, so that all will be well-baked, will rise

---

26 From the 'Simchat Yoledet, Celebrating the Birth of a Mother', in Elizabeth Resnick Levine (ed.), 1991, *A Ceremonies Sampler,* p. 17.

27 'A Pregnant Woman's Prayer', in Norman Tarnor (ed.), 1995, *A Book of Jewish Women's Prayers: Translations From the Yiddish,* New Jersey: Jason Aronson, p. 16.

nicely and will not burn, to honour the holy Sabbath (which you have chosen so that Israel your children may rest thereon) and over which one recites the holy blessing – as you blessed the dough of Sarah and Rebecca our mothers. My Lord God, listen to my voice; you are the God who hears the voices of those who call to you with a whole heart. May you be praised to eternity.[28]

The style of the *tekhinot* is pious, personal and tender, quite different from the more formal style of the official liturgy; hence they may be appropriate for wide contemporary use if they become better known precisely because ours is an era in which intense focus on the personal is approved. In addition to mentioning those areas where the rabbis have made it harder for women to participate in prayer, we should also mention one area in which they are often erroneously assumed to have made difficulties. Women's menstrual status has no bearing on their relationship to prayer. This is an area in which the rabbis quietly dropped something mandated by the Bible. While the Bible says that anything touched by a menstruating woman became unclean also, the rabbis did not implement this and they said women should pray and enter the synagogue at all times.[29]

Do women and men respond differently to rituals and liturgy? Samson Raphael Hirsch, the nineteenth-century German Orthodox thinker, certainly thought so. His explanation for women's exclusion from certain rituals such as *tefillin* was that women have an innately spiritual nature which does not require the reminders and restraints that men need, hence binding on *tefillin* is a commandment for men not women. Is this crude apologetics or does it represent some sort of truth? When I tried 'laying *tefillin*', I certainly never felt it was an observance by which I was deeply covenanted to the Almighty. I felt boxed in mentally by strapping those

---

28 'Tekhine on Baking Challah', in Diane Ashton and Ellen Umansky (eds), 1992, *Four Centuries of Jewish Women's Spirituality*, Boston: Beacon Press, p. 53.

29 Lev. 15.19–21. *Sha'arei Teshuvah* (Responsa of the Geonim) 170: 'Rabbenu Sherira of blessed memory ruled "A menstruating woman recites her prayers and blessings as usual, without any qualms. Her being forbidden to her husband, surely does not exempt her from the commandments. Did not Ravina state that a menstruating woman sets aside the priests' portion of the dough, and can this be done without reciting the blessing? What difference is there between reciting a blessing or a prayer?"' And also, *Sefer HaPardes*: 'The synagogue is a small Temple and so men and women with a discharge do not enter in a state of uncleanness? No, for we are all ritually unfit to enter the Temple and we nevertheless go to the synagogue.'

boxes on my body. The beautiful words of Hosea said while winding the *tefillin* straps round one's hand, 'I betroth you to me forever, I betroth you to me in righteousness and justice, in lovingkindness and mercy, I betroth you to me in faithfulness and you will know the Eternal',[30] were not enough to make the *tefillin* seem an expression of my love for God. Other women feel very differently – Haviva Ner David has written about the importance *tallit* and *tefillin* have for her.[31]

It is certainly true that there is a very different feel to services and prayer where only women are present but I have never been able to define precisely what makes this difference. Support for each other in taking on something new and difficult? Closeness as a group? Soprano not bass notes? The *Shechinah*, God's indwelling presence, being feminine is more comfortable in a women's group and therefore her presence is perceived more easily by all those gathered to pray beneath her wings?

Further Reading

See the Bibliography section for full details on these titles.

Diane Ashton and Ellen Umansky (eds), *Four Centuries of Jewish Women's Spirituality.*
Mary C. Boys, *Has God Only One Blessing?*
Paul Bradshaw and Lawrence Hoffman (eds), *The Making of Jewish and Christian Worship.*
Jakob Petuchowski, *Understanding Jewish Prayer.*
E. J. Smith, *Bearing Fruit in due Season: Feminist Hermeneutics and the Bible in Worship.*
Norman Tarnor (ed.), *A Book of Jewish Women's Prayers: Translations From the Yiddish.*

---

30 Hos. 2.19–20.

31 Haviva Ner David, 2000, *Life on the Fringes: A Feminist Journey Toward Traditional Rabbinic Ordination*, London: JFL Books, p. 28–65.

12 Pilgrimage

There's no discouragement
Shall make him once relent.
His first avowed intent.
To be a pilgrim.

John Bunyan, 'Who Would True Valour See'

I To Be a Pilgrim

Beryl Norman

Many Christians have had some experience of pilgrimage, perhaps some version of a 'Holy Land Pilgrim Tour'. Roman Catholics, and other denominations also, will have made pilgrimages to holy places like Lourdes, Fatima or Medugordje. We use 'pilgrimage' for our inner journeys where no travel is involved. So for example, I often say: 'I began my pilgrimage in these matters almost accidentally, one day in Birmingham ...' You, I imagine, have made and are now making pilgrimages of your own. Each year I lead a study tour of Israel for the Council of Christians and Jews. These are not strictly pilgrimages inasmuch as they are educationally based but the pilgrimage element is there as an inseparable part of the whole. In this section, I will explore the concept of pilgrimage, its history, traditions and meanings in our different faiths and the various groups within each faith. Since my own experience is mainly in Israel/Holy Land tours with both Christian and Jewish/Christian groups, most of what I say comes out of that experience.

What do we mean by the word pilgrimage? What are we doing when we engage in one? I often put this question to groups of Christian clergy when talking about Israel and Israel tours. They are surprisingly silent on the subject, and then someone suggests something like 'a journey with a religious purpose'. Unlike the Jews, and to a lesser extent the Muslims, the

[200]

Christian churches have no territorial claims on the land of Israel itself. For Christians, it is the holy sites that matter. Yet it is of course a land greatly loved and of huge importance to Christians – the land where Jesus was born, lived, taught, ministered, healed and where he died and rose from the dead. The churches have nurtured their links with these holy sites in two ways: first in churches, convents and monasteries, schools and hospitals, and second by pilgrimage.

From the earliest centuries of the Christian era people flocked to the Holy Land, making long, arduous journeys to do so. The first extant, detailed account is that of the fourth-century Spanish nun Egeria.[1] What a woman she was! I see her in my imagination as dark of hair and eye, bristling with energy and enthusiasm. Off she went over land and sea, fired by her 'desiderium' (her burning heart's desire), 'to see and touch where revelation first was'. Fortunately for the world and for us, she wrote a nightly diary in Latin and sent it back home to the sisters. What did it mean to her? She describes her experience as a personal enactment of the holy texts; the past became 'now' for her. Sacred texts and sacred place came together and she worshipped. Her faith was vivified by personal contact with those places marked by the action of God. Others later have described pilgrimage as 'encountering the trace of God in history'. Egeria's experience, and theirs, is that sometimes called *anamnesis*, a calling up into the conscious mind of something not known, or not remembered. It is Plato's word for a recalling of pre-existence. It is not the same as simply 'memory'.[2]

I have recently discovered that Orthodox Christians, when visiting sacred sites, are searching for something closer to Egeria's experience than other Christian pilgrims today.[3] For the Orthodox, it is not primarily the facts or dates which interest them, rather each site is used as a means of passing through a veil, of experiencing the Eternity which is imaged by that site and its events.[4] However, not all Christian leaders have been in

---

1 See John Wilkinson, 1981, *Egeria's Travels to the Holy Land*, Jerusalem: Ariel.

2 It is a word often used in theological discussion concerning the Eucharist/Holy Communion.

3 Timothy Ware's book *The Orthodox Church* (London: Penguin, 1963) is helpful.

4 Icons too are painted for the same purpose. They are not intended as works of art, though many become so for their great beauty and antiquity (such as those held at St Catherine's Monastery in Sinai – given by the Russian Royal family), but are for the purpose of experiencing Eternity. See John Baggley, 1987, *Doors of Perception: Icons and their Spiritual Significance*, Oxford: Mowbray.

favour of pilgrimage. Gregory of Nyssa, the great theologian of the fourth century, wrote:[5]

> What advantage is to be gained by reaching those famous places? Can one suppose that our Lord still lives there today in his body, but is absent from us foreigners? Or that the Holy Spirit is fully present in Jerusalem but cannot travel so far as to reach us?

In the Middle Ages pilgrimage to the Holy Land, as well as to other sacred sites, flourished. Later Christians regarded pilgrimage as mere 'curiositas', frivolous and without spiritual merit. Milton mocked at pilgrims who 'strayed so far to seek/ in Golgotha him dead, who reigns in Heaven.'[6] There was a proverb which said: 'He that on pilgrimage goeth ever/ Becometh holy late or never.' Martin Luther roundly criticized those who went off on pilgrimage, 'leaving wife and children at home and going to Jerusalem where they have no business'. In spite of these negative attitudes, pilgrimage flourished. For most people it was a yearning, a means of grace, and for some a penance. In Shakespeare's *Richard II*, Bolingbroke, suddenly overcome with guilt when told that the King is dead for he had partly engineered it, says, 'I'll make a voyage to the Holy Land/ To wash this blood off my guilty hand.' However it has been seen through the ages, pilgrimage has continued unbroken until this day.

What of pilgrimage among the Jewish people? For Jews, it is not the sites that are important but the Land itself. Diaspora Jews visit Israel frequently; it is the land of their long history, the land which is ultimately home, the land where most have friends and relatives. Few would describe a visit to Israel as 'pilgrimage'. It is something quite different. Yet the Jews' whole narrative of biblical faith is one of long pilgrimage. 'Go forth from your country', says God to Abraham, the man of Ur, 'from your kindred and your father's house ... to the land that I will show you.' So a people, not yet the people of Israel, answer a call to travel away from the familiar to a place known only to God, but it will be a blessing. That surely is pilgrimage. Some centuries later came the Exodus, a going out of slavery and the long wandering that followed. Another pilgrimage.

---

5 For pilgrimage at this time, see E. D. Hunt, 1982, *Holyland Pilgrimage in the late Roman Empire. AD 312–460*, Oxford: Clarendon; and P. Walker, 1990, *Holy City, Holy Places? Christian Attitudes to Jerusalem and the Holy Land in the Fourth Century*, Oxford: Clarendon.

6 Milton, *Paradise Lost*, 3.476.

It is interesting that all three of the great Pilgrim Feasts in Judaism celebrate the journey and not the entry into the Promised Land. Passover remembers the coming out of Egypt; *Shavuot* remembers Sinai and the giving of the Law; and *Sukkot* celebrates the precarious living in the desert yet the care of God in it. Reflecting these festivals, it seems that it is the wandering, the long journey and its occasions which the people of Israel remember as the paradigm for their faith. It was a time when supremely God and his people were in love – it was the honeymoon, so described by Jeremiah:

I remember the devotion of your youth, how as a bride you loved me and followed me through the desert, through a land not sown. Israel was holy to the Lord.[7]

And again, in Hosea: 'Therefore, behold, I will allure her; and bring her into the wilderness, and speak tenderly to her. There she shall answer as in the days of her youth, as at the time when she came out of Egypt.'[8] After this great experience of pilgrimage as wandering, there came a huge about-turn. The desert was abandoned, the goal of the wandering had been reached and the whole pilgrimage ethos was focused on one city – Jerusalem – and one stretch of land. The great desert throng of pilgrims, and the sense of God's presence there, were centred within the walls of one holy city, the city of David. Jeremiah's land 'not sown' had now been sown. The people were a settled people, but that is another story.

This has not exhausted all the riches of interpretation and the Pilgrim Festivals. When I once needed a Jewish voice on the inner meaning of those festivals I asked Jonathan Gorsky, one of the education officers of the Council of Christians and Jews, for his wisdom. Rashly, I attempted to answer my own questions by suggesting to him that the Exodus, Sinai and the Law, the precarious desert life were all great examples of 'You shall remember'. He was not impressed and asked me to read the original texts again. It says, 'three times a year shall all your males appear before the Lord God'. It was an encounter between the people of Israel and the God of Israel. Are we not now close to Egeria or the Orthodox churches? It is not the facts themselves that matter but the eternity imaged by those facts

---

7 Jer. 2.2–3.
8 Hos. 2.14–15.

or events. Psalm 122, a psalm of ascent (to the Temple in Jerusalem), beautifully describes the joy of arriving:

I was glad when they said to me, let us go to the house of the Lord, our feet are standing now within your gates, O Jerusalem.

After the destruction of the Temple in 70 CE came the long exile and the dispersions of 70 and 135 CE until the foundation of the State of Israel in 1948. Were there Jewish pilgrimages to the land during those centuries before 1948? There has always been a Jewish presence there even if small, and from the middle of the nineteenth century there was substantial immigration there.[9] The exiled longing for the land surely drove many to journey there – let the twelfth-century poet Yehuda Halevi speak for all:

My heart is in the East, and I am at the edge of the West
How can I taste what I eat, how can I enjoy it?
... Zion is in the domain of Edom, and I in the bonds of Arabia ...
It would be glorious to see the dust of that ruined shrine.[10]

And in his Ode to Zion:

O Zion, will you not ask how your captives are – the exiles who seek
    your welfare, the remnants of your flocks?
My heart longs for Bethel and Penuel – there the Shekinah dwelled
    within you.
If only I could roam through those places where God was revealed to
    your prophets and heralds. It would delight my heart to walk
    barefoot where your shrines once stood,
Where your Ark was hidden away, your cherubim once dwelled.[11]

Halevi set out from Moorish Spain for the Holy Land in 1140 CE. He reached Alexandria but it is not certain whether he went any further. Some reports say that he did reach Jerusalem and died there, injured by a kick from a Crusader horse. I have quoted Halevi at some length because of his Jewish longing, his 'desiderium' is so similar to that of the Christian nun Egeria eight centuries earlier. Both longed to 'see and touch where revela-

---

9 Dan Bahat (ed.), 1976, *Twenty Centuries of Jewish Life in the Holy Land: The Forgotten Generations*, Jerusalem: Ariel.

10 In T. Carmi (ed. and trans.), 1981, *The Penguin Book of Hebrew Verse*, London: Penguin, p. 347.

11 In T. Carmi (ed. and trans.), 1981, *The Penguin Book of Hebrew Verse*, p. 347.

tion had been'. For both, the real search was for the living God using holy places to facilitate that search. Halevi's approach is not one that is reflected in contemporary Jewish understandings of the land. It is not the holy sites that matter, but the land itself and the city of Jerusalem. Yet there is in Judaism, it seems to me, some sense of the holiness of certain places. In biblical Hebrew the word *makom* (place) often has a numinous, divine quality; the supreme example is that of Jacob at Bethel.[12] Awaking from his dream, he cries, '*mah nora hamakom hazeh*' – 'how awesome is this place'. Moses at the burning bush is told to remove his shoes, 'because the place (*hamakom*) where you stand is holy ground'. In both stories the holiness of the place lies in the presence there of God; it is not intrinsically in the place. It is my experience today that Jewish people do not seek to go to the Temple Mount itself because they fear to walk where once was the Most Holy Place of the Temple, where dwelt the *Shekinah*.

Finally, a few thoughts on the world of the first century CE and pilgrimage. This was the world that Jesus of Nazareth inhabited and which nurtured and moulded him. It was also the century which led to the great definitive change in Judaism which eventually formed Rabbinic Judaism. At this time there were two types of pilgrimage, side by side: the Pilgrim Feasts were the community pilgrimage par excellence:

> Every year [Jesus'] parents went up to Jerusalem for the Feast of the Passover. When he was twelve, they went up to the Feast according to the custom.[13]

That was a 'going-up' pilgrimage, but there was also a 'going-inwards' one – a quest for Wisdom, a search for the inner meaning of ancient traditions. It was the world of midrash, a spiritual reading between the lines, of Torah. Jesus' own teaching reflects this and he had learned much at the feet of the great teachers of his day in the Temple courts. The inter-testamental literature speaks explicitly of this inner journeying:

> In my youth, before I began my pilgrimage,
> I sought wisdom openly in my prayers;
> On the Temple steps I sought her
> And I will search for her until the end.[14]

---

12 Gen. 28.

13 Luke 2.41–2.

14 Ben Sirach-Ecclus. 51.13. See J. Snaith, *Cambridge Bible Commentary on Ecclesiasticus* (Wisdom of Ben Sirach), Cambridge: Cambridge University Press.

There is much more of this in The Wisdom of Solomon where Wisdom is the guide for the 'unknown journey – the glorious wandering'.[15]

Dictionaries tend to define pilgrimage as 'a journey undertaken to visit sacred places'. And so it usually is, and not only by Jews and Christians but also for Muslims with Mecca and Hindus with Benares. But has today's pilgrimage become limited to 'shrine-as-goal'? The mobile Bible study? Excellent as it is and thrilling to go on pilgrimage to sacred sites, I have sought to show here that the site itself is not the goal. That site, deeply fascinating as it is, can in the end be a vehicle for a deeper encounter with the Eternity imaged by that place.

I end, as I began, with John Bunyan and words from *The Pilgrim's Progress*: 'My sword I give him that shall succeed me in pilgrimage.'

II Pilgrimage: A Journey Towards Holiness

Rachel Montagu

I was very moved when Beryl gave her paper to the group, particularly by her insistence that pilgrimage is a journey towards holiness and that one must not confuse holiness and holy places. In my response I want to explore my feelings about Jerusalem, that place of pilgrimage par excellence.

The first time that I visited Israel, I felt nothing particular on arrival, in contrast to my excitement a few years earlier when I had visited Greece and seen the country whose literature I had read so much about at school. My father had the classic feelings of home-coming when he first went to Israel, so for some years it was a joke between us that assimilation takes seven generations – I am the seventh generation of our family to be born in this country, and he is the less acculturated sixth. During the first few months of my two years studying in Jerusalem when I felt cut off from England, I had a painful sense that my feet were rootless, stranded at pavement level, unable to make contact with the earth below because I had cut myself off from where I belonged. I could not cope with the lack of continuity in the landscape and it became part of my feelings of alienation

---

15 Wisd. 10 and 18.

because of the lack of continuity with my own life in the UK. Jerusalem is full of modern architecture and full of archaeology, but there is not much in between; and what there is, I was unable to define and date in the automatic way in which one says 'Tudor' or 'Georgian'. However, soon I came to feel deeply happy and at home there and knew that I was being awakened to things that I could never have known about in Britain. I have happy memories of my summer in Greece. Sitting under an olive tree reading Homer while listening to the sheep baaing and the goats' bells chiming further down the valley was more enjoyable than reading it in an English library, and yet what I learned in Israel is profoundly more important to who I am.

Pilgrimage and journeying are the opposite of being utterly at home and yet now, seven generations or not, as a result of my time in Israel, I live with the classic Jewish sense of ambivalence about where I am really meant to be and where my roots are. The two years that I lived and studied in Jerusalem have left me with a sense that life there reaches more spiritual heights that other cities cannot reach. Walking around the streets of Jerusalem, buying falafel, doing my weekly shopping, getting on with life, I was sometimes aware of a feeling of irritation. How can this unsophisticated town in the mountains be the centre of the spiritual universe for three religions? Yet anyone who has spent time in Jerusalem has had moments of profound awareness that this place is on some level just that. As Yehudah Amichai writes in his *Poems of Jerusalem*:

> The air over Jerusalem
> is saturated with prayers and dreams
> like the air over industrial cities.
> It's hard to breathe.[16]

For many people this is centred on the *Kotel* (the Western Wall). I used to talk disapprovingly about Kotelmania (a variation on the classic Jerusalem madness, the craziness which hits some visitors to Jerusalem), those who rush to the *Kotel* when they first arrive in the city; visit it again before they leave and feel that it is the key place. Praying *minchah* (the afternoon service) at the *Kotel* once I had the profoundest inner sense that it is an irrelevance, holy but also a potential trap, a place that can become an idol. And yet I treasure some photos I took of doves nestling in the wall

---

16 Yehudah Amichai, 1987, *Poems of Jerusalem* (a bilingual edition), Tel Aviv: Schocken.

between the kvetlach, little folded prayers stuffed into the crevices of the stones, as I treasure memories of studying all night on *Shavuot*,[17] then walking through the old city, alive in the early dawn with the footsteps of hundreds doing the same, and joining one of the many services taking place in small groups right across the entire *Kotel* plaza. We were re-enacting, as far as anyone now can, the sense of pilgrimage to Jerusalem to celebrate one of the three Pilgrim Festivals. Last time I visited Israel I saw a group of mainly Ethiopian school children visiting the *Kotel* for their *mesibat siddur* (prayer book party). When Israeli school children first learn to read, they are given a prayer book as the best book with which to celebrate their new skill; they were singing Israeli songs about prayer, their teachers encouraging them; rationally I know all the problems about the Ethiopian Jews being acculturated from their own traditions into the Israeli melting-pot, and yet it was a lovely thing to see.

Visiting the holy, there can be a sense of panic at the nearness of the unholy; my brother told me that the first time he laid *tefillin* at the *Kotel*, he suddenly found himself unable to remember how to do up the straps across his hand, something he had done countless times before with no difficulty. Elie Wiesel's autobiography describes how feelings of distress from an unsuccessful flirtation meant he forgot for the first time to say his prayers and his remorse was deepened by the fact that this happened in Israel.[18] Another moment when I was aware of the difficulties of the relationship between pilgrimage to the land of our ancestors and the complexities of political reality was when visiting the West Bank. Our guide said, 'We are walking in the footsteps of Abraham between Bethel and Ai. Israel can never give up this land. It is a crucial part of our spiritual heritage.' Valuing that historical link is good: insisting on annexing the whole of the West Bank to Israel because of it could be national suicide.

Jerusalem is a city which delights the senses. Sight: a sudden view across to the sun-soaked city walls while taking one's shopping home or the sight of a Jerusalem stone wall, that indescribable shade of pinky-cream, glowing in the afternoon sun warms the heart. The brilliant enamel-bright light whose dazzling intensity made me feel I was living behind murky dark glasses for the first year after I returned to England. Taste: the array of vegetables in the market, huge round pitta marked from the oven and the

---

17 The Feast of Weeks or Pentecost, commemorating the gift of the Ten Commandments and commemorated by all-night study sessions.

18 Elie Wiesel, 1995, *All Rivers Run to the Sea*, London: HarperCollins, p. 180.

passion with which everyone insists that their particular favourite is the best falafel in town. Smell: the intensity of the smell of jasmine or pine resin as one walks about the city at night. Hearing: the many different chants one overhears as one passes the city's synagogues. The beauty of the chanting in the Armenian cathedral. The sound of the muezzin drifting over from East Jerusalem obscured during the day but audible during sleepless nights. Touch: the intensity with which both sun and rain fall on one's body, the jerking and jolting of the city buses fighting their way through the Jerusalem traffic.

Is the intensity of what it means to a Jew now to visit Jerusalem the result of 3,000 years of history, of saying 'Next Year in Jerusalem' as we complete the Passover seder, or is it because of what is happening in Jerusalem right now? More people are studying now in Jerusalem than ever did intensive Jewish study in the past. People who are renowned scholars in diaspora communities are mere beginners in the world of Jerusalem scholarship. 'The air of Jerusalem makes wise' – is it the years of history that gives Jerusalem its flavour or is it an overspill into the atmosphere of the passionate intensive learning that fills it now? Compare Jerusalem which does have this feeling of spiritual intensity with Safed, a small city in Galilee where Jewish mysticism flourished in the late Middle Ages. One can visit the cemetery, the graves of great scholars, and go on tours of the Safed synagogues; there are a few nice painted walls, a history of mysticism, piety and poetry which began within those walls and which still influences our prayer books and the world of Jewish ideas today. Yet Safed does not have the spiritual charge in the air that Jerusalem has – at least, I did not feel it there in the same way. Whereas Jerusalem, where learning continues and expands, resonates as a result.

Beryl mentions Jews visiting friends and family in Israel, but what does the status of Jerusalem as a place of pilgrimage, a place people visit, spend a study year or a sabbatical, do to those who live there? It can often make friendships difficult, for people who live in Jerusalem have known too many people who come for a year or so and then return to their place of origin. The comings and goings, welcomes and farewells, different significances their home has for others can be unsettling for their lives. Yehudah Amichai again:

Once I sat on the steps by a gate at David's tower. I placed my two heavy baskets at my side. A group of tourists was standing around their guide and I became their target marker. 'You see that man with the baskets? Just right of his head there's an arch from the Roman period. Just right of his head.' 'But he's moving, he's moving!' I said to myself: redemption will come only if their guide tells them, 'You see that arch from the Roman period? It's not important but next to it, left and down a bit, there sits a man who's bought fruit and vegetables for his family.'[19]

I have talked about Jerusalem – what about other holy journeys in my life? I think many who have experienced the Jewish-Christian-Muslim conferences in the Hedwig Dransfeld Haus, Bendorf, Germany, will have felt as I did, a sense of pilgrimage there. The difficulties of the journey – even after I had made the journey to Germany many times there remained the shock of seeing German railway lines from the road and thinking of the cattle cars that traversed them years before. At the conference, the intensity of the encounter with Christianity and Islam, the intensity of dialogue. Each time I went, there were some people with whom it was possible to talk in a very honest, very clear and intimate way about vital religious issues which there is never time to talk about in daily life at home in a way that gave a great sense of God's presence and transcended all the difficulties of language; the food and the unspeakable rows which the organization of the conference sabbath services often generated within the Jewish group, another clear example of nearness to great holiness generating unholiness.

With the Pilgrim Festivals, there is a sense of a cycle and circuit of the year. On *Simchat Torah* we read the end of Deuteronomy, then the beginning of Genesis so the cycle of reading remains unbroken. But we also read a prophetical portion from Joshua, the account of the settling of the land of Israel, so we complete and re-start our circuit of the Pentateuch while simultaneously entering the Jewish people's journey to the present. Some people have therefore defined the spiral rather than the circle as the characteristic shape-symbol of Jewish life. The language of the Passover *seder* incorporates this dissonance between where we are and the events the liturgy describes. We are told to think of ourselves as if we, rather than our distant ancestors, are redeemed and come out of Egypt. This does stretch the imagination to the utmost. Even acid jokes about pre-Passover spring cleaning being a form of slavery do not quite bridge the gap between here and now and there and then and liturgical re-enactment of exodus is hard

---

19 Yehudah Amichai, 1987, *Poems of Jerusalem*, p. 177.

to experience as liberation, as a walk to freedom, however hard one works at making the seder as intense as possible. The Pilgrim Festivals are a significant spiral for Jewish women in another way. In biblical times we can see from the story of Hannah that going on pilgrimage to Jerusalem was optional for women rather than an obligation. Beryl quotes Leviticus: three times a year all your males shall appear before the Eternal.[20] Hannah, Peninah and Peninah's children all join the pilgrimage described at the beginning of the book of Samuel but once Samuel was born Hannah remains at home with him during the family's annual pilgrimage until he has been weaned and can be left to serve in the shrine as she had promised.[21] To compel pregnant or newly delivered women to travel to Jerusalem would not have been to their benefit. But, exemption can become exclusion, or at least a question mark over participation. Instead what we see is either the tradition affirming women as part of the community and included in the purpose of the festival or women determined to count themselves in and succeeding in doing so. Women have always been specifically included in the Passover *seder*, order of service because they were included in the miracle of redemption, even if, as Lynne says in Chapter 7, their presence is not described in the traditional *haggadah*, Passover story book; the midrash even says that 'the Children of Israel were redeemed for the sake of their women'.[22] On other festivals, Orthodox Jewish women have adopted observances from which previous generations felt they were exempt and so to be discouraged from participating, for instance the blessing of the four species during the harvest festival Succot. 'Women should be encouraged to do so. Happy are the virtuous daughters of Israel; they seek to perform commandments and bless the Eternal for the privilege.'[23] In Progressive synagogues, the idea that the celebration of festivals is in any way different for men and women – apart from women being more likely to prepare the festival meals – would be seen as bizarre. The founding Zionist leader, Theodore Herzl said about the dream of returning to the land of Israel, 'If you truly want it, it will not remain wishful thinking.' Women have wanted to participate in these observances and this has been acknowledged and recognized. The Pilgrim

---

20 Exod. 23.17.

21 1 Sam. 2.22–4.

22 Babylonian Talmud *Sotah* 11b.

23 Getzel Ellinson, 1986, *Serving the Creator: A Guide to the Rabbinic Sources*, vol. 1, Jerusalem: World Zionist Organization, p. 92.

Festivals symbolize not only our encounter with God, our redemption, revelation and living under God's protection, but our circling upward into an increased inclusion in the religious life of Judaism.

Our journey as a group has reflected some of the wider issues in dialogue. Our communication with each other has been helped by a shared sense of indignation at the way in which our respective traditions and communities treat women. As a group of friends we have found a real holiness in the time we have spent talking together, giving us a chance to study texts with friends who understand them in a similar way and a community where we, who spend a lot of time supporting others in their religious learning and growth, can come to find some support for ourselves. Our own growth in ease of communication as a group is a pilgrimage whose significance should not be underestimated. There is a prayer for saying when going on a journey; asking for God's protection from any hazards on the route:

> May it be your Will, eternal God and God of our ancestors that just as our ancestors journeyed under the shelter of your wings, so may we walk in peace and reach our desired haven in life, joy and peace. Protect us from all danger and send blessing on the work of our hands. Grant us grace, lovingkindness and mercy in your eyes and the eyes of everyone we meet.

Further Reading

See the Bibliography section for full details on these titles.

Dan Bahat (ed.), *Twenty Centuries of Jewish Life in the Holy Land: The Forgotten Generations.*

David Burrell and Yehezkel Landau (eds), *Voices from Jerusalem: Jews and Christians Reflect on the Holy Land.*

John Eade and Michael Sallmow (eds), *Contesting the Sacred: The Anthropology of Christian Pilgrimage.*

Helen P. Fry, *Christian-Jewish Dialogue: A Reader*, Chapter 5.

Lawrence Hoffman (ed.) *The Land of Israel: Jewish Perspectives.*

Robert Wilken, *The Land Called Holy: Palestine in Christian History and Thought.*

[212]

13 The Future

Will our granddaughters need to write a sequel to this book?

In this book through the sharing of personal stories, the study of biblical texts and theological discussions our voices as women have brought a rich and particular perspective which can be transformative for the way that Jewish-Christian dialogue is carried out in the future. We have recorded our voices on a range of issues that are of relevance to us both as women and as Jews and Christians. In our experience, the mixed dialogue currently does not make space for women's issues and therefore one of the primary reasons for our meeting together is to bring those concerns to the forefront of the dialogue. Our dialogue has provided, and continues to provide, an opportunity for each of us to express our religious experiences as women and this empowers us to take our insights back to the wider Jewish-Christian dialogue. In this final chapter, we will issue an affirmation statement of seven points and then from each part of the book draw together some of the insights that challenge both the women's dialogue and the wider Jewish-Christian dialogue.

Over the last 50 years the churches have issued a number of statements on Jews and Judaism and a group of Jewish scholars have issued *Dabru Emet*. None of these statements has referred to women and the contribution of women either to their respective communities or to the Jewish-Christian dialogue. Such a statement is long overdue and our group hopes that the following statement which is issued as part of our concluding reflections may provide the impetus for those involved in Jewish-Christian dialogue on an institutional level to affirm or issue a similar statement.

Point 1: We affirm that the women in the New Testament and Christianity have faced struggles for identity, leadership and authority that are parallel to those faced by women in the Hebrew Bible and Judaism.

[213]

Point 2: We affirm that women in our traditions have been marginalized and silenced and we reclaim their voices as part of the chain of tradition.

Point 3: We affirm that women's interpretations of biblical texts are providing new insights that enrich both our traditions.

Point 4: We affirm the contribution that women have made and continue to make to Judaism and Christianity.

Point 5: We affirm that women's scholarship is making a significant contribution to theology, liturgy and historical studies.

Point 6: We affirm that Judaism and Christianity are incomplete without women as equal partners who have a full public role in the life of their communities.

Point 7: We affirm the voices of women within the Jewish-Christian dialogue as a crucial and distinct part of that dialogue.

Part 1

Major advances have been made in Christian theology regarding Judaism; however, one of the challenges that remain for us as women and as Jews and Christians is whether there is a Jewish theology of Christianity. A number of Jewish scholars have written a 'Jewish response' to Christianity, but these are in a minority within the overall advances which have been made in Jewish-Christian relations over the last five decades. More recently, the statement *Dabru Emet* from predominantly American Jewish scholars has made an important start in responding to Christianity in a positive way. In it, they affirmed that Jews and Christians worship the same God and that 'through Christianity hundreds of millions of people have entered into relationship with the God of Israel', and later in the statement, which is reproduced in full in the book *Christianity in Jewish Terms*, 'Jews can respect Christians' faithfulness to their revelation just as we expect Christians to respect our faithfulness to our revelation. Neither Jew nor Christian should be pressed into affirming the teaching of the other community.'

How would a Jewish theology of Christianity be framed? There needs to be an acceptance of the principle espoused in *Dabru Emet* and by Chief Rabbi Dr Jonathan Sacks in his milestone book *The Dignity of Difference* that God is to be found for Christians in Christianity and for Jews in Judaism. A Jewish theology of Christianity cannot ignore the person of Jesus as the central figure of Christian faith; and while Jews cannot accept any incarnational claims, their own experience of God through Judaism can help them recognize the intensity of devotion to God that Jesus has kindled in Christian believers. Jewish women are particularly effective at working in a cross-communal way without being impeded by divisional boundaries and therefore it is possible that any initial progress towards a Jewish theology of Christianity may spring from women's dialogue rather than from any institutional framework. It is important for Jewish women to develop a Jewish theology of Christianity in critical solidarity with Christian women. This is certainly one area where the cross-fertilization of religious perspectives is essential.

Feminist theology and gender studies have altered the landscape of theology and must be taken into account in any broad theological vision, including that of Jewish-Christian relations. In this respect, a number of scholars are bringing feminist insights into key areas, especially theology, liturgy and biblical studies. Jewish and Christian women working together to create a feminist theology of Judaism and Christianity may be able to develop further than women of either faith could alone. One of the recurrent issues raised in Chapter 3 on messiah and Chapters 6–8 on women and Scripture (Part 2) was how Christian feminists often blame Judaism for patriarchy and the oppression of women. In response to anti-Judaism, these chapters addressed how problematic it is to see Jesus as the great liberator of women. However, one of the ongoing challenges for Christian feminist writers is how to make sense of Jesus' uniqueness in a way that does not contrast him with the Judaism of his day and in so doing, cast Judaism in an inaccurately negative light, a point which the feminist Judith Plaskow has raised. In Chapter 7 on Mary Magdalene Rachel raised a parallel point with regard to the image of the Pharisees in Christian teaching. Why is it necessary for Christians to see Christianity as better than Judaism rather than simply as good?

Holocaust studies have been significantly altered by the recent development of taking more seriously women's experiences during and after the Holocaust. The Holocaust is still not fully understood by either Jews or

Christians and may never be; however, discussing it together in our group has helped us as individuals to develop our understandings and responses, both educationally and personally. Lynne raised the painful and difficult question of whether Christians can claim the Holocaust as part of 'their story'. It is a serious question that needs to be addressed as part of the future of Jewish-Christian dialogue.

Part 2

Studying texts is a traditional religious activity in both faiths and for our group, studying texts with other knowledgeable women has blended traditional exegesis with new insights that we would not have found if we had studied only within our own faith. We have reclaimed the voices of silenced women within the Bible: Dinah, Mary Magdalene and women prophets. In so doing, their prophetic and apostolic significance has been resurrected. We have begun our textual studies by focusing on the stories of women because it is important to reclaim these women first before moving to other texts. In the future we can begin to look at wider texts, some of which may not include women's stories, for example the book of Leviticus. One of the main challenges that remain from our discussions, that is also missing from the wider dialogue, is whether Jews can accept Christian biblical interpretation as a legitimate reading of the text, even if they do not agree with it. We have studied New Testament texts together; however, the Jewish women have felt uncomfortable about giving a 'Jewish reading' of a text which is not part of their tradition. More explorations will be made in our group in the future about what it means to give a specifically Jewish reading of the New Testament and how that differs from Jews just commenting on the text. The challenges raised by reading biblical texts together are not one-sided. Can Christians also move towards an acceptance that Jewish interpretations of the Scriptures are not only 'interesting' because they explain the roots of Christian faith, but are legitimate even if Christians ultimately disagree with that interpretation? This is an area where some of the Christian women in our group are pushing the boundaries of current understandings of how we accept as valid each other's exegesis and interpretative traditions.

Part 3

In the Christian writings in this section, there was a clear sense of what Christians have learnt from Jewish liturgy; particularly an appreciation of the Jewish roots of Christian faith. One of the key areas for Jews to discuss with Christians is: what can Jews learn from Christian liturgy? Is it only a one-way process with Christians clear about what they gain from Jewish liturgy but with little possibility of reciprocal benefit? We have gained confidence to affirm a more public role for ourselves within our communities, particularly in those which do not allow for women's ministry or institutional opportunities. Our dialogue has provided an opportunity to articulate experiences and to share common human understanding – our commonality as women rather than being separated by our different traditions. Such encounter has richly deepened our own faith and spirituality as women. In the future, we will discuss the following topics: God, Israel, menopause, suffering, sexuality, Mary the mother of Jesus, purity and impurity, and feasting and fasting.

We began this chapter by asking whether our granddaughters would need to write such a book on women's voices within Jewish-Christian dialogue. The experience of our particular women's group has shown that while progress is being made by women in a number of areas of scholarship, this dialogue is in its infancy and the voices of women will need to continue to be heard. How do we make the changes that are necessary for women's voices to be heard in the wider Jewish-Christian dialogue? Religious change happens when we call for that change in a context that is willing to hear and respond to that call. Will sufficient advances have been made in our generation for our granddaughters and the daughters of our students for women's voices to be so well heard within the wider dialogue that there is no longer a need for a separate women's dialogue? Or will women still need, or simply enjoy, having a separate space and opportunity to hear each other's voice?

Glossary of Terms

agunot married women whose husbands refuse to divorce them so they are 'tied'

Amidah a set of prayers said in all the Jewish daily sabbath and festival services

apocalyptic ideas or biblical books which reveal the mysteries of the transcendent heavenly world

deicide killing God

ecclesiology the doctrine of the Church

epistemology knowledge

eschatology relating to the End Times

exegesis interpretation

Haggadah the narrative recited for the Passover

Halakah/halachah Jewish law

Hasidim ultra-Orthodox Jews

havdalah ceremony that ends the sabbath

kaddish the mourner's prayer

kashrut food laws

Lilith mythic figure, Adam's first wife

midrash commentary

Mishnah the first rabbinic code, written around 200 CE

mitzvah commandment

mohel one who carries out circumcision

Old Testament Pseudepigrapha books not included in the canon of the Old Testament

rabbinic literature the codification of Jewish Law by the rabbis after the destruction of the Temple in 70 CE

shabbat the sabbath

Shavuot the festival which celebrates the giving of the Ten Commandments to Moses on Mount Sinai

Shechinah God's indwelling presence
Simchat Torah festival called the Rejoicing of the Torah
Talmud the name given to two great compilations of academic discussions on Jewish Law called the Babylonian Talmud and the Jerusalem Talmud
Targum Aramaic translation of the Bible
Tisha b'Av mourning for the destruction of the Temple
Torah meaning 'teaching', the first five books of Moses
Yom Kippur the Day of Atonement

Bibliography

Abrams, Judith Z., 1995, *The Women of the Talmud*, New Jersey: Jason Aronson.

Adelman, Penina, 1986, *Miriam's Well*, New York: Biblio Press.

Adler, Rachel, 1983, 'The Jew Who Wasn't There: Halakhah and the Jewish Woman,' in Susannah Heschel (ed.), *On Being a Jewish Feminist: A Reader*, New York: Schocken Books.

Althaus-Reid, Marcella Maria, 2002, 'Queer I Stand: Doing Feminist Theology outside the Borders of Colonial Decency', in Charlotte Methuen and Angela Berlis (eds), *The End of Liberation? Liberation in the End? Feminist Theory, Feminist Theology and their Political Implications*, Louven: Peeters Publishers.

Amichai, Yehudah, 1987, *Poems of Jerusalem* (a bilingual edition), Tel Aviv: Schocken.

Antonelli, Judith S., 1995, *In the Image of God: A Feminist Commentary on the Torah*, New Jersey: Jason Aronson.

Appignanesi, Lisa, 1999, *Losing the Dead: A Family Memoir*, London: Chatto.

Appignanesi, Lisa, 2002, untitled essay in Ben Barkow, Katherine Klinger and Melissa Rosenbaum (eds), *Storeys of Memory*, London: The Wiener Library.

Aschkenasy, Nehama, 1994, *Eve's Journey: Feminine Images in Hebraic Literary Tradition*, Detroit: Wayne State University Press.

Ashton, Diane and Ellen Umansky (eds), 1992, *Four Centuries of Jewish Women's Spirituality*, Boston: Beacon Press.

Bach, Alice (ed.), 1999, *Women in the Hebrew Bible*, New York: Routledge.

Baggley John, 1987, *Doors of Perception: Icons and their Spiritual Significance*, Oxford: Mowbray.

Bahat, Dan (ed.), 1976, *Twenty Centuries of Jewish Life in the Holy Land: The Forgotten Generations*, Jerusalem: Ariel.

Baldovin, John F., 1991, 'Christian Worship to the Reformation', in Paul F. Bradshaw and Lawrence A. Hoffman (eds), *The Making of Jewish and Christian Worship*, Indiana: University of Notre Dame Press.

Bauckham, Richard, 2002, *Gospel Women: Studies of the Named Women in the Gospels*, London: Continuum.

Bayfield, Tony, Sidney Brichto and Eugene Fisher (eds), 2001, *He Kissed Him and They Wept*, London: SCM Press.

Bayfield, Tony, 2000, 'Response', in Marcus Braybrooke, *Christian-Jewish Dialogue: The Next Steps*, London: SCM Press.

Bechtel, Lynn M., 1994, 'What if Dinah is Not Raped?', in *The Journal for the Study of the Old Testament*, 62, p. 19–36.

Behar, Ruth and Deborah Gordon, 1995, *Women Writing Culture*, Berkeley: University of California Press.

Belenky, M. F., B. M. Clinchy, N. R. Goldberger and J. M. Tarule, 1997, *Women's Ways of Knowing*, New York: Basic Books.

Berger, David, 2001, *The Rebbe, The Messiah and the Scandal of Orthodox Indifference*, Littman Library.

Boer, E. de, 2000, 'Mary Magdalene and the Disciple Jesus Loved', in *Lectio Difficilior – European Electronic Journal for Feminist Exegesis* at www.lectio.unibe. ch/00_1/m-forum.htm.

Boer, E. de, 1996, *Mary Magdalene: Beyond the Myth*, London: SCM Press.

Bouyer, Louis, 1968, *Eucharist*, Notre Dame: Notre Dame Press.

Boyarin, Daniel, 2004, *Border Lines: The Partition of Judaeo-Christianity*, Pennsylvania: University of Pennsylvania Press.

Boyarin, Daniel, 1998, 'Gender', in Mark C. Taylor (ed.), *Critical Terms for Religious Studies*, Chicago: University of Chicago Press, p. 117–35.

Boyarin, Daniel, 1994, *Intertextuality and the Reading of Midrash*, Bloomington: Indiana University Press.

Boys, Mary C., 2000, *Has God Only One Blessing?*, New York: Paulist Press.

Bradshaw, Paul F. and Lawrence A. Hoffman (eds), 1991, *The Making of Jewish and Christian Worship*, Indiana: University of Notre Dame Press.

Braybrooke, Marcus, 2000, *Christian-Jewish Dialogue: The Next Steps*, London: SCM Press.

Braybrooke, Marcus, 1990, *Time to Meet: Towards a Deeper Relationship between Jews and Christians*, London: SCM Press.

Brenner, Athalya (ed.), 1998, *Genesis: A Feminist Companion to the Bible*, Sheffield: Sheffield Academic Press.

Brenner, A. and C. Fontaine, 1997, *Reading the Bible: Approaches, Methods and Strategies*, Sheffield: Sheffield Academic Press.

Brenner, Rachel Feldhay, 1997, *Writing as Resistance*, Pennsylvania: The Pennsylvania State University Press.

Brooten, Bernadette, 1982, *Women Leaders in the Ancient Synagogue*, Brown Judaic Studies, 36, Atlanta: Scholars Press.

Brown, Raymond, Joseph Fitzmyer and Robert Murphy (eds), 1990, *The New Jerome Biblical Commentary*, London: Geoffrey Chapman.

Brown, Raymond, 1966, *The Gospel According to John*, London: Geoffrey Chapman.

Buber, Martin, 1958, 2nd ed., *I and Thou*, Edinburgh: T&T Clark.

Büchmann, Christina and Celina Spiegel (eds), 1994, *Out of the Garden: Women Writers on the Bible*, London: Harper Collins.

Burns, Sharon, 1990, 'The Beginnings of Christian Liturgy in Judaism', in Eugene

Fisher (ed.), *The Jewish Roots of Christian Liturgy*, New York: Paulist Press.

Burrell, David and Yehezkel Landau (eds), 1992, *Voices from Jerusalem: Jews and Christians Reflect on the Holy Land*, New York: Paulist Press.

Butler, Judith, 1991, 'Imitation and Gender Insubordination', in D. Fuss (ed.), *Inside Out*, London: Routledge.

Butler, Judith, 1990, *Gender Trouble: Feminism and the Subversion of Identity*, London: Routledge.

Byrne, Lavinia, 2001, *The Journey is My Home*, London: Hodder & Stoughton.

Cantor, Aviva, 1995, *Jewish Women/Jewish Men: The Legacy of Patriarchy in Jewish Life*, San Francisco: HarperSanFrancisco.

Carmi, T. (ed. and trans.), 1981, *The Penguin Book of Hebrew Verse*, London: Penguin.

Cavaletti, Sofia, 1990, 'The Jewish Roots of Christian Liturgy', in Eugene Fisher (ed.), *The Jewish Roots of Christian Liturgy*, New York: Paulist Press.

Charlesworth, James (ed.), 1991, *Jesus' Jewishness: Exploring the Place of Jesus Within Early Judaism*, New York: Crossroad.

Charlesworth, James (ed.), 1992, *Messiah: Developments in Earliest Judaism and Christianity*, Minneapolis: Fortress Press.

Christ, Carol and Judith Plaskow (eds), 1992, *Womenspirit Rising: A Feminist Reader in Religion*, London: Harper Collins.

Clemens, Thomas and Michael Wyschogrod (eds), 1987, *Understanding Scripture: Explorations of Jewish and Christian Traditions of Interpretation*, New York: Paulist Press.

Clifford, Paula, 2001, *Women Doing Excellently: Biblical Women and their Successors*, Norwich: Canterbury Press.

Cohen, Jeremy (ed.), 1991, *Essential Papers on Judaism and Christianity in Late Antiquity to the Reformation*, New York: New York University Press.

Cohn-Sherbok, Dan, 2002, *Holocaust Theology: A Reader*, Exeter: University of Exeter Press.

Cornwell, J., 1999, *Hitler's Pope*, London: Viking.

Crawford, Robert, 2000, *The Holocaust Exhibition at the Imperial War Museum*, London: The Imperial War Museum.

Crossan, John and Jonathan Reed, 2001, *Excavating Jesus: Beneath the Stones, Behind the Texts*, London: SPCK.

Crossan, John, 1994, *Jesus: A Revolutionary Biography*, San Francisco: Harper Collins.

Crossan, John, 1991, *The Historical Jesus*, Edinburgh: T&T Clark.

Cunningham, Philip A., 1995, *Proclaiming Shalom: Lectionary Introductions to Foster the Catholic and Jewish Relationship*, Collegeville: The Liturgical Press.

Dallavalle, Nancy, 1998, 'Toward a Theology that is Catholic and Feminist: Some Basic Issues', in *Modern Theology*, 14, 4, p. 535–53.

Daly, Mary, 1988, *Webster's First New Intergalactic Wickedary of the English Language*, London: The Women's Press.

Dash, Joan, 1979, *Summoned to Jerusalem: The life of Henrietta Szold*, New York: Harper & Row.

Daube, David, *He That Cometh*, St Paul's Lecture, The London Diocesan Council for Christian-Jewish Understanding.

Davies, J., 1988, *Pilgrimage Yesterday and Today. Why? Where? How?*, London: SCM Press.

Diamant, Anita, 1997, *The Red Tent*, New York: Picador.

Donnelly, Doris *et al.*, 2001, *Jesus: A Colloquium from the Holy Land*, New York: Continuum.

Dorff, Elliott, 2001, 'Understanding Election', in Tony Bayfield, Sidney Brichto and Eugene Fisher (eds), *He Kissed Him and They Wept*, London: SCM Press.

Dunn, James, 1992, 'Messianic Ideas and Their Influence on the Jesus of History', in James Charlesworth (ed.), *Messiah: Developments in Earliest Judaism and Christianity*, Minneapolis: Fortress Press.

Dunn, James, 1991, *The Partings of the Ways Between Christianity and Judaism and their Significance for the Character of Christianity*, London: SCM Press.

Eade, John and Michael Sallmow (eds), 1991, *Contesting the Sacred: The Anthropology of Christian Pilgrimage*, London: Routledge.

Eisenstadt, O., 2001, 'Making Room for the Hebrew: Luther, Dialectics and the Shoah', in *Journal of the American Academy of Religion*, September, 69(3), p. 551–75.

Ellinson, Getzel, 1986, *Serving the Creator: A Guide to the Rabbinic Sources*, vol. 1, Jerusalem: World Zionist Organization.

Elper, Ora Wiskind and Susan Handelman, 2000, *Torah of the Mothers: Contemporary Jewish Women Read Classical Jewish Texts*, New York: Urim Publications.

Feld, Merle, 1992, 'We All Stood Together', in Diane Ashton and Ellen Umansky (eds), *Four Centuries of Jewish Women's Spirituality*, Boston: Beacon Press.

Finkelstein, Louis, 1975, *Akiva: Scholar, Saint and Martyr*, New York: Atheneum.

Fisher, Eugene (ed.), 1990, *The Jewish Roots of Christian Liturgy*, New York: Paulist Press.

Flannery, A. (ed.), 1992 rev. ed., *Vatican Council II – The Conciliar and Post Conciliar Documents*, Dublin: Dominican Publications.

Frankiel, Tamar, 1990, *The Voice of Sarah: Feminine Spirituality and Traditional Judaism*, New York: Biblio Press.

Frankl, V., 1984, *Man in Search of Meaning*, New York: Washington Square Press.

Fredriksen, Paula and Adele Reinhartz (eds), 2002, *Jesus, Judaism and Christian Anti-Judaism: Reading the New Testament after the Holocaust*, Louisville: Westminster John Knox Press.

Fredriksen, Paula, 2000, *Jesus of Nazareth King of the Jews: A Jewish Life and the Emergence of Christianity*, New York: Knopf.

Friedlander, Albert H., 1999 (revised), *Out of the Whirlwind: A Reader of Holocaust Literature*, New York: UAHC Press.

Fry, Helen P., 2002, 'Women's Dialogue, Christology and Liturgy', in Edward Kessler, John Pawlikowski and Judith Banki (eds), *Jews and Christians in Conversation: Crossing Cultures and Generations*, Cambridge: Orchard Academic.

Fry, Helen P., 1999, 'The Future of Christian-Jewish Relations', in Dan Cohn-Sherbok (ed.), *The Future of Jewish-Christian Dialogue*, Lewiston: Edwin Mellen Press.

Fry, Helen P., 1996, *Christian-Jewish Dialogue: A Reader*, Exeter: University of Exeter Press.

Fry, Helen P., 1996, *Converting Jews? From a Mission to Jews to a Mission with Jews*, unpublished PhD thesis, Exeter: University of Exeter.

Frymer-Kensky, Tikva, 2002, *Reading the Women of the Bible: A New Interpretation of Their Stories*, New York: Schocken Books.

Frymer-Kensky, Tikva *et al.*, 2000, *Christianity in Jewish Terms*, Colorado: Westview Press.

Fuchs, Esther, 1999, *Women and the Holocaust: Narrative and Representation*, New York: University Press of America.

Furlong, Monica, 1993, 'The Heart in Pilgrimage', in *The Tablet*, 6 March.

Fuss, D. (ed.), 1991, *Inside Out*, London: Routledge.

Geffen, Rela (ed.), 1993, *Celebration and Renewal: Rites of Passage in Judaism*, Philadelphia: Jewish Publication Society.

Gelerenter-Liebowitz, Shoshana, 1992, 'Growing Up Lubavitch', in Susan Grossman and Rivka Haut (eds), *Daughters of the King: Women and the Synagogue*, Philadelphia: The Jewish Publication Society.

Getty-Sullivan, Mary Ann, 2001, *Women in the New Testament*, Collegeville: The Liturgical Press.

Gilligan, Carol, 1993, *In a Different Voice*, Cambridge, Mass: Harvard University Press.

Ginzberg, Louis, 1947 ed., *The Legends of the Jews*, Philadelphia: Jewish Publication Society.

Goitein, S. D., in *The Jewish Quarterly Review*, 43, 1952/3, p. 57–76.

Gordon, Esther, 2003, *The Mass Then and Now*, London: St Paul's.

Gorenberg, Gershom, 2000, *The End of Days: Fundamentalism and the Struggle for the Temple Mount*, New York: The Free Press.

Gottlieb, Lynn, 1995, *She Who Dwells Within: A Feminist Vision of a Renewed Judaism*, San Francisco: HarperSanFrancisco.

Greenberg, Blu, 1981, *On Women and Judaism*, Philadelphia: Jewish Publication Society.

Grossman, Susan and Rivka Haut (eds), 1992, *Daughters of the King: Women and the Synagogue*, Philadelphia: The Jewish Publication Society.

[225]

Hampson, Daphne (ed.), 1996, *Swallowing a Fishbone? Feminist Theologians Debate Christianity*, London: SPCK.

Haraway, Donna, 1991, 'Situated Knowledge: The Science Question in Feminism and the Privilege of Partial Perspective', in Donna Haraway (ed.), *Simians, Cyborgs and Women*, London: Free Association Books.

Hartman, David, 1993, *Epistles of Maimonides: Crisis and Leadership and Discussions*, Philadelphia: The Jewish Publication Society.

Hebblethwaite, Margaret, 1994, *Six New Gospels*, London: Geoffrey Chapman.

Heine, Heinrich, 1823, 'Almansor. Eine Tragödie', in *Tragödien, nebst einem lyrischen Intermezzo*, Berlin: Ferdinand Dümmler.

Henry, Sondra and Emily Taitz, 1983, *Written Out of History: Our Jewish Foremothers*, New York: Biblio Press.

Heschel, Abraham J., 1962, *The Prophets*, Philadelphia: Jewish Publication Society of America.

Heschel, Susannah, 2003, 'Judaism', in Arvind Sharma and Katherine K. Young (eds), *Her Voice Her Faith: Women Speak on World Religions*, Colorado: Westview Press.

Heschel, Susannah (ed.), 1982, *On Being a Jewish Feminist: A Reader*, New York: Schocken Books.

Hilton, Michael, 1994, *The Christian Effect on Jewish Life*, London: SCM Press.

Hilton, Michael and Gordian Marshall, 1988, *The Gospels and Rabbinic Judaism*, London: SCM Press.

Hoffman, Lawrence, 2001, 'Does God Remember? A Liturgical Theology of Memory', in Michael Signer (ed.), *Memory and History in Christianity and Judaism*, Indiana: University of Notre Dame Press.

Hoffman, Lawrence A., 1987, *Beyond the Text: A Holistic Approach to Liturgy*, Indianapolis: Indiana University Press.

Hoffman, Lawrence (ed.), 1986, *The Land of Israel: Jewish Perspectives*, Notre Dame: Notre Dame Press.

Holmgren, Fredrick and Herman Schaalman (eds), 1995, *Preaching Biblical Texts: Expositions by Jewish and Christian Scholars*, Grand Rapids: Eerdmans.

Holtz, B., 1984, *Back to the Sources: Reading the Classic Jewish Texts*, New York: Touchstone.

Horbury, William, 1998, *Jewish Messianism and the Cult of Christ*, London: SCM Press.

Horsley, Richard, 1993, *Jesus and the Spiral of Violence: Popular Jewish Resistance in Roman Palestine*, Minneapolis: Fortress Press.

Hunt, E. D., 1982, *Holyland Pilgrimage in the late Roman Empire. AD 312–460*, Oxford: Clarendon.

Hyman, N., 1997, *Biblical Women in the Midrash: A Sourcebook*, Northvale.

Isaac, Jules, 1964, *The Teaching of Contempt: Christian Roots of Anti-Semitism*, New York: Holt Reinhart Winston.

Jacobs, Louis, 1973, *A Jewish Theology*, London: Darton, Longman & Todd.

Jeansonne, Sharon Pace, 1990, *The Women of Genesis: From Sarah to Potiphar's Wife*, Minneapolis: Fortress Press.

Jeremias, Joachim, 1966, *The Eucharistic Words of Jesus*, London: SCM Press.

Josipovici, G., 1998, *The Book of God*, New Haven: Yale University Press.

Kellenbach, Katharina von, 1994, *Anti-Judaism in Feminist Religious Writings*, Atlanta: Scholars Press.

Kessler, Edward, John Pawlikowski and Judith Banki (eds), 2002, *Jews and Christians in Conversation: Crossing Cultures and Generations*, Cambridge: Orchard Academic.

King, K. L., no date, 'Women in Ancient Christianity: The New Discoveries', page 4 at: www.pbs.org/wgbh/pages/frontline/shows/religion/first/women.html.

Koltun, Elizabeth (ed.), 1976, *The Jewish Woman: New Perspectives*, New York: Schocken Books.

Kraemer, Ross S. and Mary Rose D'Angelo (eds), 1999, *Women and Christian Origins*, Oxford: Oxford University Press.

Landau, Ronnie S., 1990, *Studying the Holocaust, Issues, Readings and Documents*, London: Routledge.

Leibowitz, N., 1996, *New Studies in Bereshit*, Jerusalem: Ha-Omanim Press.

Levine, Amy-Jill with Marianne Blickenstaff (ed.), 2001, *A Feminist Companion to Matthew*, Sheffield: Sheffield Academic Press.

Levine, Amy-Jill, 2001, 'Discharging Responsibility: Matthean Jesus, Biblical Law and the Haemorrhaging Woman', in Amy-Jill Levine with Marianne Blickenstaff (ed.), *A Feminist Companion to Matthew*, Sheffield: Sheffield Academic Press.

Levine, Amy-Jill, 1996, 'Second Temple Judaism, Jesus and Women: Yeast of Eden', in Athalya Brenner (ed.), *A Feminist Companion to the Hebrew Bible in the New Testament*, Sheffield: Sheffield Academic Press.

Levine, Amy-Jill (ed.), 1991, *Women Like This: New Perspectives on Jewish Women in the Greco-Roman World*, Atlanta: Scholars Press.

Levine, Elizabeth Resnick (ed.), *A Ceremonies Sampler: New Rites, Celebrations and Observances of Jewish Women*, San Diego: Woman's Institute for Continuing Jewish Education.

Lindbeck, George, 2000, 'Postmodern Hermeneutics and Jewish-Christian Dialogue', in Tikva Frymer-Kensky *et al.*, *Christianity in Jewish Terms*, Colorado: Westview Press.

Linden, Ruth, 1993, *Making Stories, Making Selves*, Columbus: Ohio State University Press.

Litvin, Baruch, 1987, *The Sanctity of the Synagogue, the Case for Mechitzah: Separation between Men and Women in the Synagogue*, New York, Ktav.

Loades, Ann (ed.), 1990, *Feminist Theology: A Reader*, London: SPCK.

Long, Asphodel, 1991, 'Anti-Judaism in Britain', in *Journal of Feminist Studies in Religion*, vol. 7, no. 2, p. 125–33.

Long, Haniel, 1969, *The Marvellous Adventures of Cabesa da Vaca*, London: Souvenir Press.

McCaffry, A., 1993, 'The Priesthood of the Teacher', in P. Jarvis and N. Walters (eds), *Adult Education and Theological Interpretation*, Malabar, Florida: Krieger Publishing Company.

McCarthy, K., 1996, 'Women's Experience as a Hermeneutical Key to a Christian Theology of Religions', in *Studies in Interreligious Dialogue*, 6 (2), p. 163–73.

McCauley, Deborah, 1988, 'Nostra Aetate and the New Jewish-Christian Feminist Dialogue', in Roger Brooks (ed.), *Unanswered Questions*, Notre Dame: University of Notre Dame Press.

McCauley, Deborah and Annette Daum, 1983, 'Jewish-Christian Feminist Dialogue: A Wholistic Vision', in *Union Seminary Quarterly Review*, vol. 38.

McEwan, Dorothea and Myra Poole, 2003, *Making All Things New: Women's Ordination, A Catalyst for Change in the Catholic Church*, London: Canterbury Press.

Magonet, Jonathan, 1991, *A Rabbi's Bible*, London: SCM Press.

Martini, Carlo-Maria, 1989, *The Woman Among her People: A Spiritual Journey into the Planet Woman*, London: St Paul's.

Meyerhoff, B., 1978, *Number Our Days*, New York: E. P. Dutton.

Meyers, Carol, Toni Craven and Ross Kraemer (eds), 2000, *Women in Scripture*, Grand Rapids: Eerdmans.

Montagu, Rachel, 2000, 'Women, Prayer and Ritual in the Bible', in Sylvia Rothschild and Sybil Sheridan (eds), *Taking up the Timbrel: The Challenge of Creating Ritual for Jewish Women Today*, London: SCM Press.

Montagu, Rachel, 1996, 'Anti-Judaism in Christian Feminist Theology', in Jonathan Romain (ed.), *Renewing the Vision: Rabbis Speak out on Modern Jewish Issues*, London: SCM Press.

Montagu, Rachel, 1987, 'With God-like Struggles I have Wrestled with My Sister and Prevailed', *European Judaism* 87:1.

Morton, N., 1985, *The Journey Is Home*, Boston: Beacon Press.

Munro, Eleanor, 1987, *On Glory Roads: A Pilgrim's Book About Pilgrimage*, New York: Thames & Hudson.

Murray, Robert, 1991, 'Revelation (Dei Verbum)', in Adrian Hastings (ed.), *Modern Catholicism: Vatican II and After*, London: SPCK.

Ner David, Haviva, 2000, *Life on the Fringes: A Feminist Journey Toward Traditional Rabbinic Ordination*, London: JFL Books.

Neusner, Jacob, 1984, *Messiah in Context: Israel's History and Destiny in Formative Judaism*, Philadelphia: Fortress Press.

Newsom, C. A. and S. H. Ringe (eds), 1992, *The Women's Bible Commentary*, London: SPCK.

Novick, Peter, 1999, *The Holocaust in Collective Memory*, London: Bloomsbury.

Ofer, Dalia and Lenore Weitzman (eds), 1998, *Women in the Holocaust*, New Haven: Yale University Press.

Oppenheimer, Aharon, 1997, 'Leadership and Messianism', in Henning Graf Reventlow (ed.), *Eschatology in the Bible and in Jewish and Christian Tradition*, Sheffield: Sheffield Academic Press.

Orenstein, Debra (ed.), 1998, *Lifecycles: Jewish Women on Life Passages and Personal Milestones*, vol. 1, Woodstock: Jewish Lights.

Orenstein, Debra and Jane Litman (eds), 1997, *Lifecycles: Jewish Women on Biblical Themes in Contemporary Life*, Vermont: Jewish Lights Publishing.

Oxford Dictionary of the Christian Church, Oxford: OUP, 1983.

Papacostaki, Maria and Harry Brod, 1991, 'Weaning Ceremony', in Elizabeth Resnick Levine (ed.), *A Ceremonies Sampler: New Rites, Celebrations and Observances of Jewish Women*, San Diego: Woman's Institute for Continuing Jewish Education, p. 39–41.

Pavlov, Holly, 2000, *Mirrors of Our Lives: Reflections of Women in Tanach*, Southfield: Targum Press.

Pawlilowski, John and Hayim Goren Perelmuter, 2000, *Reinterpreting Revelation and Tradition: Jews and Christians in Conversation*, Wisconsin: Sheed & Ward.

Pawlilowski, John, 1982, *Christ in the Light of the Jewish-Christian Dialogue*, New York: Paulist Press.

Peskowitz, Miriam and Laura Levitt (eds), 1997, *Judaism since Gender*, London: Routledge.

Petuchowski, Jakob, 1972, *Understanding Jewish Prayer*, New York: Ktav.

Plaskow, Judith, 1991, 'Feminist Anti-Judaism and the Christian God', in *Journal of Feminist Studies in Religion*, vol. 7, no. 2.

Plaskow, Judith and Carol Christ (eds), 1989, *Weaving the Visions: Patterns in Feminist Spirituality*, London: Harper Collins.

Plaskow, Judith, 1983, 'The Right Question is Theological', in Susannah Heschel (ed.), *On Being a Jewish Feminist: A Reader*, New York: Schocken Books.

Plaut, W. G., 1967, *The Torah*, New York: Union of American Hebrew Congregations.

Porter, Jack Nusan (ed.), 1995, *Women in Chains: A Sourcebook on the Agunah*, New Jersey: Jason Aronson.

Primavesi, Anne, 1991, *From Apocalypse to Genesis*, London: Continuum.

Prior, Michael, 2002, 'Ethnic Cleansing and the Bible: A Moral Critique', in *Holy Land Studies*, vol. 1, no. 1, p. 37–59.

Pui-Lan, Kwok, 1995, *Discovering the Bible in the Non-Biblical World*, Maryknoll: Orbis Books.

Pui-Lan, K. and Elisabeth Schüssler Fiorenza (eds), 1998, *Women's Sacred Scriptures: Concilium 1998/3*, London: SCM Press.

Raphael, Melissa, 2003, *The Female Face of God in Auschwitz*, London: Cassell.
Raphael, Melissa, 1999, 'When God Beheld God', in *Feminist Theology*, vol. 21.
Ricci, C., 1994, *Mary Magdalene and Many Others*, Minneapolis: Fortress Press.
Rittner, Carol and John Roth, 1993, *Different Voices: Women and the Holocaust*, New York: Paragon House.
Rittner, Carol and John Roth (eds), 1991, *Memory Offended*, New York: Praeger.
Roberts, M., 1984, *The Wild Girl*, London: Methuen.
Rosenzweig, Franz, 1994 ed., 'Scripture and Luther', in Martin Buber and Franz Rosenzweig, *Scripture and Tradition*, Bloomington: Indiana Press (first published 1926).
Roth, Joel, 1988, in Simon Greenberg (ed.), *The Ordination of Women as Rabbis: Studies and Responsa*, New York: Jewish Theological Seminary.
Rothschild, Sylvia and Sybil Sheridan (eds), 2000, *Taking up the Timbrel: The Challenge of Creating Ritual for Jewish Women Today*, London: SCM Press.
Rothschild, Sylvia, 1994, 'Undermining the Pillars of the Women's Gallery', in Sybil Sheridan (ed.), *Hear Our Voice: Women Rabbis Tell Their Stories*, London: SCM Press.
Ruether, Rosemary Radford, 1987, 'Feminism and the Jewish-Christian Dialogue', in John Hick (ed.), *The Myth of Christian Uniqueness*, London: SCM Press.
Ruether, Rosemary Radford, 1981, *To Change the World: Christology and Cultural Criticism*, London: SCM Press.
Ruether, Rosemary Radford, 1974, *Faith and Fratricide*, New York: Seabury Press.

Sacks, Jonathan, 2002, *The Dignity of Difference: How to Avoid the Clash of Civilisations*, London: Continuum.
Sanders, E. P., 1993, *The Historical Figure of Jesus*, London: Penguin.
Sanders, E. P., 1985, *Jesus and Judaism*, London: SCM Press.
Sandmel, David, Rosann Catalano and Christopher Leighton (eds), 2001, *Irreconcilable Differences?*, Colorado: Westview Press.
Santayana, George, 1905, *The Life of Reason*, vol. I:12, New York: Scribners.
Sarah, Elizabeth, 1994, 'Rabbiner Regina Jonas 1902–1944: Missing link in a broken chain', in Sybil Sheridan (ed.), *Hear Our Voices: Women Rabbis Tell their Stories*, London: SCM Press.
Schiff, Hilda (ed.), 1995, *Holocaust Poetry*, London: HarperCollins.
Schneiders, Sandra, 1999, *The Revelatory Text: Interpreting the New Testament as Sacred Scripture*, Collegeville: The Liturgical Press.
Schneiders, Sandra, 1991, *The Revelatory Text: Interpreting the New Testament as Sacred Scripture*, San Francisco: Harper San Francisco.
Schneiders, Sandra, 2001, in *Selling All: Commitment, Consecrated Celibacy and Community in Catholic Religious Life*, New Jersey: Paulist Press.

Scholefield, Lynne, 1999, *A Tale of Two Cultures: A Dialogical Study of the Cultures of a Jewish and Catholic Secondary School*, University of London, unpublished PhD thesis.

Scholz, Susanna, 1998, 'Through Whose Eyes? A Right Reading of Genesis 34', in Athalya Brenner (ed.), *Genesis: A Feminist Companion to the Bible*, Sheffield: Sheffield Academic Press.

Schreier, Helmut and Matthias Heyl (eds), 1997, *Never Again! The Holocaust's Challenge for Educators*, Hamburg: Kramer.

Schüssler Fiorenza, Elisabeth, 1994, *Jesus. Miriam's Child, Sophia's Prophet: Critical Issues in Feminist Christology*, London: SCM Press.

Schüssler Fiorenza, Elisabeth (ed.), 1993, *Searching the Scriptures: A Feminist Introduction*, New York: Crossroad.

Schüssler Fiorenza, Elisabeth, 1984, *In Memory of Her: A Feminist Theological Reconstruction of Christian Origins*, London: SCM Press.

Sheres, Ita, 1990, *Dinah's Rebellion: A Biblical Parable for our Time*, New York: Crossroad.

Sheridan, Sybil (ed.), 1994, *Hear Our Voice: Women Rabbis Tell Their Stories*, London: SCM Press.

Shermis, Michael and Arthur Zannoni (eds), 1991, *Introduction to Jewish-Christian Relations*, Mahweh: Paulist Press.

Siegele-Wenschkewitz, Leonore, 1991, 'The Discussion of Anti-Judaism in Feminist Theology: A New Area of Jewish-Christian Dialogue', in *Journal of Feminist Studies in Religion*, vol. 7, no. 2, p. 95–9.

Signer, Michael (ed.), 2001, *Memory and History in Christianity and Judaism*, Notre Dame Indiana: University of Notre Dame Press.

Simon, Marcel, 1986, *Verus Israel*, Oxford, The Littman Library of Jewish Civilization.

Smith, E. J., 1999, *Bearing Fruit in Due Season: Feminist Hermeneutics and the Bible in Worship*, Collegeville: The Liturgical Press.

Snaith, J., *Cambridge Bible Commentary on Ecclesiasticus* (Wisdom of Ben Sirach), Cambridge: Cambridge University Press.

Solomon, Norman, 1991, *Judaism and World Religion*, London: Macmillan.

Spark, Muriel, 1965, *The Mandelbaum Gate*, New York: Avon.

Starbird, M., 1999, 'Mary Magdalene: The Beloved', at: www.magdalene.org/belovedessay.htm.

Stark, Rodney, 1995, 'Reconstructing the Rise of Christianity: The Role of Women', in *Sociology of Religion*, vol. 56, no. 3, p. 229–44.

Sered, Susan Starr, 1992, 'The Synagogue as Sacred Space for Elderly Oriental Women in Jerusalem', in Susan Grossman and Rivka Haut (eds), *Daughters of the King, Women and the Synagogue*, Philadelphia: Jewish Publication Society.

Taitz, Emily, 1992, 'Women's Voices, Women's Prayers: The European Synagogues of the Middle Ages', in Susan Grossman and Rivka Haut (eds), *Daughters of the King, Women and the Synagogue*, Philadelphia: Jewish Publication Society.

Tarnor, Norman (ed.), 1995, *A Book of Jewish Women's Prayers: Translations From the Yiddish*, New Jersey: Jason Aronson.

Tatman, Lucy, 2002, 'Western European-American Feminist Christian Theologians: What It Might Mean to Take Ourselves Seriously', in Charlotte Methuen and Angela Berlis (eds), *The End of Liberation? Liberation in the End? Feminist Theory, Feminist Theology and their Political Implications*, Louven: Peeters Publishers.

Theissen, Gerd and Annette Merz, 1998, *The Historical Jesus: A Comprehensive Guide*, London: SCM Press.

Trible, Phyllis, 1982, 'Feminist Hermeneutics and Biblical Studies', in *The Christian Century*, 3–10 February.

Trible, Phyllis, 1978, *God and the Rhetoric of Sexuality*, Philadelphia: Fortress Press.

Trible, Phyllis, 1984, *Texts of Terror*, Philadelphia: Fortress Press.

Tuckett, Christopher, 1987, *Reading the New Testament*, London: SPCK.

Umansky, Ellen M. and Dianne Ashton (eds), 1992, *Four Centuries of Jewish Women's Spirituality*, Boston: Beacon Press.

Vermes, Geza, 2000, *The Changing Faces of Jesus*, London: Penguin.

Wacker, Marie-Theres, 1991, 'Feminist Theology and Anti-Judaism: The Status of the Discussion and Context of the Problem in the Federal Republic of Germany', in *Journal of Feminist Studies in Religion*, vol. 7, no. 2, p. 109–16.

Walker, P., 1990, *Holy City, Holy Places? Christian Attitudes to Jerusalem and the Holy Land in the Fourth Century*, Oxford: Clarendon.

Wardi, Dina, 2003, *Auschwitz: The Limits of Dialogue*, New York: Paulist Press.

Ware, Timothy, 1963, *The Orthodox Church*, London: Penguin.

Wegner, Judith R., 1988, *Chattel or Person? The Status of Women in the Mishnah*, Oxford: Oxford University Press.

Weinberg, Matis, 1999, *FrameWorks: Exodus*, Boston: The Foundation for Jewish Publications.

Wiesel, Elie, 1995, *All Rivers Run to the Sea*, London: HarperCollins.

Wiesel, Elie, 1982, *The Gates of the Forest*, New York: Schocken.

Wilken, Robert, 1992, *The Land Called Holy: Palestine in Christian History and Thought*, New Haven: Yale University Press.

Wilkinson, John, 1981, *Egeria's Travels to the Holy Land*, Jerusalem: Ariel.

Williamson, Clark (ed.), 1992, *A Mutual Witness: Towards Critical Solidarity Between Jews and Christians*, St Louis: Chalice Press.

Williamson, Clark M., 1989, *When Jews and Christians Meet: A Guide for Christian Preaching and Teaching*, St Louis: CBP Press.

Witherell, Carol and N. Noddings (eds), 1991, *Stories Lives Tell*, New York: Teachers College Press.

Wollaston, Isabel, 1996, *A War Against Memory?*, London: SPCK.

Yerushalmi, Yosef Hayim, 1982, *Zakhor* (Jewish History and Jewish Memory), Philadelphia: The Jewish Publication Society of America.

Zornberg, Avivah Gottlieb, 2001, *The Particulars of Rapture: Reflections on Exodus*, New York: Doubleday.
Zornberg, Avivah Gottlieb, 1995, *Genesis: The Beginning of Desire*, Jerusalem: The Jewish Publication Society.

Church Documents and Statements

Catholic-Jewish Relations: Documents from the Holy See, London: The Catholic Truth Society, 1999.
Faith and Order Paper No. III, 1982, Geneva: World Council of Churches, 1982.
A. Flannery (ed.), 1992 rev. ed., *Vatican Council II – The Conciliar and Post Conciliar Documents*, Dublin: Dominican Publications.
Pontifical Biblical Commission, 2002, *The Jewish People and their Sacred Scriptures in the Christian Bible*, The Vatican: Libreria Editrice Vaticana, English edn.

Jewish Documents and Statements

Dabru Emet, September 2000, *The New York Times*. Also in Tikva Frymer-Kensky *et al.*, 2000, *Christianity in Jewish Terms*, Colorado: Westview Press.
Women in the Jewish Community: Survey Report, 1994, London: Office of the Chief Rabbi.
Women in the Jewish Community: Review and Recommendations, 1994, London: Office of the Chief Rabbi.

Index of Names and Subjects